GENDERING THE FAIR

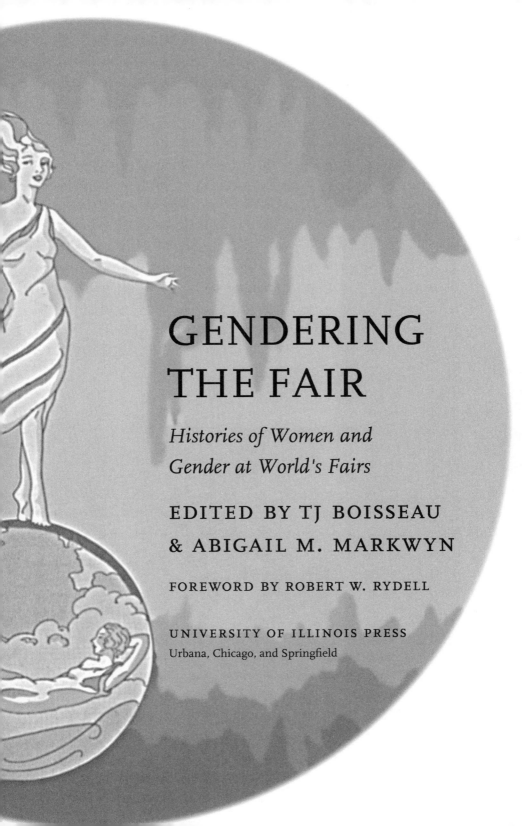

GENDERING THE FAIR

*Histories of Women and
Gender at World's Fairs*

EDITED BY TJ BOISSEAU
& ABIGAIL M. MARKWYN

FOREWORD BY ROBERT W. RYDELL

UNIVERSITY OF ILLINOIS PRESS
Urbana, Chicago, and Springfield

Library of Congress Cataloging-in-Publication Data
Gendering the fair : histories of women and gender at world's fairs /
edited by TJ Boisseau and Abigail M. Markwyn ; foreword by Robert W. Rydell.
p.   cm.
Includes bibliographical references and index.
ISBN 978-0-252-03558-6 (cloth : alk. paper)
ISBN 978-0-252-07749-4 (paper : alk. paper)
1. Exhibitions—History—19th century. 2. Exhibitions—History—20th century.
3. Exhibitions—Social aspects—History—19th century. 4. Exhibitions—Social aspects—
History—20th century. 5. Women—History—19th century. 6. Women—History—
20th century. 7. Women—Public opinion—History—19th century. 8. Women—Public
opinion—History—20th century. 9. Sex role—History—19th century. 10. Sex role—
History—20th century. I. Boisseau, Tracey Jean. II. Markwyn, Abigail M.
T395.G35   2010
907.4—dc22   2010016580

CONTENTS

FOREWORD

Robert W. Rydell

Between London's 1851 Crystal Palace Exhibition and the 1939–40 New York World's Fair, nearly one billion people visited many dozens of world's fairs (as they are called in the United States) or universal expositions or world expos (as they are called everywhere else). Since the Second World War, well over 500 million visits have been recorded through world expo turnstiles, and that number will only increase with the 2010 World Expo in Shanghai, expected to attract 80 million visitors.[1] The manifest importance of these events for shaping the modern world, in everything from architecture to patterns of globalization to fundamental matters of human identity, is why their study is so important.

Over the past two decades a rich body of documentary and theoretical scholarship has emerged about the changing forms and functions of world's fairs. Historians, anthropologists, social scientists, and performance studies scholars have set their sights on expositions, arguing that these spectacles have been mirrors that reflect as well as laboratories that shape the societies that host them. The scholarly literature about expositions is increasingly vast, and this fact alone underscores the need for a volume like this—one that at once assesses and advances arguments about how better to think about these multiplexes of modernity in terms of gender.

To date, most of the scholarly attention devoted to world's fairs has emphasized technology, architecture, imperialism, and race. Despite some notable treatments of gender, this crucial aspect of exposition history is only beginning to receive its due. What this volume makes clear is that rereading expositions in terms of gender deepens not only our understanding of expositions but also our comprehension of the cultural construction of gender in modernizing societies around the globe.

Readers who might be expecting documentary accounts of exhibits in the various "women's buildings" at world's fairs will be immediately impressed by the alternative approach taken here. Authors examine gender as an instrument of power and resistance, as a strategy for rethinking the meaning of cosmopolitanism, as well as a critical category for thinking about the construction of national and colonial identities. For these authors, in other words, gender seeped into and structured the discursive mapping of expositions in their entirety. This is one of the chief lessons of this book.

With so much scholarship underway on women's efforts through expositions to advance political and economic equality, better health care, and international peace and cooperation, it is important to call attention to a related effort occurring in the realm of historic preservation. In San Antonio, Texas, home of the 1968 Hemisfair, one of the few surviving women's buildings from any world's fair is still standing in Hemisfair Park—a world's fair landscape still dominated by the exposition's (masculinist) Tower of the Sun. Fortunately, fundraising efforts, spearheaded by the Women's Pavilion at Hemisfair Park, Inc., are being pursued to preserve this structure—a legacy from the 1968 fair that embodies the cumulative struggles of so many women over time to improve the social, political, and economic position of women in the modern world.

The chapters in this volume focus on the so-called "golden years" of world expos, between the mid-nineteenth and mid-twentieth centuries. Analyses such as these will advance the study of both world's fairs and the academic study of gender. I am also hopeful that they will have another application as well—namely, to the planning of future world expos. Most Americans believe that world's fairs are no longer held, but this erroneous belief is symptomatic of Americans' ignorance of world affairs (world of fairs?) more generally. Countries continue to host world expos. The 2010 Shanghai event, dedicated to the theme of "Better Cities/Better Lives," will likely be the biggest world's fair ever conducted, in terms of attendance as well as exhibition space. Additional fairs are planned for Korea (2012) and Milan (2015), with bids coming in from multiple countries for the right to hold the 2020 exposition.[2] It is precisely because world expos will map the course of the twenty-first century that planners of upcoming world's fairs, whether Americans or not, would be well advised to learn from this book that any world expo that ignores gender is representing something less than the world.

NOTES

1 Paul Greenhalgh, *The Modern Ideal: The Rise and Collapse of Idealism in the Visual Arts from the Enlightenment to Postmodernism* (London: Victoria and Albert Museum, 2005), 119; and John E. Findling and Kimberly D. Pelle, *Encyclopedia of World's Fairs and Expositions* (Jefferson, N.C.: McFarland, 2008), 414–17.

2 Information about upcoming world expos is available from the Paris-based Bureau of International Expositions.

ROBERT W. RYDELL

GENDERING THE FAIR

World's Fairs in Feminist Historical Perspective

TJ Boisseau and Abigail M. Markwyn

Gendering the Fair presents a wide array of original scholarship aimed at enriching and deepening our appreciation for the gendered dimensions of world's fairs, as well as for the roles played by particular women or groups of women in molding the meanings generated by these mass-attended events. As our contributors demonstrate, an interrogation of the significance of gender—that ultimate organizing principle of identity, key ideological precept, and foundational shaper of lived experience—in the creation and reception of fairs is vital to our estimation of their enduring cultural power. Some contributors to this volume seek to illuminate the consequential ways in which nation-states deployed gender in the presentations of their nations. Others direct our attention to the opportunities that world's fairs presented to women as actors seeking to re-envision womanhood in specific national and international contexts. Still others present the reader with a front-row seat to fair organizers' more or less successful manipulation of fairgoers' experience of the fairgrounds as gendered space. Interdisciplinary in approach and fully mindful of the intertwined nature of gender in the construction of racial, class, national, and colonial relations of power, the scholarship offered here illustrates the indispensability of women's and gender history to the study of world's fairs. They also offer persuasive evidence of how germane an appreciation of world's fairs is to our study of women's and gender history.

World's fairs and expositions represent the most important international mass events of the modern era. This assertion may be commonplace, yet the extent to which this is so bears repeating. Predating the theme parks and mass attractions of the post–World War II era, international expositions held in the nineteenth century in Europe, North America, Asia, and Latin America occasioned the first global gatherings of mass numbers of people, with many expositions attracting upwards of ten million, twenty-five million and, by the mid-twentieth century, as many as fifty million visitors to events that usually spanned five or six months. Apart from the communication technologies that would eventually permit masses of people to "virtually" gather together—and often presaging (if not introducing) these same technologies—expositions helped produce a globalized mass public and permitted regional publics to form within nation-states. In recognition of the vast potential of world's fairs and international expositions[1] to shape public opinion, governments as well as every variety of community organization have attempted to control the representation of themselves and their constituents at these events. Invariably, the results of their efforts comprised elaborate displays of organizing and power brokering, generated innovative public-relations campaigns, and honed new forms of propagandistic strategizing. At fairs, government and commercial sponsors introduced cross-class, multiracial, mixed-sex, and international audiences to major technological breakthroughs and scientific ideas as well as revolutionary design concepts ascendant in art, architecture, media, and entertainment culture. Fairs helped cross-pollinate ideas and technologies central to agriculture, labor, social science, communication, transportation—the list of areas of engagement that world's fairs entailed is endless. Furthermore, the unusually replete quality of the extant historical record documenting many world's fairs places them squarely within the historical researcher's purview. The capacity for such evidence to shed light on how public perceptions were formed or new initiatives forged at particular moments around important topics and issues has made world's fairs and international expositions inescapably relevant to all fields of historical inquiry.

World's fairs and expositions hold particular interest for historians of women. Generally locked out of control over most forms of mass media, nineteenth- and early-twentieth-century fairs provided a venue for organized groups of women to communicate to a mass and often international public a vision of themselves as constituent members of particular nations and a newly collective consciousness of themselves as a sex. Examination of their efforts reveal the

TJ BOISSEAU AND ABIGAIL M. MARKWYN

limits and capacities of women's organizing in this era and expose the internal rivalries and politicized struggles between women of different races, classes, and nations in these years.

The re-envisioning or reinforcing of gender as framing device and as lived experience at world's fairs has made these events especially interesting to historians of gender. Since the first modern international exposition was held in London in 1851, gender has been a crucial component of world's fair designs and prime framework for the impressions that fair visitors took away with them. Further, world's fairs have tended to annunciate racial, class, and national identity in highly gender-specific ways. With scholars increasingly choosing to interrogate popular culture through gender as a "category of analysis," world's fairs represent supremely convenient vehicles by which to explore this intersection—resulting in a recent upsurge in feminist research focusing on fairs.[2] *Gendering the Fair* seizes this productive moment in scholarly output to present important new work that promises to enliven debates over the meaning and significance of world's fairs and their relevance to our understanding of the history of women and gender.

Finding Women at the Fair

As a look at the first few decades of publishing and symposia on world's fairs might bear out, world's fair researchers only sporadically acknowledged the participation or contribution of women to the organizing of expositions. This remained true long after the emergence of women's history as a serious field of scholarly inquiry, a development that triggered a minor explosion of feminist-inspired research of world's fairs in the 1970s.[3] In these years, feminist scholars—particularly art historians—searching for women in the historical record found ample evidence of women's public activism at expositions. Regardless of how little this early research seemed to inform masculinist perspectives on world's fairs, in the 1970s feminist scholars trained in art, architectural, social, political, and labor history eagerly entered into dialogue with one another concerning the meaning that world's fairs in the past had held for women.

Viewed in hindsight as milestones of progress for women and typically accepted by contemporaries as harbingers of modernity, world's fairs seemed to hold boundless interest for feminist historians newly attuned to the need to bring attention to women's historic interventions in the public sphere. In particular, the 1893 Columbian Exposition's Board of Lady Managers and the impressive Woman's Building it oversaw in Chicago that year offered ample material for feminist analysis. It is to this fair that U.S. feminist historians first turned to chart American women's officially sanctioned debut into the public life of the nation.[4] As scholars sought to bring to light the almost forgotten contributions of women as fair organizers, inventors, intellectuals, and artists, these early works generally focused on female accomplishment. Among the most pressing and illuminating of topics to explore were women's struggles to assert and control their representation within fair administrations. This is not to say that these early histories were uniformly celebratory in tone or content. Immediately and with bitter irony, feminist researchers exposed the redoubled discrimination black women experienced at the hands of white female organizers at these same American fairs.[5] Complete with detailed descriptions of infighting that drew lines between women of different races, regions, classes, and political allegiances, Jeanne Madeline Weimann's comprehensive and illustrated coffee table book, *The Fair Women*, documented the full extent of women's participation in the 1893 Columbian Exposition.[6] Weimann's meticulous research, set within an accessible descriptive framework, inspired more in-depth and scholarly analysis of the efforts of "organized womanhood" to promote themselves and their causes at world's fairs.[7] An article published in 1984 by Karen J. Blair, for instance, stands out not only for its focus on "the limits of sisterhood" but also for its early insistence on connecting women's political organizing at U.S. world's fairs to larger questions of American reform and the Progressive movement.[8]

Research into the complexity of world's fairs held in the United States, both in terms of their organizing and their public reception, was spurred on that same year by the publication of Robert Rydell's comprehensive *All the World's a Fair: Visions of Empire at American International Expositions, 1876–1916*. Building on Alan Trachtenberg's cultural analysis of the "White City" at the 1893 Chicago World's Fair, Rydell showed how, by the late nineteenth century, fairs generally served to accustom white American fairgoers to seeing their racial identity as structured in concert with the new set of colonial or neocolonial relationships that the United States was forging in this period.[9] The work of Rydell and his cohort raised an obvious question for historians of women: what were the nationalist, racialist, and colonialist implications of women's participation at world's fairs, and how did gender function to support or undermine such projects? One of the first scholars to tackle that question was Gail Bederman, whose brief but insightful discussion of Ida B. Wells-Barnett's role at the 1893 Chicago World's Fair (drawing on Hazel Carby's trenchant analysis of the rhetorical strategizing that characterized Barnett's anti-lynching campaign) went beyond noting the Board of Lady Managers' racist policies of exclusion.[10] Her work fleshed out the significance of race and sexuality in the presentation of gender as inscribed especially by exhibits and performances held on the "midway," or the exotic entertainment zone, of the Columbian Exhibition. Bederman's discussion of these topics reflected a cultural turn that the discipline of history had taken—

one that would have profound implications for women's and gender history as well as the study of world's fairs in the next decade.

In the 1990s, scholars' new preoccupation with questions of power, agency, representation, and resistance—and the degree to which these sorts of questions hinge on cultural manifestations of gendered ideology—represented a general transformation in humanities and social science research. A new wave of feminist scholarly attention broke over the 1893 Columbian Exhibition with art historians again at the forefront of rethinking the meaning of world's fairs and the complex ways in which gender and other axes of identity informed one another at these events.[11] Following their lead, social historians also took a new look at the complexities of race and colonialist ideology informing women's participation and experience of world's fairs. Often, with the 1893 Woman's Building and the complex organizing that produced it firmly centered in researcher's sights, such scholars demonstrated an increasing interest in gender as much as women and displayed a firm commitment to seeing gender, race, class, and nationalist ideologies as necessarily shaping one another.[12] Fairs other than the 1893 Chicago World's Fair yielded different insights—ones that challenged earlier interpretations of the limits of women's fair organizing and strengthened our appreciation of the key role played by gender at world's fairs.[13] A new recognition of the way meaning was organized through visual iconography and of the gendered politics of space—both architecturally conceived and ideologically produced—has infused recent feminist scholars' analyses of expositions.[14] Amateur and professional photographic representations of fairs, sculptural presentations, and painting exhibits all have come under scrutiny informed by trends shaping the new cultural history such as those coming from subaltern studies, performance theory, and psychoanalysis.[15] Others drawing from the self-reflective criticism of anthropologists have recognized in the coerced performances of colonized peoples resistance to their often feminized and sexualized presentation on midway zones.[16] Most recently, Cheryl Ganz has brought questions emanating from performance studies, design theory, and social history to bear on a comprehensive study of the 1933 Chicago World's Fair that neither remarginalizes women's participation nor ignores the gendered messages conveyed as a whole by this fair's nationalist and eugenicist vision of the future.[17]

The accumulation of feminist scholarship on world's fairs produced in the past decade illustrates just how fruitful the scholarly quest, initially undertaken in the hope of finding women at world's fairs, has proven. It also demonstrates the degree to which world's fair scholarship has contributed to an expansion of the boundaries of women's history to include an accounting for gender as shaper of ideological and material reality. A leaning toward cultural treatments of nationalism, racialism, and colonialism in Anglophone scholarship has had particular influence on studies of expositions held in Britain, Canada, the United States, and Australia, but a long scholarly tradition supports world's fair scholarship published in German, French, Dutch, Swedish, and many other languages as well.[18] Indeed, the internationalist orientation of world's fairs—the largest and most significant of them also necessarily multinational in terms of audience as well as participants—has given world's fair scholarship superlative value as a bridge between national histories.[19] The unique contribution *Gendering the Fair* makes is to place considerations of women and gender at the center of this cross-national and cross-disciplinary dialogue.

Gendering the Fair

This collection builds on the scholarship described above while it pushes our gender analysis of world's fairs forward. Given the advanced state of women's history scholarship and feminist theorizing about culture, the authors in this volume are not in the position of early women's historians of needing simply to chronicle women's achievements and failures either in terms of their presence or their exclusion at world's fairs. Instead, contributors to *Gendering the Fair* critically analyze the significance of women as planners and visitors, organizers and administrators, performers and workers, guides, journalists, and pundits. These scholars, trained in gender analysis, move easily between examining women's experiences, considering the role that gender plays in shaping the fabric of particular world's fair cultures, and assessing world's fairs' impact on gender as a relation always in formation. Readers will find that gender figures in these works less as a substitute code for women than as a relation such that masculinity, masculinism, and men's particular positioning and experiences at fairs also are set firmly within analytical frameworks. And as so much of what feminist and postcolonial scholars have accomplished in the past fifteen years has shown, gender is a constituent part of nationalist and colonialist ideology and institution building just as much as the reverse. Concomitantly in the scholarship included in this volume, women as agents are not isolatable from considerations of gender as an effect and producer of ideology. Neither are considerations of gender artificially separated from questions of racial, class, national, or colonial identity.

The contributors to this collection work from within several national historical traditions of Europe as well as those of Canada and the United States. Their training represents the respective and overlapping outlooks of scholars working in the fields of architecture and design, literature and art history, visual and performance studies, religious studies, public history, labor history, and women's history. They offer insight and analysis of the historical records

TJ BOISSEAU AND ABIGAIL M. MARKWYN

preserved from many world's fairs, particularly that of fairs which have seen little previous study and on topics that have been unwisely neglected up to now. The variety of approaches as well as fairs taken up by our contributing authors belie a previous tendency in world's fair scholarship to center on a very few well-known fairs or, in the case of U.S. women's history, an all-too-often exclusive focus on the Woman's Building of the 1893 Chicago World's Fair. This collection reveals instead the ever-widening range of topics, themes, and disciplinary approaches currently at the forefront of world's fair scholarship. The point of such diversity, however, is not only to sample the best of research from several fields of study but also to provide a venue for cross-disciplinary feminist dialogue about world's fairs. The schema of *Gendering the Fair*—a tripartite sectioning of chapters respectively focused on national identity formation, women's activism, and the visual and spatial dimensions of fairgoers' experience of fairs—is not intended to compartmentalize these issues under disparate and artificial rubrics of analysis but to highlight particularly germane themes explored by world's fair scholars and to generate insight into the complex ways that gender enters into all facets of the world's fair experience.

In part 1, "Woman, Gender, and Nation," scholars call attention to the centrality of gender and of women—their visual representation, ideas associated with their "essence" and sexuality, and nationally specific visions of social advancement for women—to nation-states' self-presentation at world's fairs. In chapter 1, "'Little Black Rose' at the 1934 *Exposição Colonial Portuguesa*," Isabel Morais untangles the complicated strands of erotics, race, and colonialism woven into fair organizers' design of the 1934 *Exposição Colonial Portuguesa* (First Portuguese Colonial Exhibition) held in Oporto, where 1.3 million visitors attended the event specifically "to see the blacks" and, in particular, to eye the young Balanta beauty queens on display. Morais explains how a public sexualizing and idealizing of African women such as "Rozinha," or "little black Rose," helped broaden the appeal of Salazar's colonial philosophy and ambition to forge a new Portuguese national identity based on a positive appraisal of African women as desirable sexual partners and symbolic mothers to a miscegenated Portuguese nation. To similar ends but with a reverse gendered and racial strategy, iconic visual evidence from San Francisco's 1915 Panama-Pacific International Exposition permits Sarah J. Moore in "Manliness and the New American Empire at the 1915 Panama-Pacific Exposition," the last chapter of part 1, to demonstrate how fairgoers' experiences of this fair were saturated with masculinist and imperialist meaning in the service of an emerging new American imperial hegemony over the Western hemisphere and Pacific rim. Foregrounding and metaphorically inscribing the male body, fair organizers built upon the masculinist rhetoric of Theodore Roosevelt to create a tangible world of empire in miniature for visitors to the 1915 exposition. In the case of the 1934 Oporto fair, the centering of African women's highly sexualized bodies in the sightlines of fairgoers was meant to look backward to a historic imperial grandeur in the hope of re-establishing Portugal's status as a world power in the future. In the case of the 1915 fair held in San Francisco, the United States and the city of San Francisco looked westward to the Pacific to provide a new focal point for Americans in the re-envisioning of themselves as an emerging world power with extracontinental territorial possessions. In the case of both, however, hypersexualized visual presentations of gender—of black women in Oporto and of white men in San Francisco—supplied the most germane vehicle for the remaking of colonialist national identities.

The middle two chapters in part 1, "The New Soviet Woman at the 1939 New York World's Fair," by Alison Rowley, and "Japan—Modern, Ancient, and Gendered at the 1893 Chicago World's Fair," by Lisa K. Langlois, illuminate the way in which nation-states—namely, Japan and the Soviet Union—countered negative international propaganda through an assertion of the unique national character of their women and nation-specific gender relations between men and women. Lisa Langlois explains how the Japanese Lady's Boudoir and the Phoenix Hall at the 1893 Chicago World's Fair helped legitimize Japanese sovereignty by marking cultural production with particular gender ideologies—both modernist and traditionalist in tone. Her work illustrates the complexity of such representations. The Japanese contribution to this fair negotiated the paradoxes of modernity by presenting itself as a modern nation deserving of inclusion within the great powers of the moment on the basis of having a unique national past steeped in traditions, the most telling of which were explicitly patriarchal in tone and content. Japanese women, she tells us, bore the burden of proving that Japan was an "ancient" nation by performing a patriarchalism that excluded them from the modern or contemporary moment. The opposite strategy was employed by Soviet fair organizers in New York in 1939 who, taking good advantage of a prewar thawing of tensions between the United States and the USSR to intervene in American conceptions of life in the Soviet Union, presented the "New Soviet Woman" as a fully actualized equal of Soviet men. Alison Rowley's research focuses our attention on the significance of material souvenirs, particularly educational booklets produced by the Soviets for distribution at this fair, in shaping fairgoers' experiences of the fair. Drawing implicit but stark contrasts between American society and Soviet society, these promotional materials outlined a full range of political rights and economic opportunities available to women under Soviet socialism. Just as Moore's and Morais's work highlights the usefulness of gender as a race-specific and highly sexualized tool of empire, Rowley's and Langlois's research illuminates widely differing representational strategies yet firmly points to the centrality of women to the self-presentation of nation-states at world's fairs.

Part 2, "Women in Action," refocuses some of these same concerns through the prism of women's activism. In contrast to part 1, authors in part 2 document ways that women strove to overcome their manipulation as inert signs of national identity, taking charge of their own representation at world's fairs often toward explicitly political ends. In chapter 5, "Mormon Women, Suffrage, and Citizenship at the 1893 Chicago World's Fair," Andrea G. Radke-Moss considers how Mormon women's religious identity was reconciled with American national identity by way of prominent Mormon women's deliberate and organized interventions at the 1893 Columbian Exposition. Her research illuminates the way women of the Church of Jesus Christ of Latter-day Saints used this fair as an opportunity to present themselves as liberated members of what she calls "an increasingly American" church leading not only to the gaining of statehood for Utah in 1896 but, with it, suffrage for Utah women. With a more broadly global context in mind, Anne Clendinning's work on the International Council of Women (ICW) at the World's Fair of 1924 held in Wembley, England, exposes in chapter 6 ("Internationalist Peace Activism at the 1924 British Empire Exhibition") the central underlying paradox of international expositions as manifesting inherently nationalist expressions of internationalism. Deepening our appreciation of this paradox, Clendinning shows how the ICW furthered its mission of bringing women together, across national boundaries, to work for education and peace and to express its message of transnational feminism within a realm saturated with imperial iconography and rhetoric, despite the fact that the ICW espoused an elitist feminism arguably out of touch with the new politics of mass democracy in 1920s Britain.

World's fairs did not always enshrine internationalism as a central preoccupation. World's fairs held in the United States often provided useful venues for localized groups of women to articulate their particular understandings of their relation to larger forces and movements. As editors we have been more interested in what the idea and format of a world's fair meant to different sets of organizers and constituencies who applied the term themselves to the events they organized—the scope of which may have fallen short of the grandest of international expositions—than in proposing or applying an extradiegetic definition of "world's fair" based on an artificial set of criteria (whether hinging on scale or period). The remaining two chapters in part 2, for instance— "The Woman's World's Fairs (or The Dream of Women Who Work), Chicago 1925–1928," by TJ Boisseau, and "Memorializing the 1897 Tennessee Centennial Woman's Building," by Elisabeth Israels Perry—refuse to parse the definitional aspects of world's fairs. Instead, they direct our attention to the substantive efforts of women exerted at regional or localized fairs or through local women's organizing at more internationally significant expositions to establish themselves in the public mind. Boisseau rediscovers a set of fairs that has gone virtually unnoticed by scholars of both women's history and world's fairs. Despite their size relative to other expositions, the Woman's World's Fairs held in Chicago every summer for four years in a row starting in 1925 present a view onto the way that women, when unencumbered and unlimited by men's assumptions about women or by corporate influences, used the structure and formatting of a world's fair to present themselves to the public and to promote their own ideas about women. Boisseau concludes that the cross-class celebration of women's productivity as workers undermines prevailing ideas held by historians that women in the United States fully embraced a consumerist ethic and rejected a consciousness of themselves as a sex in the years immediately following the gaining of suffrage. With a similar set of goals in mind, Perry uncovers a memorial, erected in 1904, to women's participation at the 1897 Tennessee Centennial and International Exposition that shines a light on the ambiguous status and philosophies spurring a generation of women to public activism in the late Gilded Age. Her cogent discussion of the politics of public history and commemorations reminds us how easily displaced, covered over, and forgotten have been the public interventions made by women operating locally to resituate themselves and establish a legacy of women's activism.

Part 3, "Gendered Spaces," offers scholarship on world's fairs that reminds us that such events were not just rhetorical but primarily experiential in nature. Rather than communicating its ideas through purely oral or written channels, world's fairs presented visual lessons and comprised spatial manifestations of ideology. In chapter 9, "Encountering 'Woman' on the Fairgrounds of the 1915 Panama-Pacific Exposition," Abigail M. Markwyn's exploration of the many ways in which visitors to the 1915 Panama-Pacific Exposition would have encountered ideas about women as political actors, representatives of their race, and constituent members of the nation simply by visiting the fairgrounds overturns the glib assumptions that women's activism declined following the closing of the 1893 Columbian Exposition. This chapter brings a dialogue begun by Sarah J. Moore in part 1 full circle as Markwyn counters Moore's emphasis on the hypermasculinity of the Panama-Pacific Exposition with an emphasis on the way that women—both activist women and average fairgoers—actually used and experienced the spaces of the fairgrounds, carving out niches for themselves as well as for explicitly feminist causes. As Markwyn's research evinces, ideas about women were built into the design of the fairgrounds rather than segregated into spaces that fairgoers could choose to engage with or opt out of as they might have been if a "Woman's Building" had been erected. However, this does not mean, as Markwyn is careful to point out, that fairgoers did not encounter "Woman" as a racialized and nation-specific concept. Both emphases—Moore's on hypermasculinity and Markwyn's on expressions of women's agency—converge to paint a picture of the Panama-Pacific exposition as firmly rooted in a highly racialized and newly imperial sense of self that animated U.S. expressions of national identity in this period.

As Markwyn's work amply demonstrates, women's self-segregated spaces at world's fairs, some specifically designed as "woman's buildings," deserve our attention. In chapter 10, "Woman's Buildings at European and American World's Fairs, 1893–1939," architectural historian Mary Pepchinski's cross-national and comparative analysis of Woman's Buildings—the definition of which itself embodies a set of interesting contradictions and silences—encourages us to reconsider accepted notions of modern architecture as they have been informed by ideas regarding representation of "the feminine." Arguing that the story of the Woman's Buildings proposes that the instability and conflicts which inform feminine representation are both integral to how we think categorically about buildings, and their sites, Pepchinski points to the crucial role played by women at fairs as well as that played by world's fairs in the construction of "the feminine" in mass culture. Pepchinski's chapter comparing architecture featured at European and American fairs over a span of several decades makes the most of the opportunity that world's fairs as internationalist venues offer to the scholar for cross-national analysis.

The final chapter in part 3, Anne Wohlcke's "Policing Masculine Festivity at London's Early Modern Fairs," shifts our attention from the gender-specific spaces of Woman's Buildings and experiences of female fairgoers to those of male attendees to fairs, and fairs as repressively policed gendered spaces. Assessing the relative freedom and agency available to fairgoers at an early moment in the formation of the urban-sited fair—in eighteenth-century London—Wohlcke's research charts the emergence of a hegemonic sensibility dictating men's behaviors, eventually producing the fair as a "predictable slate on which visions of the present and future could be drawn." Wohlcke's work confirms the centrality of gender in design and surveillance mechanisms deployed at urban-sited fairs—fairs that charted the way for the first modern world's fair held in London in 1851—arguing that "gendering fairs was the first step in making fairgrounds useable venues for the promotion of national or economic interests." Rejecting the often overly narrow parameters (whether of period or scale) placed around scholarly interest in world's fairs, this chapter permits readers to appreciate the development of intentional techniques, strategies, and formats meant to reproduce fairs as orderly spaces where visitors would take in sights, sounds, and meanings in predictable and controlled ways. As Wohlcke's work demonstrates, fairgrounds were destined to become highly contested spaces where gender served both as a prime vehicle and an explicit target of political struggle.

The inclusion of Wohlcke's work on fairs held during a nascent period in the history of world's fairs—arguably a period that predates "world's fairs" properly defined as modern phenomena—along with Boisseau's essay on the relatively diminutive Chicago Woman's World's Fairs should signal the reader that *Gendering the Fair* positions itself a bit differently than many compendiums of essays, facts, descriptions, and bibliographies of world's fairs. The editors of and contributors to *Gendering the Fair* treat world's fairs and international expositions not as belonging to a categorical box that we care about policing but instead see them as convenient vehicles able to generate comparative frameworks of analysis and permitting the exploration of themes and questions that are central to feminist inquiry. Certainly the chapters included in *Gendering the Fair* negate the notion that the point of scholarship featuring world's fairs is simply to parade their intrinsically fascinating facets or, worse, to find new ways of parsing the definitional or statistical elements of what constitutes a world's fair—in both cases primarily to satisfy the antiquarian's curiosity about these events.

Nor is our purpose limited to showcasing the ways in which women were excluded, hampered, or triumphant in their efforts to participate as active agents at world's fairs. Instead, these chapters read in concert with one another make clear that what is compelling about world's fairs to a current generation of serious students of women's history and feminist scholars in many fields is the fairs' unparalleled capacity to articulate the gender status quo at particular moments, their historic role in shaping the terms of gender transformation and women's activism, and their inevitable participation in the reframing of gender to encompass the racial, class, and colonial agendas of nation-states. Our most ambitious aim is to permit the significance of this crucial—but what might otherwise comprise an overly scattered body of work on gender—to be appreciated fully for the first time as a coherent field of study by students, scholars, and aficionados of world's fairs alike. We hope this volume will supply an indispensable point of reference not only for those who study and research world's fairs as such, but also for feminist scholars working in fields that inevitably bring world's fairs into their field of vision.

NOTES

1 For purposes of this book, the terms "world's fair" and "international exposition" are interchangeable.

2 The phrase is Joan W. Scott's, from "Gender: A Useful Category of Historical Analysis," *American Historical Review* 91, no. 5 (1986): 1053–75. See also the most recent ventilation of the usefulness of this concept in *AHR* Forum, "Revisiting: Gender a Useful Category of Analysis," *American Historical Review* 113 (2008): 1344–1430.

3 This explosion includes works such as Duncan R. Jamieson, "Women's Rights at the World's Fair, 1893," *Illinois Quarterly* 37 (1974): 5–20; Joelynn Snyder-Ott, "Woman's

Place in the Home (that she built)," *Feminist Art Journal* 3 (1974): 7–8, 18; Wayne Falke, "Samantha at the Centennial," *Hayes Historical Journal* 1 (1977): 165–71; Jeanne Madeline Weimann, "A Temple to Woman's Genius: The Woman's Building of 1893," *Chicago History* 6 (1977): 23–33; Terree Grabenhorst-Randall, "The Woman's Building," *Heresies* 1, no. 4 (Winter 1978): 1, 44–46; Deborah J. Warner, "Women Inventors at the Centennial," in *Dynamos and Virgins Revisited: Women and Technological Change in History,* ed. Martha Moore Trescott (Metuchen, N.J.: Scarecrow, 1979); Deborah Grand Golomb, "The 1893 Congress of Jewish Women: Evolution or Revolution in American Jewish Women's History?" *American Jewish History* 70, no. 1 (1980): 52–67; William Stephenson, "How Sallie Southall Cotton Brought North Carolina to the Chicago World's Fair of 1893," *North Carolina Historical Review* 58, no. 4 (1980): 364–83.

4 This early period of writing on women's history at world's fairs also often encompassed women's fight against exclusion from the 1876 Philadelphian Exposition and either implicitly or explicitly contrasted women's roles at the two fairs. See, for instance, Judith Paine, "The Women's Pavilion of 1876," *Feminist Art Journal* 4, no. 4 (1976): 5–12; William D. Andrews, "Women and the Fairs of 1876 and 1893," *Hayes Historical Journal* 1 (1977): 173–83; Frances K. Pohl, "Historical Reality or Utopian Ideal?" *International Journal of Women's Studies* 5 (1982): 289–311.

5 Ann Massa, "Black Women in the 'White City,'" *Journal of American Studies* 8 (1974): 319–37; Erlene Stetson, "A Note on the Woman's Building and Black Exclusion," *Heresies* 2 (1979): 45–47. See also work published in succeeding decades, such as Paula Giddings, *When and Where I Enter: The Impact of Black Women on Race and Sex in America* (New York: Bantam, 1984), 85–89; Hazel Carby, *Reconstructing Womanhood: The Emergence of the African American Woman Novelist* (New York: Oxford University Press, 1987), 107–19; Anna R. Paddon and Sally Turner, "African Americans and the World's Columbian Exposition," *Illinois Historical Journal* 88, no. 1 (1995): 19–36.

6 Weimann's *The Fair Women* (Chicago: Academy, 1981) remains the fullest treatment of women's participation in and experience of the 1893 fair.

7 Works published in the 1980s that expand on Weimann's book to consider the efforts of white elite women organizers especially at the 1876, 1893, and 1904 Louisiana Purchase Expositions include Virginia Grant Darney, "Women and World's Fairs: American International Expositions, 1876–1904," (PhD diss., Emory University, 1982); for a more sophisticated analysis, see Mary Francis Cordato, "Representing the Expansion of Woman's Sphere: Women's Work and Culture at the World's Fairs of 1876, 1893 and 1904" (PhD diss., New York University, 1989), and Cordato, "Towards a New Century: Women and the Philadelphia Centennial Exhibition, 1876," *Pennsylvania Magazine of History and Biography* 107, no. 1 (1983): 114.

8 The phrase "organized womanhood" is contemporary to the period. Its significance to world's fairs has been best explored by Karen J. Blair in "The Limits of Sisterhood: The Woman's Building in Seattle, 1908–1921," *Frontiers: A Journal of Women's Studies* 8, no. 1 (1984): 45–52. More recent works examining the dimensions of organized women's efforts at world's fairs include that of Ann Firor Scott, *Natural Allies: Women's Associations in American History* (Urbana: University of Illinois Press, 1992), 128–31; Sidney Bland, "Women and World's Fairs: The Charleston Story," *South Carolina Historical Magazine* 94, no. 3 (1993): 166–84; Carol Cornwall Madsen, "The Power of Combination: Emmeline B. Wells and the National and International Councils of Women," *Brigham Young University Studies* 33, no. 4 (1993): 646–73; Gayle Gullett, "'Our Great Opportunity': Organized Women Advance Women's Work at the World's Columbian Exposition of 1893," *Illinois Historical Journal* 87 (1994): 259–76; Kristie Miller, "Of the Women, For the Women, and By the Women," *Chicago History* 24, no. 2 (1995), 58–72;

Sylvia Yount, "A 'New Century' for Women: Philadelphia's Centennial Exhibition and Domestic Reform," in *Philadelphia's Cultural Landscape*, ed. Katharine Martinez and Page Talbott, 149–60 (Philadelphia: Temple University Press, 2000).

9   Alan Trachtenberg, "White City," in *The Incorporation of America: Culture and Society in the Gilded Age* (New York: Hill and Wang, 1982), 208–33; Robert Rydell, *All the World's a Fair: Visions of Empire at American Expositions, 1876–1916* (Chicago: University of Chicago Press, 1984). Rydell's singular focus on world's fairs and the racial, national, and ethnic dimensions of the spectacle they presented encouraged more work in this vein by Neil Harris and James Gilbert. See Neil Harris, *Cultural Excursions: Marketing Appetites and Cultural Tastes in Modern America* (Chicago: University of Chicago Press, 1990); James Gilbert, *Perfect Cities: Chicago's Utopias of 1893* (Chicago: University of Chicago Press, 1991).

10 Gail Bederman, *Manliness and Civilization: A Cultural History of Gender and Race in the United States, 1880–1917* (Chicago: University of Chicago Press, 1995), 31–41. See also Carby, 107–16.

11 Examples of art historians' work on world's fairs published in the early 1990s include, most notably, Judy Sund, "Columbus and Columbia in Chicago, 1893: Man of Genius Meets Generic Woman," *Art Bulletin* 75, no. 3 (1993): 443–66; John Hutton, "Picking Fruit: Mary Cassatt's Modern Woman and the Woman's Building of 1893," *Feminist Studies* 20, no. 2 (1994): 318–48; Carolyn Kinder Carr and Sally Webster, "Mary Cassatt and Mary Fairchild MacMonnies: The Search for Their 1893 Murals," *American Art* 8, no. 1 (1994): 52–69.

12 TJ Boisseau dissects the rhetorical strategies deployed by the Board of Lady Managers, finding "white queenliness"—or a reliance on a set of racialized contrasts between "modern" and "civilized" women and colonized or "backward" women—to be a central organizing trope of elitist women's organizers at this fair. See "White Queens at the Chicago World's Fair: New Womanhood in the Service of Class, Race, and Nation," *Gender and History* 12, no. 1 (2000): 33–81. For more on the generation of racial meanings reliant on gendered representations, see Micki McElya, *Clinging to Mammy: The Faithful Slave in Twentieth-Century America* (Cambridge: Harvard University Press, 2007). McElya's work draws in part on that of Kimberly Wallace Sanders, whose 1998 essay on Aunt Jemima also addressed the role of Nancy Green and compared it to the rhetoric of the black women who appeared at the World's Congress of Representative Women: "Dishing Up Dixie: Recycling the Old South in the Early-Twentieth-Century Domestic Ideal," in *Burning Down the House: Recycling Domesticity*, ed. Rosemary Marangoly George, 215–31 (Boulder: Westview, 1998). For how internationalist ideas about women at the 1893 Exposition hinged on nationalism and colonial agendas, see Noël Valis, "Women's Culture in 1893: Spanish Nationalism and the Chicago World's Fair," *Letras Peninsulares* 13, no. 2–3 (2001): 633–64.

13 For examples of scholarship on fairs other than the Columbian Exhibition, bracketing the era of emerging work on world's fairs that integrate gender, race, and class into their analyses, see Zeynep Çelik and Leila Kinney, "Ethnography and Exhibitionism at the Expositions Universelles," *Assemblage* 13 (1990): 34–59; and Cheryl Ganz, *The 1933 Chicago World's Fair: A Century of Progress* (Urbana: University of Illinois Press, 2008), especially her chapters on "women's spaces" and African American women's fair organizing, 85–122.

14 On the gendered politics of space at world's fairs, see Laura Rabinovitz, "The Fair View: The 1893 Chicago World's Columbian Exposition," in *For the Love of Pleasure: Women, Movies, and Culture in Turn of the Century Chicago*, 47–67 (New Brunswick: Rutgers University Press, 1998); and Andrew E. Wood, "Managing the Lady Managers: The

Shaping of Heterotopian Spaces in the 1893 Chicago Exposition's Woman's Building," *Southern Communication Journal* 69, no. 4 (2004): 289–302.

15 Examples of works focusing on painting include Erik Trump, "Primitive Woman— Domesticated Woman: The Image of the Primitive Woman at the 1893 World's Columbian Exposition," *Women's Studies* 27, no. 3 (1998): 215–58; and Ruth Iskin, *Modern Women and Parisian Consumer Culture in Impressionist Painting* (New York: Cambridge University Press, 2007), 184–224. On sculpture, see Melissa Dabakis, *Visualizing Labor in American Sculpture: Monuments, Manliness and the Work Ethic, 1880–1935* (Cambridge: Cambridge University Press, 1999), 62–82. On photography, see Julie Brown, *Contesting Images: Photography and the World's Columbian Exposition* (Tuscon: University of Arizona Press, 1994); Laura Wexler, *Tender Violence: Domestic Visions in an Age of U.S. Imperialism* (Chapel Hill: University of North Carolina Press, 2000), 262–90; and Deborah Willis and Carla Williams, "The Black Female Body in Photographs from World's Fairs and Expositions," in "Race, Photography, and American Culture," *exposure* 33, no. 1/2 (Daytona Beach: Society for Photographic Education, 2000). On performance, see Amy Taipale Canfield, "Discovering Woman: Women's Performances at the World's Columbian Exposition Chicago, 1893" (PhD diss., The Ohio State University, 2002).

16 See Gertrude M. Scott, "Village Performance: Villages of the Chicago World's Columbian Exposition of 1893" (PhD diss., New York University, 1990), 297–98; Annie Coombs, *Reinventing Africa* (New Haven: Yale University Press, 1994), 187–213; Charles A. Kennedy, "When Cairo Met Main Street: Little Egypt, Salome Dancers, and the World's Fairs of 1893 and 1904," in *Music and Culture in America, 1861–1918*, ed. Michael Saffle, 271–98 (New York: Garland, 1998); Bernth Lindfors, ed., *Africans on Stage: Studies in Ethnological Show Business* (Bloomington: Indiana University Press, 1999), noting especially Robert Rydell, "'Darkest Africa': African Shows at America's World's Fairs, 1893–1940," 135–55. The list of scholarly works tacking in these directions is rapidly expanding and includes Patricia O. Afable, "Journeys from Bontoc to the Western Fairs, 1904–1915: The 'Nikimalika' and their Interpreters," *Philippine Studies Quarterly* 52:4 (2004), 445–73; Cherubim Quizon, "Two Yankee Women at the St. Louis Fair: The Metcalf Sisters and Their Bagabo Sojourn in Mindanao," *Philippine Studies* 52, no. 4 (2004): 527–55; Adria Imada, "Aloha America: Hawaiian Entertainment and Cultural Politics in the U.S. Empire" (PhD diss., New York University, 2003); Nancy J. Parezo and Don D. Fowler, *Anthropology Goes to the Fair: The 1904 Louisiana Purchase Exposition* (Lincoln: University of Nebraska Press, 2007). See also works cited in notes 11–13 for additional important work focused on people racially deemed "other" on the midway zones of world's fairs.

17 Ganz, *1933 Chicago World's Fair*. See especially her chapter "Sally Rand and the Midway" for an excellent example of nuanced interpretation informed by class, race, and gender analysis as well as enlightening methodological attention to the visual register and Rand's performative strategies (7–27).

18 For examples of German-language scholarship, see Gunda Barth-Scalmani and Margret Friedrich, "*Frauen auf der Wiener Weltausstellung von 1873: Blick auf die Bühne und hinter die Kulissen*" [Women at the Vienna World Exhibition of 1873: View of the Stage and behind the Scenes], in *Bürgerliche Frauenkultur im 19. Jahrhundert*, ed. Brigitte Mazohl-Wallnig, 175–232 (Vienna: Böhlau, 1995); Manuela von Miller, "Philadelphia 1876–Chicago 1893–Paris 1900: Amazonen der Kunst; Frauen erobern die Weltausstellungen" [Philadelphia 1876–Chicago 1893–Paris 1900: The Amazons of Art: Women Conquer World Exhibitions] (PhD diss., *Universität Salzburg*, 1998); Marjan Groot, *Vrouwen in de vormgeving, 1880–1940* [Women in Design in the Netherlands, 1880–1940] (Rotterdam: 010 Publishers, 2007). Comprehensive bibliographies representing mul-

tiple national traditions of world's fair scholarship are available online: see Alexander C. T. Geppert, Jean Coffey, and Tammy Lau, "International Exhibitions, Expositions Universelles, and World's Fairs, 1851–1951: A Bibliography," available at http://www.tu-cottbus.de/theoriederarchitektur/wolke/eng/Bibliography/ExpoBibliography.htm (accessed January 12, 2010).

19 For a cross-national perspective, see Paul Greenhalgh, *Ephemeral Vistas: The Expositions Universelles, Great Exhibitions, and World's Fairs, 1851–1939* (Manchester: Manchester University Press, 1988), 174–97. A more recent strong example of comparative work on international expositions is Peter H. Hoffenberg's *An Empire on Display: English, Indian, and Australian Exhibitions from the Crystal Palace to the Great War* (Berkeley: University of California Press, 2001), 215–18. And, in this volume, see chap. 10, "Woman's Buildings at European and American Fairs, 1895–1939," by Mary Pepchinski.

TJ BOISSEAU AND ABIGAIL M. MARKWYN

PART I
Woman, Gender, and Nation

"By arriving next to her, my dear reader, you will see that Rozinha is a sphinx-like soul, she gives you a sideward glance, smiling, always smiling, but she does not offer anything else to your curiosity but white teeth, bright eyes, and such undulations that make you think that if Africa is like that, lovely will be the life in the bush."
—ELÍSIO GONÇALVES, CHRONICLER OF *O COMÉRCIO DO PORTO-COLONIAL*, 1934[1]

CHAPTER I

"Little Black Rose" at the 1934 *Exposição Colonial Portuguesa*

Isabel Morais

According to the recollections of dozens of visitors to the *Exposição Colonial Portuguesa* (First Portuguese Colonial Exhibition) held in the city of Oporto in 1934, nothing they encountered there equaled the impression made by a young Balanta woman who was called Rozinha, or "Little Rose."[2] As the epigraph to this chapter reveals, Rozinha was an enigmatic figure—one whose blank expressions inspired the white male fantasy of satisfying sexual engagement with readily available colonized black women. Unlike at other fairs, where half-naked women danced to great fanfare as well as considerable disapproval in the entertainment zones, the display of Rozinha and the other Balanta women in Oporto in 1934 was not a byproduct of commercial interests relegated to the geographical outskirts or ideological margins.[3] Rozinha was specifically promoted by organizers and state officials to catch the attention and spark the imagination of Portuguese men, with the goal of motivating them to support or even embark themselves on colonialist ventures in the outlying areas of the Portuguese empire. To large effect, their strategy succeeded. Rozinha not only attracted great notice among the general Portuguese public "eager to see the blacks," she also came to represent a touchstone for Portuguese intellectuals, pundits, and members of the high bourgeoisie who considered this iconic African woman's "true type of beauty" uniquely able to invoke the past greatness of the Portuguese empire and to extend that greatness into the future.[4] The high profile of Rozinha and the other two dozen or so Balanta women displayed at the *Exposição* more than challenged old canons in a country that had long rendered black African women invisible or associated them with mere servitude. As declared in the caption of a popular postcard sold at the fair, featuring on its front a photo of Rozinha, naked, and looking directly at the camera with arms raised and breasts prominently displayed, Rozinha ensured and literally embodied "O Sucesso da Exposição de 1934" ("the Success of the 1934 *Exposição*").

Fig. 1.1. Rozinha, the Success of the Exhibition. Souvenir postcard. Photo by Domingos Alvão, Porto, 1934, Arquivo de Fotografia do Porto—CPF/MC, nº AL013103.

Fig. 1.2. Colonial Exhibition. Commemorative stamp edition. Author's private collection.

This sentiment was widely shared. By the end of the *Exposição,* many credited Rozinha with the fair's financial and cultural success. Even the official stamp issued at the fair featured a stylized image of Rozinha.

The celebration of Balanta beauty in Oporto in 1934 seemed the clearest enunciation of the new spirit of optimism regarding the future of Portugal and its colonies under the *Estado Novo,* or the "New State" of Prime Minister António Salazar. The official commissioner of the 1934 *Exposição* in a commentary on the exhibition attendees stated, "Some say: 'Let's see the Blacks!' [B]ut those who had just come to see the Blacks . . . had seen something else, and had felt a healthy, intimate pride . . . because they were not inhabitants of a small country."[5] Among all the many attractions during the four months of summer that the *Exposição* remained open, Rozinha—deemed the most ideal representative of the Balanta women from Guinea as well as the single greatest symbol of a newly miscegenated empire-republic imagined by Salazar—reigned supreme.

This chapter explores the complex ways that gender, sexuality, and empire came together in the summer of 1934 in Oporto, in the form of a world's fair. The promotion of Rozinha in 1934 presaged the emergence and championing in the next decade of *Lusotropicalism*—a racialized understanding of empire promoted by Salazar and other influential Portuguese figures that hinged on the celebration of black women as uniquely desirable sexual partners for Portuguese men. Lusotropicalism advocated miscegenation between Portuguese men and colonized black women as a way to solidify and enhance the Portuguese empire throughout the world and especially in Africa. It was at the 1934 *Exposição* that African women were first introduced to a mass Portuguese public, presented as the women best able to inspire and realize both Portuguese men's sexual desire and Portuguese imperial ambitions. Any analysis that seeks to capture the political significance of this fair as a tool of propaganda deftly wielded by Salazar must necessarily focus on the gendered, even overtly sexual meanings purposefully and with determination produced by the *Exposição*'s organizers and achieved with the "cooperation" of Balanta women imported from Africa.

The 1934 *Exposição:* Celebrating Salazar's Colonial Vision

The 1934 *Exposição* was the first colonial exposition and also the largest exposition ever held in Portugal.[6] It inaugurated a series of large-scale public events culminating in the grandiose *Exposição do Mundo Português* (Portuguese World's Exposition) held in Lisbon in 1940. These two fairs, along with an intense public relations effort made by Salazar during the same decade, represented Salazar's determination to enhance Portugal's international reputation as a world power and to reshape Portuguese public opinion in ways that would allow him to pursue his colonial ambitions, particularly in Africa. Prior to Salazar's reign, and apart from a small contribution to an early exhibition held in Paris in 1855, Portugal had displayed little interest and expended minimal efforts to participate in international expositions, compared with the United States or other European nations such as France and Great Britain. Under Salazar, and in light of his *Estado Novo,* world's fairs seemed suddenly far more relevant to the national agenda.

The interwar period was crucial for Portugal and for Salazar's consolidation of his political power over the country. After coming to power in 1933, following the 1926 right-wing military coup and the fall of the first democratic republic in Portugal, Salazar's military dictatorship (supported by a bourgeoisie with commercial investments and interests in Angola) remained unchecked for much of the next three decades and paved the way for the authoritarian state, *Estado Novo* (1933–74). Salazar imposed strict controls over the country's social, cultural, and economic life and made wide use of mass media to spread his nationalist propaganda. The pompous 1934 *Exposição* was part of a large-scale ideological program of propaganda promoting Portuguese colonialism and leading directly to the development of ethnographic museums, popular art, architecture, and films. Salazar's *Estado Novo* aimed at nothing less than a revising of the map in ways meant to enhance Portugal's influence and outweigh its seemingly small size. For instance, the *Carta do Império Colonial e de Portugal* (Map of the Colonial Empire and Portugal) exhibited at the 1934 fair intended to show an indivisible empire twenty-two times the size of metropolitan Portugal, stretching "from Minho to Timor."[7] The map showed Mozambique superimposed over part of France and Spain; Angola superimposed over the Third Reich and part of the central and Eastern Europe. The map makes clear Salazar's intention for Portugal to reclaim its place as a great European power on the basis of its imperial domain. Key to the promotion of Salazar's *Estado Novo* was his cultural program, and prominent in this program were expositions—particularly the 1934 *Exposição*—where a great mass of illiterate Portuguese were presented with a picture of national cohesion by way of a demonstration of the glory of the Portuguese Colonial Empire.[8]

The 1934 *Exposição* was officially opened on August 16, 1934, by the President of the Republic, General Oscar Carmona. Salazar followed the project closely. He not only visited the construction work in progress, but he attended it incognito, posing as a typical visitor. At the fair in Oporto, national authorities and local elites helped the masses to envisage a restoration of national pride.[9] Brazil's successful bid for independence in 1822 and the humiliating British Ultimatum of 1890, which forced Portugal to withdraw from the "rose" regions of Africa (the area from Angola to Mozambique typically outlined in pink on maps of Africa), continued to prick at Portuguese chauvinistic pride even in the

1930s. The exposition held in Oporto was meant to trigger a national determination to recover Portugal's full glory as a colonial power.

As early as 1930, the city's wealthy bourgeois industrialist and businessmen established the so-called *Grupo Pró-Colónias* (Pro-Colonies Group), the purpose of which was to amass sufficient funds to underwrite the fair.[10] The organization emulated forms of entertainment and facilities that had proved successful in other international expositions, in particular with a coterminous fair held in the United States, the 1933–34 Chicago Centennial Exhibition—specifically in terms of showcasing modern technology, ethnic villages, and exotic female attractions. The official commissioner of the 1934 *Exposição*, Henrique Galvão, had prior world's fair experience, having served as director of Colonial Exhibitions and Fairs for Portugal at the International Colonial Exhibition held in Paris in 1931.[11] Galvão and other organizers chose the *Palácio de Cristal* (Crystal Palace)—a replica of London's Crystal Palace and the centerpiece of arguably the first world's fair held in 1851, to which Portugal contributed a notable exhibit—to host the event due to its location, availability of an exhibition hall associated with international exhibitions, wide space, and gardens.[12]

Between 1931 and 1934, architects, designers, and engineers aimed to transform the architecture, public spaces, and gardens of the *Palácio de Cristal* into a realistic venue for educational exhibits portraying the grandeur of the Portuguese Empire and great moments in its colonial past. The architectural style, the decoration, and the white colors of the buildings asserted the influence of Modernism in this moment. Several pavilions asserted Portugal's mission in the realms of military, evangelization, education, and corporation. The "Official Section" presented the "History and the Work of Portuguese Colonization"—a historical perspective of Portuguese colonial ventures of the previous forty years. The Military Room displayed information about the Portuguese military campaigns in every colony as well as conquest memorabilia, while the Hunting Pavilion was devoted to showcasing taxidermic animals from Africa. The Ethnographic Museum displayed a vast collection of various sorts of crafts from every colony. Housed in a chapel, an Iconographic Museum celebrated the educational work of the Catholic missions. Dioramas in wood portrayed missionary nuns from different congregations helping female natives in domestic activities (such as sewing, cooking, and raising poultry). These representations of devout domesticity and labor of young native women demonstrated the merits of the evangelization work of the Roman Catholic missions, work that that led to their successful conversion and presumably to their cultural assimilation as well. Modern commercial entertainment and facilities for visitors included the aerial cable, which crossed above the lake to transport the public from the exterior to the interior of the *Exposição*, the switchback railway for the internal circuit of the precincts of the fair, the fountain waterworks, an amusement park with a

Ferris wheel, a "Wall of Death" (where two performers drove motorcycles), a flea circus, the official cinema and theater, restaurants, a library of informative books about Portugal's colonies, a colonial historic archive, a post office, and a health center to provide assistance to the natives who were brought for the exhibition. In sum, the fair focused visitors' attention on the elaborate and long-established services and institutions Portugal had set up in its colonial possessions. The overall impression fairgoers were meant to take away was the effectiveness of Portugal's "civilizing mission" in the colonies and the enormous benefits that the colonized peoples reaped, thanks to Portuguese colonial administration.

The *Exposição,* like other contemporary world's fairs, displayed 324 "natives," including men, women, and children brought from every Portuguese colony, all of whom became, as the journalist Hugo Rocha noted, "the greatest attraction, the popular attraction par excellence."[13] In 1933, the year prior to the opening of the fair, Portuguese Minister of the Colonies Armindo Monteiro addressed a letter to the governors of every colony asking them to send "typical indigenous families" to Oporto to be displayed at the *Exposição* in "an environment as close as possible to [their] natural environment."[14] In this letter, Monteiro also spelled out the purposes of the fair, explaining that it should display the "great possibilities and accomplishments of the empire" and be "didactic" in order to "constitute a lesson of colonialism for the Portuguese people"[15] The people sent from Portugal's colonies were on constant display, day and night, housed in prefabricated villages in a specialized precinct on the fairgrounds. The *Exposição* goers could admire naturalistic settings such as rainforests, the desert, the bush, a zoo with wild animals, and many other lifestyle simulations, including the natives' traditional *batuques* (dances performed to the rhythm of African drums), craftsmanship, and military parades of the colonial army. There were also "oriental" streets echoing the streets of India and China, as well as replicas of the *Arco dos Vice-Reis* (Arch of Viceroys), the *Guia Lighthouse* and *Camoes's Grotto* (replicas of those found in then Portuguese-controlled Goa in India and Macau in China). Indigenous villages, the so-called *Casa do Colono* (Colonizer's House), and a typical Portuguese colonial farm surrounded the main white building, the *Palácio das Colónias* (Palace of Colonies).

The *Palácio* exhibited sleek and linear modernist design principles yet was capped by a huge elephant that symbolized the power and might of colonial possessions in Africa. The exhibits inside were meant to reinforce the grandeur of Portugal, past, present, and future, and paid homage to Oporto's economic and social progress and its business and industrial elite.

The *Exposição* was so popular among lower and working classes that, according to Juliano Ribeiro, summer Sundays became known as *Os Domingos na Exposição* (Sundays at the Exposition). As the one day off work for men and women

Fig. 1.3 Palace of the Colonies. Souvenir postcard. Photo
by Domingos Alvão, Porto, 1934, Arquivo de Fotografia do
Porto—CPF/MC, n° AL04789 .

who worked in factories and for farming people from the countryside, Sunday
was the day that the fairgrounds swelled with their numbers.[16] As they could not
afford the expensive restaurants of Oporto, these folks often brought their own
food and made picnics in the gardens of the *Exposição*.[17] Cheap tickets aimed
at all pockets were made available by way of private initiatives and government-
supported associations. Students, scouts groups, and regional folklore groups
among many other associations were offered tours that included a combination
of reduced train fares and cheap entrance fees. With such incentives, the poor,
middle, and affluent classes from every corner of the country departed from their
homes to make a visit to the *Exposição* that summer. Not only national visitors
but also visitors from neighboring Spain, as well as foreign personalities such
as the Prince of Wales and the ministers of Spain and Belgium, were drawn to
Oporto that summer, finding resonance with its colonialist themes, best epito-
mized by the ethnic villages so central to its colonial message.

Among the representations of ethnic groups on display were thirty-two pyg-
mies from the Makankala tribe of Angola; it was the first time such people were
displayed at a European exposition. The representation from Guinea included
sixty-three Africans of different ethnic groups (Balantas, Bigajós, Mandigas,
and Fulas) and some tribal chiefs who had become allies of the Portuguese by
suppressing revolts among other tribes. There was also a village on view, representing the Archipelago of Bigajós from the West African colony of Guinea-
Bissau. This village was placed on an island in the middle of a manmade lake
where at night a fountain, imported from Germany especially for this event,
offered a colored-light show, further enticing fairgoers to look in its direction.[18]

The so-called process of *pacificação* (pacification) in 1915 of Guinea-Bissau's peoples lasted longer than in the other colonies.[19] However, it seems that fair organizers were determined to turn even Portugal's least successful colonial ventures into causes for celebration of national prowess. Determined to relocate Portugal at the center of the great powers of Europe through an emphasis on empire, Salazar and the organizers of the 1934 *Exposição* put colonized people at the center of fairgoers' experience.

Lusotropicalism, or the New Portuguese Colonial Imaginary under Salazar

The display of colonized people at the 1934 *Exposição* was the most tangible manifestation of a colonial ideology—which would become known as Lusotropicalism—underlying Salazar's visions for Portugal in this period. While the ideas of such would be most famously disseminated at fairs like the *Exposição*, the tenets of this philosophical outlook were developed within the official academic and executive institutions of the state.

In 1933, a young Portuguese academic, António Ferro, gained national prominence as director of the *Secretariado de Propaganda Nacional* (SPN), the national propaganda secretariat of the *New State* created in the same year.[20] Ferro, together with other Portuguese intellectuals and political elites, had affinities with Portuguese modernists and their counterparts in the rest of Europe as well as in Brazil. They shared a fascination with ethnic forms of African-inspired art that exploded onto the art scenes of world's fairs and also the discursive field among the modernists in Europe in the 1930s and 1940s. Ferro's agency, modeled on Hitler's and Mussolini's cultural fascist propaganda, developed the so-called *política do espírito* (politics of spirit), associating a popular cultural policy to nationalism through the control of cultural events, cinema, theater, press, radio, and censorship until 1950. Ferro and Galvão incarnated an idealized example of a modern Portuguese-African "hero," equally versatile in a European as well as in an African milieu, the sort of characters portrayed in Galvão's emblematic novels regarded as the epitome of Portuguese colonial literature.[21]

In the 1930s, the flamboyant Galvão, after his return from the African colony of Angola, where he served as governor of Huila in 1919, submitted an official report to the government wherein he devised an efficient public administration in the African colonies through economic cooperation between the metropolis's economic interests and Angola. His political strategy aimed to create a new Brazil in Angola through a massive colonization by Portugal due to the scarcity of whites. At the *Exposição* in Oporto in 1934, Galvão launched his work *No Rumo do Império* (*On the Footsteps of the Empire*) inspired by his earlier report, where he claimed that "the Portuguese were the first colonizers in the modern world and the only ones that always placed their human and spiritual interests above their commercial ones."[22] By emphasizing Portugal's exceptionable colonization, Galvão seems to echo Gilberto Freyre's *Lusotropicalism* well before it was officially adopted by the regime, reminding and attempting to persuade his readers that there was, in fact, already a sort of *proto-lusotropicalist* sensibility in Portugal dating back to the eighteenth century.[23]

The 1934 *Exposição* served the *Estado Novo*'s purpose of stimulating the commitment of future colonizers to Africa. The idea of the resurgence of a Portuguese empire was taking shape during the interwar period, when totalitarian regimes were extending their influence: Adolph Hitler and Benito Mussolini had already assumed power in Germany and Italy, respectively, while Spain teetered on the edge of civil war between the Republicans and the Fascists. Portugal's rivalry with these European nations held distinct consequences for its colonial agenda, particularly as its participation in the First World War had been aimed at the defense of Angola against German attacks. Thus, Portugal felt this was a crucial and opportune moment to reaffirm its role as an Old Empire able to take its place among other imperial nations. Rather than likening Portugal to its rivals in terms of racial and colonialist strategies, under Salazar's influence Portugal attempted to carve out a unique niche within the European empires by distinguishing itself in these same terms.

The 1934 *Exposição* was the regime's first grandiose exhibition and gave the colonial elites their first opportunity to find a new direction for the empire using intellectual and propaganda productions to consolidate the Portuguese presence in the colonies under Portuguese rule. It also served as a way to reeducate the public at both elite and non-elite levels. They aimed to reassert the concept of the exceptionalism of Portuguese colonization—the Portuguese people's ability to both colonize and to enjoy privileged interethnic relations with the colonized, which, allied to issues related to miscegenation, started to gain appeal at the *Exposição*. Admittedly, despite all sorts of intellectual and cultural antecedents cited by proponents of colonial miscegenation (as if it were a constituent element of the history of Portuguese colonialism), the *Exposição*'s new prescriptive emphasis on miscegenation and wholesale celebration of it also met with some opposition from those who feared the undermining of a social order otherwise organized around the tenets of white supremacy.

Supporters of "white supremacist" theories, particularly those infused with eugenic perspectives on the races as best kept distinct and unamalgamated, saw the fair as an occasion demanding a response, and they staged their own event near the end of summer. As the *Exposição* drew to a close on September 30, the *Primeiro Congresso de Antropologia Colonial Nacional* (First Congress of National Colonial Anthropology) was held at the *Palácio das Colónias* from September

22 to 26, with the participation of "colonial agents" (scholars, military leaders, colonial officials, and religious figures). Mendes Correia, head of the Institute of Anthropology and Ethnology in Oporto and chair of the Executive Commission of the Congress, together with Eusébio Tamagnini, who created the *Sociedade Portuguesa de Eugenia* (Portuguese Society of Eugenics) in Coimbra in 1934, opposed the celebration of miscegenation at the *Exposição*.[24] As had happened in the 1870 world's fair in Paris, when members of the French Anthropological Society used natives brought from French colonies for their research, Correia coordinated a research team to conduct anthropometric studies and perform aptitude tests on the natives displayed at the 1934 *Exposição*.[25] The ethnographic findings obtained contributed to Mendes Correia's work aiming to establish an index of racial "efficiency"—one that "proved" miscegenation between the "white" Portuguese and black colonized peoples would weaken the nation.[26] Wholly denying the importance or even presence of miscegenation already existing in Portugal, both Correia and Tamagini conceded that miscegenation was "inevitable" in the colonies, but they presaged that this would produce a "*quebra da continuidade histórica*" (a break in the historical continuity) of the Portuguese people, and its consequences would be "disastrous."[27] Despite these authoritative voices of dissent, however, Salazar's support for the pro-miscegenation scientists swung the emphasis of the *Exposição* in that direction, and miscegenation would continue to comprise a constant focus of Portuguese anthropology in the following decades. Several factors, such as the abstruse language and technical nature of the eugenicists' exhibits and speeches as well as the timing of the conference—held as it was in the last week of the *Exposição*—relegated the eugenicists to the margins of the fair and confined the debate they hoped to spark to narrow official, scientific, and religious audiences.

The *Exposição* served as a doorway opening onto a colonial vision of an empire where Africa appeared as an idealized place for harmonious racial coexistence and, ultimately, miscegenation. Once a place perceived solely as a destination for banished criminals, exiled convicts, and political opponents, in the first quarter of the twentieth century—and indeed from the time of the 1934 *Exposição* onward—Africa emerged as a desirable, even irresistible, land of opportunity for economic, social, and sexual gain—an Edenic "new Brazil." The ideas about race that permeated the fair generated material changes. In the late 1940s and 1950s the Portuguese government embarked on a project of promoting white immigration and the creation of Portuguese *colonatos* (colonates) in two great colonial territories Angola and Mozambique. The *Exposição* occurred at a moment of "crystallized" debate on miscegenation and by doing so legitimated an entire area of research. By contributing to setting the debate in motion, the event gave rise to later articulations with repercussions for later policies.

For the first time, ordinary Portuguese men were offered an opportunity to look beyond their country's narrow borders, to participate actively in the winning of the empire and the subjugation/assimilation of other races. They were encouraged especially to encounter black women firsthand and to see these women as attractive and appropriate sexual mates. No single event of the fair was more effective in achieving this goal than the celebratory display of Balanta women. The public memorializing of the beauty of Balanta women helped broaden the appeal of *Lusotropicalism* beyond the literate classes of Portugal to include non-elites within its purview. Indeed, eroticism wielded as a Foucauldian "instrument of power" was being deliberately created around the Portuguese colonies, making them a more desirable place for prospective settlers.[28] The display of eroticism and fetishization of black women at the *Exposição* successfully displaced dominant scientific discourse regarding the superiority of the white race and its need to remain pure. As Gilberto Freyre explained, this subversion of an ideology rampant throughout Europe and North America could be only understood by pointing to the exceptionalism of the Portuguese process of colonization, which had created a uniquely harmonious empire by embracing and making good use of "the love of a man for a coloured woman and for a hot country."[29] The public excitement spurred by the presence of the natives, mainly the high profile and well-received representations of Balanta women at the *Exposição,* gave shape to this type of thinking and fueled popular receptiveness to miscegenation in Portugal in this period.

Gendered Visions of Empire: The Balanta Beauties

Despite a few weak voices condemning miscegenation at the conference held near the end of the *Exposição,* the fair overwhelmingly celebrated miscegenation as the unique contribution of the Portuguese nation to the world and the project of empire. To make this point, black women brought from Africa were the singular emblematic attraction of the fair. Their sexualization became the fair's most potent lure to bring in the crowds and formed an embodied pedagogy promoting eroticized understandings of empire. As indicated at the outset of this chapter, one African woman, "Rozinha," was chosen to provide a focal point for all the erotic yearnings of Portuguese men for the return of imperial grandeur as well as sexual dominance over black women's bodies. It was Rozinha's body more than any other onto which this dual fantasy was projected.

Rozinha was given the title of "Black Venus"—a term associated with black female nudes dating back to the 1781 anonymous poem "The Sable Venus: An Ode" or to Saartjie, or Sarah Baartman, from one of South Africa's ethnic groups

Fig. 1.4. Rozinha, the Black Venus.
Souvenir postcard. Photo by Domingos
Alvão, Porto, 1934, Arquivo de Fotografia
do Porto—CPF/MC, n° AL02399.

(Khoi or San) who was exhibited between 1810 and 1815 in London and Paris as the famous "Hottentot Venus."[30]

Many black women became popularized at world's fairs, such as at the 1889 World's Fair in Paris, where Senegalese native women were displayed, and at the 1893 World's Columbian Exposition in Chicago, where eight bare-breasted Dahomey women and girls were shown. However, unlike these earlier exhibits of black womanhood, at the *Exposição* the representations of the female flesh of African women, while not totally devoid of stereotypes, were associated with images of beauty and eroticism and supplanted the more negative images of black womanhood prevailing in the colonial memory, thus opening the door to a discourse generating assimilation policies.

The presentation of Rozinha and her female compatriots differed from the presentation of Balantan and other African men at the *Exposição*. Unlike their male companions who preserved their native or Islamic names, Rozinha and her other female companions were given Christian-sounding names—like "Inês" and "Isabel"—implying that they had probably been baptized into the Church, and thus were marriageable. Domingos Alvão, one of Oporto's well-known professional photographers who had already received awards at the International Fair of Leipzig in 1914, was the official photographer at the *Exposição*. His photos, like the overwhelming majority of the published photographs of the *Exposição*, illustrate the idyllic life of the native people on display, in particular that of Rozinha, and were published in an album with a preface by Galvão.[31] This iconography consists of beautiful, postcard-like photographs ranging from individuals to groups of Africans and Asians, as part of the Portuguese Colonial display at the exposition. Rozinha was persistently captured on film at the *Exposição,* and what distinguishes her photographs from others depicting Africans is the constant inclusion of a caption with her name. The fact that in so many of the photographs only one person is named, with the adoption of a Portuguese name, exemplifies one of the criteria for the assimilation.

Although Rozinha, as we have seen, was imagined to be the "success of the exhibition," the discourse on Rozinha was a discourse on a woman who did not have a voice of her own. No visible efforts were made to interview her through translators, as was the case with her male companions. What she had to say was irrelevant: she was there to "appear," not to be heard. Rozinha was essentially "mute" and never verbally interacted with the "her" public, which in a certain way contributed to her aura of mystery and exerted great attraction over white males. As far as we know, Rozinha did not take any initiative of her own; perhaps she was not even completely aware of the impact of her presence. Unlike the two most talked-about female performers appearing at Chicago's two prominent world's fairs (Sally Rand who wowed audiences with her nearly nude feather dance in 1933–34, and "Little Egypt," or Farheda Mazar, whose 1893 veiled belly dance would be recreated at every subsequent major U.S. world's fair through the first half of the twentieth century), both of whom gave interviews and purposely sought fame for themselves, Rozinha remained always voiceless and was presumed to harbor no such personal ambition. Details about her identity, like those of other Balanta women, were completely silenced. Even her participation in the "live shows," where the African group dancers performed, is hardly described except in general terms. Based on these reports and photographic evidence, it remains unclear whether the entirety of Rozinha's performance amounted to anything more than holding still and smiling while posing for photographers and the admiring visitors to the fair.

Unlike Sally Rand's, Farheda Mazar's, and other exoticized and eroticized performances of feminine sexuality at world's fairs, Rozinha's allure was not the result of her appearing to "perform" at all. Instead, her stillness and voicelessness created an awe-inspiring aura around her and contributed to a sort of idolatry, a mélange of sexuality and platonic admiration, that lasted throughout the exhibition and inspired highbrow odes to be written in her honor as well as politicized cartoons lampooning her mesmerizing effect on fairgoers. Elísio Gonçalves, the chronicler of *O Comércio do Porto* described the general admiration of the public: "Hundreds, thousands of people pass by the village where she lives . . . and stand there half an hour, an hour, who knows! Just waiting that Rozinha will show up and confirm that the admiration that they have for her is welcomed and understood."[32] And while extensive press coverage, publicity, and recollections popularized Rozinha as overtly sexual, she was also perceived as an image of patriotism and veneration. Rozinha and other Balanta representations clearly demonstrate how eroticism was being deliberately associated with

Portuguese African colonies, making them more desirable places for prospective colonizers. One of the most emblematic photos shows a bare breasted Balanta woman holding Portugal's national flag under the protection of white colonizer woman and man figures represented at the *Monumento ao Esforço Colonizador* (Monument to the Colonizer's Effort) erected at the entrance of the *Exposição*. The caption is elucidative. It reads, in Portuguese: "A Guinea's svelte and gentle woman in a tableau of patriotic exaltation." The Balanta woman's photo speaks volumes as a metaphor about Africa, where a desirable black woman assumes a symbolic dimension as sexual partner and possible mother to a miscegenated nation. Her representation may well be seen as a dominion metaphor over colonized women and the African territories.

Rozinha's image was reproduced in many ways—sold as individual photographs or as postcards for dissemination beyond the fair. A series of somewhat soft-core pornographic images of a naked Rozinha and other Balanta women was made for the exposition and accommodated the "colonial desire" of a male public eager to get souvenirs. In many of the photographs representing moments of daily life at the village, there is an obvious eroticization of Rozinha, who seems to have clearly been instructed to pose in particular ways. The photographer composed his images of Rozinha in a style immediately reminiscent of famous American pin-ups' erotic poses. The young, bare-breasted woman is shown with both arms raised and hands holding her head at the center of the image with her face looking directly at the male's colonial gaze, as an indication of her sexual availability. As at the 1889 World's Fair in Paris, where the Senegalese native women were forced to display their nudity inside the fairground but got dressed outside it, Rozinha, during the *Exposição*, also wore a "civilized" dress when she was awarded the title of Queen of the 1931 *Exposição*. One of the best-known department stores in Oporto, *Armazéns Cunhas*, "dressed" the Queen and used her as advertisement on a souvenir postcard with the name of the department store. The commercialization of Rozinha's body and image—her assimilation into the colonial order of the Portuguese empire-nation—would continue throughout the exhibition and outlive it in the material form of these postcards, advertisements, and photographs.

These mass-produced images of the Balanta women, and in particular those of Rozinha, endured in the national collective memory. Most people in Oporto still remember the event through the oral history of the city, and the images preserved by postcards and photos continue to be reproduced in new editions on the exhibition and are even featured on internet blogs.[33] The author of *Porto 1934—A Grande Exposição de Azevedo*, published in 2000, did not hesitate to call Rozinha the "sorceress" who broke the hearts of half of Oporto's men seven decades ago, while Paulo Valada, the author of the preface, still recalls the excess of emotion he experienced when he visited the exposition as a child and his mother sent him to kiss Rozinha.[34]

For many visitors who attended the event, Rozinha and the Balanta women embodied a new spirit of optimism regarding the future of Portugal and its colonies under the *Estado Novo*. The presence of the Balanta women provocatively challenged old canons as they reincarnated and refashioned the eroticized female object. The enthusiasm with which they were received anticipated an emergent tolerance for interracial sex and partnering and helped prepare the ground for more widespread acceptance of *Lusotropicalism* in Portugal.

Conclusion

On September 9, 1934, after four successful months, the *Exposição* ended in a spectacular parade. The *Cortejo Colonial* (Colonial Parade) was meant to symbolize the *Exposição*'s theme of the greatness of the Portuguese empire and the unique ability of the Portuguese to integrate with different peoples to create multiracial societies.[35] The parade exhibited *tableaux vivants* of the history of Portugal. It was composed of cars emblazoned with allegorical illustrations representing the historical periods of Portuguese conquests and "discoveries," the most famous navigators of the colonies of Brazil and Africa, and former soldiers of the colonial army. Colonial subject peoples were portrayed according to socioeconomic and racial hierarchy. Their mode of dress depended on their degree of "assimilation" to the dominant culture. Guinea's allegorical bright yellow car, for example, showed the *Régulo* (local ruler) of Guinea seated on a throne, and at his feet were Rozinha and Isabel wearing crowns. With such displays, the organizers of the 1934 *Exposição* identified and corresponded to an impoverished population's wish to improve their living conditions by luring them to be future colonizers, exploiting the opportunities waiting for them across the oceans in distant lands. They were able to instill national pride, confidence, and a sense of adventure under the guidance of a paternalistic regime. They wrapped national ideology and sensuality with the most modern technology, architecture, art, and advertising.

The *Exposição*'s organizers and intellectuals appropriated the Balanta women, most effectively Rozinha, to transmit specific messages to attract the visitors to lands bursting with promise. She represented the land that the Portuguese must fully possess to better dominate. Metropolitan Portugal contributed to a better knowledge and awareness that could arouse the curiosity of the population and ultimately would stimulate the commitment of future colonizers to Africa. With such strategies, they set the agenda and strategies for the colonies to continue to become places of sexual indulgence, but in ways that did not pose a threat to colonial rule. The 1934 *Exposição* amplified the erotic politics of the exotic and paved the way to a more general acceptance of the discourse on miscegenation. Above all, notwithstanding the obvious objectification of the black female body, the representation of the Balanta woman Rozinha, and the emphasis on interracial eroticism, the 1934 *Exposição* created the first iconic images of black women introduced to Portugal, which contributed to removing them from obscurity and elevating them to be associated with sexual desire and the imperial ambition of a nation.

NOTES

1 "Chegando ao pé dela, leitor, verá que a Rozinha é uma alma esfíngica, que te olha de soslaio, sorrindo, sorrindo sempre, mas não oferecendo mais à tua curiosidade que dentes brancos, uns olhos vivos, e uns requebros que te levam a pensar que se a África é assim, adorável será a vida do sertão." Quoted by Ercílio Azevedo, *Porto 1934—A Grande Exposição* (Edição do Autor, 2003), 147. This and all other translations of Portuguese into English that follow are the author's.

2 Ibid.

3 Rozinha's popularity evokes two most talked-about attractions of the Chicago World's Fair, which took place in 1933 and again in 1934, Sally Rand's feather dance and Farheda Mazar (or "Little Egypt"), the belly dancer at the 1893 World's Columban Exhibition, held in Chicago. Chery Ganz, *The 1933 Chicago World's Fair: A Century of Progress* (University of Illinois Press, 2008), 7–27; Charles A. Kennedy, "When Cairo Met Main Street: Little Egypt, Salome Dancers, and the World's Fairs of 1893 and 1904," in *Music and Culture in America 1861–1918,* ed. Michael Saffle, 271–98 (New York: Garland, 1998).

4 Azevedo, *Porto 1934,* 148.

5 Alguns diziam: "Vamos ver os Pretos! . . . mas aqueles que tinham vindo só para ver os Pretos . . . tinham visto mais alguma coisa . . . tinham sentido um orgulho íntimo e sadio . . . porque não eram habitants de um país pequeno." Ibid., 200.

6 Portugal was present in several successive international exhibitions: in Paris (1855, 1867, 1879, and 1931), London (1862 and 1921), Vienna (1873), Philadelphia (1876), San Francisco (1915), Rio de Janeiro (1922), Seville and Barcelona (1929), and Antwerp (1930).

7 Minho is in northwest Portugal, and Timor was the most distant Portuguese colony in the Asia-Pacific region.

8 The level of literacy in Portugal was 38 percent in the 1930s. António Candeias e Eduarda Simões, "Alfabetização e Escola em Portugal no Século XX: Censos nacionais e estudos de casos (Alphabetization and School in Portugal in the Twentieth Century: National Census and Case Studies), *Análise Psicológica* 1, no. 17 (1999): 157. Between the 1930s and 1940s, there were state-sponsored exhibitions and commemorations like the *Exposição do Mundo Português (Exhibition of the Portuguese World)* and *Comemoração do Duplo Centenário da Fundação da Nacionalidade e da Restauração (Commemoration of the Double Centenary of the Foundation of Nationality [1940] and the Restoration [1640]).*

9 After the Berlin Congress in 1884–85 and consequent partitioning of Africa among the colonial powers, Portugal's claim to the so-called *Mapa Cor-de-Rosa (Rose-Colored Map),* a vast territory stretching from Angola to Mozambique, culminated with the British "ultimatum" in 1890, which forced Portugal to withdraw from that region.

10 Azevedo, *Porto 1934,* 20.

11 In 1947, Galvão ultimately became one of Salazar's most vocal critics. Facing a prison sentence, he escaped to South America, where he joined other dissidents. In 1961, he hijacked an airplane in order to express opposition to Salazar, and in 1962 he also organized and took part in the hijacking of the Portuguese liner *Santa Maria* off the coast of South America with the objective of creating an opposition government in Angola. The plan failed and the hijackers accepted asylum in Brazil. He died in Brazil in 1970, the same year Salazar passed away in Lisbon. Henrique Galvão, *My Crusade for Portugal* (Cleveland: World Publishers, 1961).

12 Henrique Galvão, *Álbum Comemorativo da Primeira Exposição Colonial Portuguesa (Commemorative Album of the First Portuguese Colonial Exposition)* (Porto: Litografia Nacional, 1934), 7–9. In the 1950s, the *Palácio de Cristal* was torn down to make room for the Pavilion to hold the International Championship of Hockey. Yet today the gardens in the area are still known as *Palácio de Cristal*.

13 ". . . atracção maior, atracção popular por excelência." Hugo Rocha, *Ultramar, Orgão Oficial da Exposição Colonial,* no. 10 (1934): 2.

14 Translated. Quoted by Cláudia Castelo, "*O modo português de estar no Mundo—o luso-tropicalismo e a ideologia colonial portuguesa (1933–1961)*" (The Portuguese Way of Being in the World—Lusotropicalism and Portuguese Colonial Ideology) (Porto, Edições Afrontamento, 1999), 118.

15 Ibid.

16 Juliano Ribeiro, "Os Domingos na Exposição" (Sundays at the Exposition), in Azevedo, *Porto 1934,* 165.

17 Ibid., 166.

18 Ibid.

19 L. Amado, "A Literatura Colonial," *Revista ICALP* 20:5.

20 In 1944, the *Secretariado de Propaganda Nacional* (SPN) changed its designation to *Secretariado Nacional de Informação, Cultura Popular e Turismo* (SNI) (National Information, Popular Culture and Tourism Secretariat); Ferro was appointed as its head.

21 Henrique Galvão was awarded three Colonial Literature prizes in 1932, 1934, and 1936. These Portuguese, who had direct experience of work and control over the colonies, collectively represented what Benedict Anderson calls an "imaginary community." This community played an important role in the political culture of the regime. Benedict Anderson, *Imagined Communities: Reflections on the Spread of Nationalism* (London: Verso, 1983).

22 Henrique Galvão, *No Rumo do Império (On the Footsteps of the Empire)* (Porto, Palácio de Cristal: Litografia Nacional do Porto, 1934).

23 Cristiana Bastos, "Race, Medicine and the Late Portuguese Empire: The Role of Goan Colonial Physicians," *Institute of Germanic and Romance Studies* 5, no. 1 (2005): 25. Malyn Newitt, *Portugal in Africa: The Last Hundred Years* (London: Hurst, 1981), 184.

24 The Portuguese Society of Eugeny remained active until 1974. M. L. Areia and M. T. Rocha, "Ensino da antropologia," in *Cem Anos de Antropologia em Coimbra, 1885–1985 (One Hundred Years of Anthropology in Coimbra),* ed. M. L. Areia, 22 (Instituto de Antropologia, Coimbra: UC/IA, 1985).

25 William H. Schneider, *An Empire for the Masses: The French Popular Image of Africa, 1870–1900* (Westport, Conn.: Greenwood, 1982), 124–201. Correia's anthropological field observations were conducted on 305 adults and 19 children at the colonial exhibition and comprised 59 anthropometric measurements. António Mendes Correia, "Valor psico-social comparado das raças coloniais" (A Comparative Psychosocial Value of Colonial Races), in *Trabalhos do primeiro Congresso Nacional de Antropologia Colonial* (Porto: Setembro de 1934, Editora 1ff Exposição Colonial Portuguesa), 385–93.

26 Ibid.

27 Ibid., 1:62.

28 Michel Foucault, *The History of Sexuality*, Vol. 1, trans. Robert Hurley (New York: Random House, 1978).

29 Gilberto Freyre, *The Portuguese and the Tropics*, trans. Henel M. D'O. Matthew, and F. de Mello Moser (Executive Committee for the Commemoration of the Fifth Centenary of the Death of Prince Henry the Navigator, Lisbon, 1961), 46.

30 Janell Hobson, *Venus in the Dark: Blackness and Beauty in Popular Culture* (New York: Routledge, 2005).

31 *Álbum Fotográfico da 1ff Exposição Colonial Portuguesa-101 Clichés de Alvão—Porto, fotógrafo oficial da Exposição Colonial* (*Photographic Album of the First Portuguese Colonial Exposition*) (Porto: Litografia Nacional, s.d.).

32 ". . . Centenas, milhares de pessoas passam pela aldeia onde ela vive .ΛS.ΛS. e ficam ali paradas meia hora, uma hora—que sei eu! À espera que a Rozinha apareça e lhes dê testemunho de que a admiração que lhe votam é agradecida e compreendida." Quoted by Azevedo, *Porto 1934*, 147.

33 Brito Ribeiro "Uma Visita à Exposição Colonial Portuguesa" (A Visit to the Portuguese Colonial Exposition), *WebBlog Vila Praia de Âncora*, http://vilapraiadeancora.blogs.sapo.pt/28447.html (accessed May 12, 2008).

34 Paulo Valada, preface to Azevedo, *Porto 1934*, 8.

35 *Ultramar*, October 1, 1934.

CHAPTER 2

The New Soviet Woman at
the 1939 New York World's Fair

Alison Rowley

Despite the upsurge in feminist scholarship on world's fairs of late, Soviet contributions to international exhibitions in the twentieth century remain wholly unstudied apart from analyses of architecture that give little consideration to questions of gender or women's experiences.[1] Yet even the most cursory survey of the extant textual record documenting Soviet world's fair exhibits and displays can reveal a heavy and explicit emphasis placed by Soviet officials on the presentation of women's roles and Soviet gender relations. This chapter focuses on the contents of the fifty-five pamphlets distributed at the Soviet Pavilion during the first season of the 1939–1940 New York World's Fair. These pamphlets—distributed en masse at a fair that attracted tens of millions of visitors—conveyed some of the most important themes Soviet fair organizers wished to drive home to fairgoers. Among the most prominent was the role of women in an idealized Soviet society. Since, as one promotional publication released by American fair organizers put it, "Women's participation was a first thought in the planning of the New York World's Fair of 1939," exhibits showcasing the accomplishments of women and messages concerning the prescribed or future roles for women were meant to pervade the entire fair.[2] The Soviet government readily embraced this approach and considered the New York World's Fair a prime opportunity to showcase the "New Soviet Woman" to a largely American audience.

Souvenirs—material items that communicate and even embody the central themes of expositions—represent invaluable sources for historians seeking to understand the constructions of gender and national identity that underlay visitors' experiences of fairs. Pamphlets and other ephemeral items present the public face of a nation as particular regimes intend it to be viewed. In this case, Soviet officials viewed souvenir pamphlets as a prime way of engaging directly with an otherwise hard-to-reach American public. Given the central control of publishing in the USSR, the booklets distributed at the Soviet Pavilion should be considered official statements of Soviet ideology, and it was these texts that presented the "New Soviet Woman" to the American public in 1939.

The pamphlets represent another salvo in the long propaganda war of words the Soviets had been waging since the October Revolution of 1917. Official statements about the "New Soviet Woman" were meant to counter popular (mis) conceptions rife within the American media. The new Soviet government's quick passage of laws that made divorce easier to obtain, legalized abortion, and made marriage a civil affair sparked some wild exaggerations and rumors in the American press. In October 1918, for instance, an item in the *New York Times* reported that young women in some parts of Soviet Russia had to register at government-run "bureaus of free love."[3] The idea that the Bolsheviks had somehow "nationalized women" also spread rapidly, repeated as it was in speeches by U.S. politicians like Sen. Lawrence Sherman of Illinois in January 1919.[4] Even once these specific notions had been disproved, many mainstream and conservative American commentators continually repeated the idea that attempts to enshrine a principle of women's autonomy within Soviet law represented an attack on the institution of the family as they conceived of it.

The Soviet government defended its policies by going on the offensive. Implicit criticism about the way Western societies treated women permeated the Soviet exposition materials, in the process suggesting that Soviet socialism offered a more advanced as well as a more just socioeconomic system than Western capitalism. Consistently presenting American fairgoers with female role models who found self-fulfillment by putting work ahead of family, the Soviets implied that the American system deprived women of similar career opportunities and chances for personal happiness and, by doing so, retarded social and national progress. The benevolent role of the state, in contrast to a lack of social services provided by the U.S. government, was underscored whenever the pamphlets addressed the question of Soviet family life, especially in the areas of childcare provisions. Finally, Soviet superiority was further underlined in celebratory stories of minority women that portrayed the supposed elimination in the USSR of discrimination based on ethnicity—a clear dig at the racial divisions evident in American society.

Participation in the 1939 New York World's Fair offered the Soviet government an unprecedented opportunity to reach a much bigger and more diverse American audience. More than 25 million visitors came to the fair in its first season. The Soviets were the first foreign nation to sign up to participate, and Gallup polls conducted during the fair indicated that, by the close of that first summer, the pavilion they built had proved to be one of the most popular.[5] Visitors marveled at the main Soviet pavilion made of marble and granite, and they eagerly explored its two floors divided into seven themed sections, housing a restaurant, cinema, and a complete working replica of a Moscow metro station. In front of the main pavilion, the Soviets built a 259-foot red marble column that held a 79-foot statue of a worker holding a giant red star (visible from most of the fairgrounds). A second, smaller pavilion devoted to Soviet arctic exploration was built next to the main pavilion, and the Soviets also contributed an exhibit to the Hall of Nations. Soviet contributions to the fair were engineered not to be overlooked, nor the USSR's central messages aimed at the American public to be ignored.

To heighten the appeal of its pavilion and draw visitors in to see their exhibits, Soviet fair organizers recruited students, particularly young attractive female students, from Soviet universities and the Institute of Foreign Languages.[6] Greetings from smiling and well-spoken young women likely added impact to the emphasis on egalitarian relations between the sexes found within. In exhibitions such as those included in the Hall of Culture and Leisure, visitors to the Soviet pavilion could see, among other things, a bronze statue of a Soviet sportswoman and photographs of pregnant women receiving government-provided prenatal care. Other images, like the one found in the background in figure 1, showed smiling women holding their children. Smiling women, represented in the exhibits as well as guiding visitors through them, drove home a central theme of the Soviet pavilion that life was simply better under socialism.

No materials on offer by the Soviet government at the 1939 World's Fair, however, contained as much power to have a lasting impact on visitors as those that fairgoers took home with them. Souvenir pamphlets presented a unique opportunity for the Soviet government to convey explicit information and perspectives on life in the USSR, and fair organizers took good advantage of it, producing and distributing millions of these tangible reminders of what fairgoers experienced in the pavilion itself. And no message contained in these brochures was more central to the competition between the nations or more intriguing to an American public than the notion that Soviet women had advanced past American women in the race to achieve modern womanhood.

Fig. 2.1. Hall of Culture and Leisure in the Soviet Pavilion. Postcard. Author's collection.

Souvenirs at Work

More than eighty years after the first fair souvenirs were sold, the distribution of all kinds of items to fairgoers was an established practice at international expositions. Indeed, material items comprised an essential strategy aimed at ensuring that fairgoers would remember their experiences and share them with others. A successful souvenir campaign could, in no small part, determine which experiences would be generalized to lend meaning to the fair overall. Edward J. Orth, who visited the New York World's Fair as a twelve-year-old boy and who went on to become a major collector of fair memorabilia, exclaimed over the prodigious number of pamphlets and free written paraphernalia urged upon fairgoers at this exhibition. "The code word was 'booklets,'" he explained, "and whenever I visited an exhibit I would make it my business to ferret out some 'booklet' souvenir. A 'booklet' was a postcard, leaflet, book, folder, pamphlet, brochure, free sample, or whatever else was given to the exhibit visitor for free. Had no choice, folks; I had no money to spend on souvenirs or such."[7] These items drove Orth's lifelong passion for the 1939 event, as well as that of many others who continue to collect and trade these materials. Official written sources of information on particular booths, exhibits, and structures at the 1939 World's Fair presented the public face of the regimes that created them. The historical narratives, facts, figures, and photographs included were carefully and consciously pruned to paint an idealized portrait of each nation.

Visitors to the Soviet Pavilion at the New York World's Fair were encouraged to select among fifty-five different booklets at the pavilion bookstore as well as at two Soviet-sponsored booths located respectively in the Hall of Culture and the Hall of Nations.[8] The booklets were compact but replete with information and ideas. All were published by the main provider of Soviet materials to the rest of the world, Moscow's Foreign Languages Publishing House.[9] Since all aspects of publishing in the USSR were at that time under state control, the brochures were official statements of the Soviet government. Their authors were often leading experts in their fields, and some names, like that of film director Sergei Eisenstein, would have been recognizable to many American visitors. Idealizing Soviet life with pictures of gleaming new cities and happy citizens as well as masses of impressive-sounding statistics, these encyclopedic treatments offered an implicit comparison with what the Soviets assumed life in the United States was like. Whatever misunderstandings on which pavilion paraphernalia may have been based, the dialogue between cultures that a visit to the Soviet Pavilion and perusal of its brochures inspired reveals key points of political and cultural distinction. In an overt effort to appeal to American women, representations of the "New Soviet Woman" occupied a prominent position in this invented dialogue.

The "New Soviet Woman" at Work

The working woman, although never a rarity in America where the first industrialized workers were female textile loom operators, was perennially discussed in the U.S. mainstream media as a novelty and subject of sometimes acrimonious debate. In the 1930s, with unemployment soaring, as many as 25 percent of adult American women worked outside the home for wages, a figure that does not count the many women and children who performed hidden "home" or "piece" work inside their homes for remuneration.[10] Women workers in the United States were hit hard by the Depression but were not wholly excluded from the labor force, in part because they were often concentrated in jobs that were the least well-paid and, in many cases, had become feminized in the eyes of men. This kind of stereotyping reflected American popular beliefs about the value of women's skills as well as ideas as to what kinds of work were suitable for women to perform. Employment distinctions were also made on the basis of marital status. The vast majority of Americans—82 percent in a 1936 Gallup poll—thought that (white) married women should not engage in paid labor if their husbands could support them.[11] In general, U.S. courts and state governments upheld policies and laws barring married women from employment.[12] Given this atmosphere, the Soviet celebration of women workers may have appeared to many Americans as unconventional, even strange. The Soviet pamphlets distributed at the New York World's Fair presented a world where it was expected that women would work outside the home, excel at it, and take pleasure in doing so. This vision of women as workers left no room to debate whether women could combine job responsibilities with family life; it was simply assumed that they would do so and that they could perform both roles handily.

For the Soviets, the history of the Russian revolution could be symbolized by women's transformation—a transformation that was usually presented in binary terms, where women suffered gender and material oppression in the tsarist period but were liberated by socialism. After embracing work outside the home, often in a job that had previously been restricted to men, the "New Soviet Woman" forged a new identity for herself and became a role model to others, both at home and abroad. *The Soviet Press,* a booklet distributed at the fair, used the life story of Praskov'ia Pichugina to convey this story of upward female social mobility to fair visitors. Pichugina evolves from being an unskilled worker to a skilled mechanic, and she eventually leaves the workbench for a white collar Communist Party position. As the booklet's triumphantly florid prose indicates, her story symbolizes the path that countless other Soviet women have trodden since the revolution. "Comrade Pichugina," this "true daughter of the people," the brochure assures us, was "typical of many gifted people who had formerly been brow-beaten and stifled by tsarism and had found application for their abilities only under the Soviet system."[13] Other stories of liberation, personal fulfillment, and upward social mobility (complete with similar rhetorical flourishes) appear in all of the booklets that referred to Soviet women.

These brochures placed similar emphasis on the egalitarian nature of the Soviet system. Equality between the sexes was singled out as a characteristic of Soviet life and a facet of Soviet society that should be emulated. The pamphlets trumpeted the fact that young women in the USSR had the same educational opportunities as men. Photographs showed them in classes together, studying such disparate subjects as civil engineering, aerodynamics, and mathematics. According to these pictures, women were active learners, listening intently to their instructors and not afraid to answer questions in front of their classmates. Lest a skeptical reader conclude that such illustrations represented only a symbolic commitment or an overly optimistic goal, statistical data supporting the conclusion that egalitarianism had already been achieved under socialism reinforced illustrated claims. For instance, in a pamphlet devoted to student life in the USSR, the author noted, "In the Soviet Union, 43 per cent of the college and university students are women."[14] The overall impression conveyed by the booklets was that higher education was now the norm for Soviet citizens, particularly for younger workers, and that women faced no discrimination should they want to improve their qualifications. This idealized world contrasted with perceived American reality where only a small minority of women could hope to attend college and where there were quotas restricting the number of women admitted to law and medical schools.[15]

This propaganda promised that once in the labor force, gender discrimination did not stand in the way of career success for Soviet women either. Instead, pamphlet after pamphlet featured descriptions of women entering professions that had previously been dominated by men. For instance, the story of Zinaida Troitskaya, the first Soviet female locomotive driver, was repeated in three booklets.[16] One pamphlet used her story to highlight the emancipation of women as workers that the revolution had augured. "For many years," this pamphlet decried, "women were not allowed to drive locomotives in the U.S.S.R., for this work was considered too difficult for them. Troitskaya was the first to prove that women can do this job no worse than men and today hundreds of women are employed as locomotive drivers." The pamphlet went on to assert the institutionalization of programs aimed to broaden employment opportunities for women, noting that "many study courses have been established for women who wish to become locomotive drivers or assistant drivers."[17] Even in what may have been seen as among the most manly of occupations—steering that massive icon of industrialized progress, the railway locomotive—Soviet women were encouraged to think of themselves as entirely up to the task.

The discourse of liberation and gender equality was extended to rural women as well, although in their case a slightly different historical narrative was presented to the American public. The evils of the tsarist period continued to be emphasized, but now the "last fetters" of peasant women were said to have been broken by the collectivization of agriculture in the late 1920s.[18] Prior to collectivization, the male head of each household controlled the family's financial resources, and women were not guaranteed to receive any remuneration for their work. The collective farms introduced a new pay structure—one that paid each individual member for his or her labor. Hence, as the pamphlets underscored, peasant women had gained financial independence from men. Their growing importance in the Soviet countryside was further signaled by references to women assuming leadership positions in the collective farms and becoming agricultural machinery operators or shock workers.[19] In other words, here too the booklets celebrated women who broke with traditional gender norms and stereotypes.

The story of Leah Lishnyansky is illustrative of the type of prose that was commonly employed to tell the life stories of the "New Soviet Woman." It is included in D. Bergelson's pamphlet on the establishment of Birobidzhan, a

Jewish autonomous region within the borders of the Soviet Union. Bergelson writes, "Among the builders of Birofeld is the Lishnyansky family." Despite this opening reference, Bergelson immediately narrows the focus to only one person: "The wife—Leah Lishnyansky—the best milkmaid on the collective farm—is now a member of the Soviet Parliament, a Member of the Supreme Soviet of the U.S.S.R. She was one of the first settlers and has set many examples of great devotion to the cause of building up the Jewish Autonomous Region."[20] Lishnyansky's husband is not named, nor are his work achievements mentioned. Instead, Bergelson continues: "Leah Lishnyansky's eyes look grave and thoughtful as she now recalls her own and her husband's first steps on the virgin land here amid the taiga. Every step was beset with difficulties. But she and her husband, together with the other collective farmers of their village, overcame all difficulties and obstacles."[21] These three sentences underscore women's equality with men as well as women's overall importance to Soviet agriculture. The story assigns Lishnyansky a pivotal role in forging the new society; it is her identity as a working woman, rather than as wife or mother, that is foregrounded.

In the materials distributed by Soviet officials at the 1939 fair, women's active participation in politics was singled out as the ultimate expression of Soviet revolutionary ideology. The most successful Soviet women were described as women who combined meaningful employment with political work. Nine booklets made some kind of textual or photographic reference to a woman then serving in the Supreme Soviets—on paper the highest organs of national and republican government in the USSR. One particularly striking image was included in the booklet *Women in the U.S.S.R.* In a clear reversal of traditional gender norms and expectations about power and influence in the public sphere, this booklet showed a male constituent coming to seek the assistance of his female representative to the Supreme Soviet.[22] Praskov'ia Pichugina told her American audience that the Soviet Union "has given the woman equal rights with man to administer the state" and gives details in support of this assertion. "There are 189 women among the Members of the Supreme Soviet of the U.S.S.R.," she reports, and "among the Members of the Supreme Soviets of the Union Republics there are 848 women, and 578 women are Members of the Supreme Soviets of the Autonomous Republics. Over 1,500,000 women actively participate in the work of Village and City Soviets."[23] The use of statistics was a common tactic of Soviet propaganda of the era. Quantification lent a solidity to their claims meant to squash potential skepticism even if such figures overlooked salient factors—such as the fact that women were excluded from the ruling clique around Stalin and tended to be ghettoized into less significant positions within the Communist Party hierarchy.

When the pamphlets turned to the "New Soviet Minority Woman," the texts relied heavily on the use of such binary oppositions as advanced/backward and modern/traditional. These binarisms hinged on the idea that progressive change rejected not only the values and social structure of the Russian tsarist regime but also eschewed the rural patriarchal traditions that predominated in the far-flung, "ethnic," or "Eastern" corners of the Soviet Union. Included were frequent statements asserting a radical transformation under socialism for women in these rural districts. "The Soviet state," as one brochure put it, "solicitously assists the formerly most backward peoples in the relatively more rapid development of their economy and culture so that they may be on a par with the more advanced peoples and republics of the Soviet Union."[24] References to the evils of the tsarist era were joined by others singling out patriarchal families and religion as the root causes of "ethnic" (meaning "non-ethnically Russian") women's oppression. C. Aslanova in *The National Question Solved* described the stubborn backwardness sometimes exhibited by misogynist cultures before the revolution. "Among most of the Eastern peoples," she claimed, "women enjoyed no rights whatsoever. Woman was looked down upon. She was the docile slave of her husband, father or brother." Folk sayings, like "Don't mix into men's affairs with your dough-covered hands," reportedly said by men to women in Azerbaijan, were included to prove her argument.[25] In the eyes of the Soviets, the attitudes that lay behind such comments provided ample justification for their own campaigns to "liberate" those they saw as oppressed minority women.

The cornerstones of Soviet policy vis-à-vis Muslim women were attacks on the veil and arranged marriages. These were described as "manifestations of cultural backwardness" and "survivals of tribal customs" in Aslanova's booklet.[26] The second half of the 1920s saw campaigns against both practices. The attack on the veil, for instance, culminated in a series of mass unveilings between 1927 and 1929.[27] The subject had long been a favorite of Soviet propaganda, so its inclusion in the fair booklets was consistent with the line that Moscow had taken since the 1920s.[28] Ideas of progress and female emancipation were linked with the secularization and Sovietization of minority groups. Transitional images, like the photograph in figure 2 that showed a group of minority men and women receiving ballots to vote in the elections for the Supreme Soviet of the Turkmen SSR, occasionally appeared in the fair materials.[29] I refer to this image as a transitional one because while the people shown wear traditional dress—thereby indicating that they had not entirely embraced a Westernized way of life—they are in the process of voting in an election—in other words, participating in a political ritual introduced by the Soviet government. This mechanism was one way the Soviets increased the political rights of minority women and sought to give them louder voices within their communities. Although the people in that picture wore traditional dress, they were not engaged in traditional behavior. Similar images are included in the booklet *Cultural Progress among the Non-Russian Nationalities of the U.S.S.R.* In it, a photograph of Turkmen teenagers in a classroom was placed just after a passage damning the state of ethnic women's education in Russia prior to the revolution. The picture underscored the claim that, now, young women were being educated in the same classrooms as their brothers.

A slightly different narrative was suggested by the images and textual references depicting minority women who had already fully assimilated into mainstream (meaning ethnically Russian or more cosmopolitan) Soviet culture. They adopted Western dress and came to be defined by professions, technical prowess, and work-related upward mobility rather than by marriage, faith, or family. Maijura Abdurakhmanova, a young Uzbek woman whose life story was outlined in *Light Industries of the U.S.S.R.,* was one such example. The author pointed out that Maijura "saw a machine for the first time in her life in 1934."[30] However, that did not prove to be an insurmountable obstacle, for she decided to embrace industrial work and became a spinner. Implicit in this choice was the notion

Fig. 2.2. Turkmen voting in elections to the Supreme Soviet. Photograph in *The National Question Solved* (Foreign Languages Publishing House, 1939). Author's collection.

ALISON ROWLEY

that Maijura rejected the types of work traditionally assigned to Uzbek women by their communities and families in favor of pursuing a Soviet-style career. However, becoming a spinner who worked with industrial machinery rather than a woman engaged only in cottage-type production was only the first step. Ultimately, her productivity singled her out for further advancement: Maijura was elected to the Supreme Soviet of the USSR and enrolled at the Industrial Academy so that she could train to become a mill manager. Her story was not unique. Other examples that contained the same elements connecting Sovietization with upward mobility were included in all booklets that addressed the position of minorities in the Soviet Union. The sum of these narratives ultimately allowed one author to conclude decisively that "only Soviet power brought the women emancipation." This author goes further to credit the Soviet system with helping "Eastern" women in all areas of Soviet life to achieve equality with men: "Under the beneficent rays of the Soviet national policy thousands of women in the East have developed and become statesmen, doctors, engineers, fliers, teachers, agricultural experts, etc."[31] In other words, thousands of women had become shining examples of the "New Soviet Minority Woman."

The "New Soviet Woman" at Play

Just as Soviet women were expected to take their rightful positions in the factories or the fields of the collective farms, so too were they expected to assume center stage on the nation's playing fields. The Bolsheviks saw leisure as a state and political issue rather than as a private matter. In domestically produced propaganda, the Soviets connected sports participation with greater work productivity and military preparedness, rejecting ideologically "incorrect" forms of leisure—religious worship or drinking parties—as counterrevolutionary behaviors.[32]

A conscious, careful difference in emphasis is revealed in the materials created for American visitors to the New York World's Fair. Gone are references to sport replacing religion and omitted are the defense-related applications of some popular Soviet sports. Given that the fair opened at the end of April 1939 as the winds of war were already gathering in Europe, this is not surprising. The Soviets wanted to use their presence at the event to create a positive impression, and they did not want to alienate visitors by showing the "New Soviet Woman" transgressing too far beyond acceptable American norms or calling to mind military conflicts. Hence, while the booklets celebrated women breaking into masculine realms such as aviation, this was carefully contextualized within a spirit of daring and action, firmly delinked from militarism. Aviation was an area of adventurism particularly emphasized, as it was thought to resonate well with Americans who had become accustomed to hearing about the exploits of Amelia Earhart, Anne Morrow Lindbergh, and other well-known aviatrixes of the period.

A conscious rendering of female heroics is abundantly evident in the attention devoted to the most famous Soviet female pilots: Polina Osipenko, Marina Raskova, and Valentina Grizodubova. In 1938 these women undertook a record-breaking long-distance flight in a plane called the *Rodina* (*Motherland*). References to the women, as well as to the *Rodina* flight, were sprinkled across a number of the booklets. A more lengthy discussion was included in *Outstanding Flights by Soviet Airmen*, by M. Vodopyanov, and Osipenko tells her own story in *The Soviet Far East*. The story of the *Rodina* flight was manipulated in a number of ways to disconnect possible military implications from adventurism. Vodopyanov's booklet, for example, reproduced a photograph of the *Rodina* crew, in full flight gear next to the plane.[33] The caption below contained two details of note: it mentioned the "Hero of the Soviet Union" designation that was awarded to all three women in recognition of their contributions to Soviet aviation, and it referred in passing to the military rank held by two of them.[34] Other booklets did not include information about this military connection. While hundreds of thousands of Soviet women received some kind of paramilitary training in the 1930s, it was still exceedingly rare for women to actually serve in the military. This aspect of Osipenko's and Raskova's careers seems to have been deliberately downplayed for American audiences. Instead, Vodopyanov went on to provide statistical information about the distance and duration of the flight and connected it to the friendly aerial competition that existed between nations in the 1930s.

Osipenko's booklet, on the other hand, associated the *Rodina* flight with Soviet control of the country's peripheral regions. Her narrative of events, including the rescue operation after the women crashed in Siberia, was interspersed with sections describing changes to life in the Far East once it came under Soviet control. She underscored the heroism and determination of the women throughout her narrative: she described threats from fog, cold, and frozen instruments. After the crash, Osipenko and Grizodubova had to use rifle shots to drive off curious bears, while Raskova was left wandering around the taiga on her own with only chocolate bars to stave off hunger and eighteen cartridges to fend off bears. The dramatic tone of the story spoke volumes about the grit of the ideal Soviet woman, but it was not used to imply that there had been a mass movement into aviation by the female half of the Soviet population or that women had any role to play in the defense of the nation. Indeed, the only mention of Osipenko's military rank in her booklet came in the publisher's note that was tucked into the front—a note made necessary since Osipenko and fellow pilot Anatolii Serov were killed in a training exercise in May 1939.[35]

The 1939 materials distributed at the Soviet pavilion also showed women enjoying more traditional sports in their spare time. Great pride was expressed in the records set by Soviet women and, in the case of parachuting, they were credited with introducing it as a sport in the USSR.[36] The activities of sports-women were typically discussed alongside those of their male counterparts, with the language used in the texts conveying a sense of balance and gender equality, as we can see in this example from Andrei Starostin's *Sport in the U.S.S.R.*: "Millions of schoolchildren, lads and girls, adult men and women and even middle-aged people are proud bearers of the 'Labor and Defense' Badges."[37] In addition, photographs showed men and women exercising alongside one another. Because Soviet propaganda did not equate sport with either reproductive health or increased physical beauty and attractiveness to the opposite sex, such scenes of mixed groups exercising together were intended simply to convey the equal access that women had to sport.

However, this notion may not have resonated well, for some of the images presented women's bodies in clothes that American audiences would have considered risqué. In the 1930s, exercise programs in the United States, like those offered by the YMCA, were strictly segregated. Moreover, as David Gelernter notes, "In 1939, just under two-thirds of the [U.S.] population holds it to be indecent for a woman to appear on the street in shorts."[38] Hence, images like figure 3, which showed women with their leg and neck muscles bulging, might have been viewed as unfeminine and immodest.[39] Or perhaps American readers might have been willing to overlook these transgressions because the prose found in the same booklet so deliberately desexualized Soviet women's participation in sport. Starostin, in particular, emphasized that sport was a family affair. He did so by dwelling at length on the example of the Kochetkov family. The Kochetkovs, headed by their fifty-year-old mother, all entered events at a cross-country meet in Kuibyshev. The mother, three daughters, two sons, and a son-in-law won several events and collectively "endowed a family prize for the best showing in cross-country running."[40] By making the mother (whose age was noted in the text with the implication that she was past childbearing years) the central figure in the story, it eliminated any suggestion that sexuality played a role in her participation in sport. Rather, sport was depicted as a form of leisure wholesomely adopted by an idealized Soviet family.

The New Soviet Family

A final detail stood out in the story of the Kochetkovs: the absence of a father. In her work on Soviet motherhood, Olga Issoupova argues that in the 1930s Soviet men saw their roles as husbands and fathers marginalized by the

Fig. 2.3. Soviet sportswomen. Photograph in *Sport in the U.S.S.R.*
(Foreign Languages Publishing House, 1939). Author's collection.

state.[41] By forming a supportive alliance with Soviet women, the regime was able
to take the place of men in the family unit. Fathers were excluded from childcare
responsibilities and nurturing behavior, while women were bombarded instead
with images emphasizing social services like state-run childcare institutions.
Eliminated from upbringing, fathers were only assigned financial obligations
to their children in the form of the payment of child support. This marginalization began when a new family law code was issued in 1936 and reached its
apex when the "Mother Heroine" awards were created in 1944.[42] As Issoupova
notes, "The title 'hero father' was not introduced. The state gave the title and
the money to the mother, and thus developed a direct relationship with her as
the producer of the children, and the man was excluded from this relationship
as an insignificant figure (if not as a competitor for the woman's loyalty)."[43]

The process was readily apparent in the propaganda materials that the Soviets developed for foreign consumption as well. Maternity was an issue of
special concern in the souvenir booklets given out at the New York World's
Fair, for the Soviet government had to counter lingering doubts and persistent
rumors concerning state attitudes and intentions vis-à-vis the family as well as
the morality of Soviet women. As a result, at least a dozen souvenir booklets
included references to the new family code and its application in practice. The
issue of the recriminalization of abortion was addressed directly in *Public Health
Protection in the U.S.S.R.* The author, after explaining the new restrictions on
access to abortion, argued that the measures were progressive and reflected the

desires of Soviet women themselves. Here, the Soviets presented a line that they expected to resonate well with American Christians, who because of earlier family policies, suspected the Soviet government of encouraging what they viewed as immoral behavior and attitudes toward reproduction and family relations.

State support for, and some might say control of, mothers was signaled in several additional ways. It is worth bearing in mind that almost nowhere did the materials suggest that a woman might want to stay home with her children.[44] Instead, it was assumed that all mothers were working mothers who would make use of state benefits and institutions. Hence a great deal of emphasis was placed on the level of state spending on maternity benefits, hospitals, and daycare centers. The final page of *Work and Wages in the Soviet Union*, for instance, included such figures. The numbers were meant to appear staggeringly large, particularly since by omitting any exchange-rate information, American readers would have had no sense of the comparative value of the ruble. Readers were told that "maternity benefits granted by the state in 1937 amounted to 1,145,000,000 rubles" and that the "expenditure of the state in 1937 on maternity homes was 488,000,000 rubles."[45] Numbers that took up that much room on the page must surely have amounted to a major financial commitment, or so the propagandists hoped Americans would believe.

The emphasis on state-organized social services, which implicitly suggested the American government was less diligent in looking after its population, continued as the propaganda shifted to the subject of prenatal care. American readers were informed that pregnant women were expected to register with health officials who would monitor their conditions and instruct them "in the care of the child, its regime, diet and proper upbringing."[46] This supervision continued after a child had been born as well, since all children were to be registered at a district child-welfare center and, more important, it was expected that mothers would make use of spaces in crèches when they returned to work. This was the norm presented by Soviet propaganda. As author M. Ilin rhetorically queried: "How is it possible to reconcile the child and a factory machine, the child and the steering-wheel of an airplane, the child and a microscope, the child and a Deputy's seat?" He answered, "The state must help the woman, must take over the care of the child during the time the mother is working or studying."[47] The opinions and policies encapsulated in Ilin's words were further reinforced in the kinds of photographs used in the booklets. Simply put, women were never pictured caring for their own children or in family-style portraits. Instead, Soviet children were always shown away from their parents in institutional-type settings, and married couples were not pictured together either.

This particular vision of maternity and child rearing had implications for the depiction of fathers in Soviet propaganda. American fathers of the 1930s were an assumed part of life in most families, if only as primary breadwinners and disciplinarians. The contrast between American and Soviet expectations of fathers was stark. Soviet fathers were invisible. Only three booklets contained photographs of a man with a child, and the word father appeared less than a handful of times in all of the booklets combined.[48] Unmentioned and unseen, their position was co-opted by Communist Party leaders. Nowhere was that more apparent than in the final illustration in *Sport in the U.S.S.R.* (fig. 4).[49] The image was bursting with symbolic meanings and implications. At first glance, it shows a group of women participating in a physical culture parade. However, the visible features of the architectural landscape make it apparent that the women are marching on Red Square—in other words, that they are participating in a ritual at the very center of Soviet power. The women carry their children on their shoulders as they march under the watchful gaze of the Soviet leadership, whose figures incidentally are out of proportion in the image. The male Communist Party leaders are the only men included in the photograph. The replacement of fathers by party surrogates is further suggested by a final detail: a reproduction of an iconic portrait of Stalin with Gelya Markizova, the daughter of a high-ranking Communist Party official from Buriat-Mongolia, that appears behind the marchers. This image was widely circulated in the late 1930s as the regime began to present Stalin as the symbolic father of the nation.[50]

Gender equality brought with it certain obligations, according to these materials, including the assumptions that all women would seek work outside the

Fig. 2.4. Soviet women marching in parade on Red Square.
Photograph in *Sport in the U.S.S.R.* (Foreign Languages Publishing House, 1939). Author's collection.

ALISON ROWLEY

home and that minority women would adopt Sovietized identities. Although couched in the language of emancipation and liberation, these notions in effect limited the choices of the "New Soviet Woman," particularly concerning family life. Motherhood and marriage always came a distant second to the needs of the Soviet economy. At a time when the American public was debating whether women should, or even could, combine work with domestic responsibilities, Soviet propaganda depicted a world where that question had already been settled.

Conclusion

At the end of the 1939 season, the Soviet Union withdrew from the New York World's Fair. Widespread condemnation of the pact with Hitler as well as the invasion of Finland meant that American visitors were no longer receptive to anything the Soviets had to say. Memory of the fair, however, lived on. Historians have sought to recapture some of this lost world by examining photographic records of the pavilions and exhibits or by scouring the pages of accounts written by visitors. Overlooked in the historical scholarship on this fair, however, have been the souvenirs and materials produced and distributed by the Soviet government itself in an effort to shape American understandings of Soviet life and revolutionary ideology. A close reading of the titles distributed by Soviet fair organizers shows how important the "New Soviet Woman" was to their narrative of social, economic, and political transformation. The stories of women embodied the transformation of everyday life undertaken by the Soviet government—a transformation meant to appeal to an American audience still feeling the effects of the Great Depression. This effort to convince the American public of the attractions of socialism failed, and relations between the two countries remained strained in the ensuing decades. Ultimately, the fears spawned by the Cold War in the late 1940s and 1950s led the vast majority of Americans to anathematize the Soviet Union and all that its leaders had to say on any subject, including gender relations.

NOTES

1 Anthony Swift, "The Soviet World of Tomorrow at the New York World's Fair, 1939," *Russian Review* 57 (1998): 364–79.
2 Quoted in David Gelernter, *1939: The Lost World of the Fair* (New York: Free Press, 1995), 129. At earlier American fairs, women's exhibits were often segregated in specific multinational pavilions. See Tracey Jean Boisseau, "White Queens at the Chicago World's Fair," *Gender and History* 12 (2000): 33–81; Judith Paine, "The Women's Pavilion of 1876," *Feminist Art Journal* 4 (1976): 5–12; and Cheryl Ganz, *The 1933 Chicago World's Fair: A Century of Progress* (Urbana: University of Illinois Press, 2008).
3 Peter Filene, *Americans and the Soviet Experiment, 1917–1933* (Cambridge, Mass.: Harvard University Press, 1967), 46.

4 Filene, 46.

5 Nicholas Cull, "Overture to an Alliance: British Propaganda at the New York World's Fair, 1939–1940," *Journal of British Studies* 36 (1997): 326.

6 See Swift, 369, and David Nye, "European Self-Representations at the New York World's Fair, 1939," in *Cultural Transmissions and Receptions*, ed. R. Kroes, 60 (Amsterdam: Free University Press, 1993).

7 Quoted in Jon Zachman, "The Legacy and Meaning of World's Fair Souvenirs," in *Fair Representations*, ed. R. W. Rydell and N. Gwinn, 205 (Amsterdam: VU University Press, 1994).

8 The layout of the Soviet Pavilion as well as mention of the booths and bookstore can be found in the brochure *Union of Soviet Socialist Republics New York World's Fair (Pavilion of the USSR at the New York World's Fair, 1939)*.

9 All of the booklets were published by Foreign Languages Publishing House in 1939, so I have opted to list only the authors and titles of the booklets in these notes.

10 Susan Ware, *Holding Their Own* (New York: Twayne Publishers, 1982), 21.

11 Ibid., 27.

12 Sheila Rowbotham, *A Century of Women* (New York: Viking, 1997), 203.

13 Vera Golenkina, *The Soviet Press*, 29–30.

14 S. Kaftanov, *Soviet Students*, 9.

15 In the 1930s, the number of American women who attended college varied between 10.5 and 12.2 percent. See Ware, 57.

16 See P. Krivonoss, *The Stakhanov Movement on Soviet Railroads*, 7, 27; V. Obraztsov, *The Railroads of the U.S.S.R.*, 13, 28; and S. Sobolev, *Soviet Youth at Work and Play*, 20.

17 Krivonoss, 27.

18 The expression comes from V. F. Molyakov, *The Countryside, Past and Present*, 31.

19 Shock worker (*udarnik*) was the title given to workers who regularly over fulfilled their production quotas. They were rewarded with higher wages, priority access to goods in short supply, and other privileges. See Hiroaki Kuromiya, *Stalin's Industrial Revolution* (Cambridge: Cambridge University Press, 1990); and Lewis Siegelbaum, *Stakhanovism and the Politics of Productivity in the USSR, 1935–1941* (Cambridge: Cambridge University Press, 1990).

20 Leah Lishnyanskaya's name has been anglicized to Leah Lishnyansky. D. Bergelson, *The Jewish Autonomous Region*, 33.

21 Bergelson, 33.

22 P. Pichugina, *Women in the U.S.S.R.*, 22.

23 Pichugina, 24.

24 Yanka Kupala, *Cultural Progress among the Non-Russian Nationalities of the U.S.S.R.*, 8.

25 C. Aslanova, *The National Question Solved*, 27–28.

26 Aslanova, 27.

27 The unveiling campaign had violent results. In Uzbekistan alone, more than two thousand women were killed for shedding their veils. See Adrienne Edgar, "Bolshevism, Patriarchy, and the Nation: The Soviet 'Emancipation' of Muslim Women in Pan-Islamic Perspective," *Slavic Review* 65, no. 2 (2006): 266.

28 See Fanny Bryan, "Anti-Islamic Propaganda: *Bezbozhnik*, 1925–35," *Central Asian Survey* 5 (1986): 29–47.

29 Aslanova, 7.

30 D. Khazan, *Light Industries of the U.S.S.R.*, 17.

31 Aslanova, 28.

32 Alison Rowley, "Sport in the Service of the State: Images of Physical Culture and

Soviet Women, 1917–1941," *The International Journal of the History of Sport* 23 (2006): 1314–40.

33 M. Vodopyanov, *Outstanding Flights by Soviet Airmen*, 21.

34 The members of the *Rodina* crew were the only women to be given this title prior to World War II. See the list in Iu. N. Ivanova, *Khrabreishie iz prekrasnykh zhenshchiny Rossii v voinakh (Valiant Exploits by Outstanding Russian Women in Warfare)* (Moscow: Rosspen, 2002), 247–54.

35 *Rabotnitsa* 15 (1939): 6–7.

36 Iakov Moshkovsky, *Parachute-Jumping and Gliding: Popular Soviet Sports*, 9.

37 Andrei Starostin, *Sport in the U.S.S.R.*, 11. The badges were awarded for meeting sports targets.

38 Gelernter, 215.

39 Starostin, 25.

40 Ibid., 16, 19.

41 Olga Issoupova, "From Duty to Pleasure? Motherhood in Soviet and Post-Soviet Russia," in *Gender, State and Society in Soviet and Post-Soviet Russia*, ed. S. Ashwin (London: Routledge, 2000).

42 Excerpts are available in Rudolf Schlesinger, *The Family in the USSR* (London: Routledge, 1949).

43 Issoupova, 33.

44 I found only one reference to stay-at-home mothers in the booklets. See M. Ilin, *The Little Citizen of a Big Country*, 29.

45 I. Gudov, *Work and Wages in the Soviet Union*, 22.

46 N. Propper-Grashchenkov, *Public Health Protection in the U.S.S.R.*, 17–18.

47 Ilin, 25–26.

48 See Aslanova, 31; Krivonoss, 13; and M. Vodopyanov, *Moscow-North Pole-Vancouver, Wash*, 27.

49 Starostin, 29.

50 See Hans Günter, "Wise Father Stalin and His Family in Soviet Cinema," in *Socialist Realism without Shores*, ed. T. Lahusen and E. Dobrenko (Durham, N.C.: Duke University Press, 1997). On the picture of Stalin with Markizova, see David King, *The Commissar Vanishes* (New York: Metropolitan, 1997), 153.

We have been accustomed to regard [Japan] as uncivilized, or half-civilized at best, but we found [at the 1876 Centennial Exposition] abundant evidences that it outshines the most cultivated nations of Europe in arts which are their pride and glory, and which are regarded as among the proudest tokens of civilization.[1]

—*CENTENNIAL CLIPPINGS*, HISTORICAL SOCIETY OF PENNSYLVANIA

Siam and Ceylon are here, anxious to take their places in line with the nations . . . hoping that the Exposition of '93 will do for them what the Centennial did for Japan.

—THOMAS PALMER (COLUMBIAN EXPOSITION PRESIDENT). WILLIAM E. CAMERON, *THE WORLD'S FAIR, BEING A PICTORIAL HISTORY OF THE COLUMBIAN EXPOSITION* (1893)

CHAPTER 3

Japan—Modern, Ancient, and Gendered at the 1893 Chicago World's Fair

Lisa K. Langlois

The hopes of Ceylon and Siam that they might follow the path laid by Japan in 1876 were eclipsed by the spectacular impression Japan created at the 1893 Columbian Exhibition. As a result of Japan's triumph that summer, pundits, recognizing in Japan's exhibits a unique articulation of modernity, raised Japan above all other Asian nations—pronouncing it the "Great Britain of the Asia," the "Paris of the Asia," and the "Chicago of the Orient."[2] No other nation outside Europe and its former settler colonies, such as the United States, would draw such praise—praise that aided Japan's efforts to call for renegotiation of the unequal treaties it had brokered earlier in the century with Western powers, including its first, the Treaty of Peace and Amity, signed with the United States in 1854.[3] The successful reintroduction of Japan by the Meiji government (1868–1912) to the millions who visited Chicago in 1893 substantively strengthened its hand, and in 1894 Japan signed the first of several new treaties that in

56

time returned judicial and tariff autonomy to the Japanese state.[4] This chapter will show to what degree these representations, Japan's most potent weapons at a key moment of diplomacy, hinged in the end on the way women were figured within them. By presenting Japanese women as signs of a particularly Japanese past, fair organizers wielded an effective reverse logic that overturned the notion of Japan as latecomer to reposition it as an ancient civilization poised to make a unique contribution to modernity. However paradoxical it might seem, an ability to demonstrate a specifically Japanese patriarchal past at this fair through the display of women still mired in that past permitted Japan to carve out an authentic national presence within Western-defined modernity.

Japanese commissioners convinced an international audience of Japan's right to full national sovereignty and the justice of its cause through a two-pronged approach: on the one hand, exhibits in the Japanese Lady's Boudoir in the Woman's Building (fig. 1) reinvented what "Japanese women" meant to an international audience. The architectural setting, furnishings, and two publications aptly portrayed "ancient" and "modern" womanhood.[5] By eliding distinctions in historic time, exhibits presented all Japanese women as simultaneously traditional and modern. On the other hand, Japanese exhibits elsewhere in the fairgrounds made clear distinctions between historical and modern Japan, both of which were characterized as masculine. The Phoenix Hall, Japan's national pavilion, legitimized Japanese sovereignty by presenting a highly compressed history of previous regimes and praiseworthy accounts of past male rulers. Modern Japan competed in industry and commerce in the White City. By contrasting a completed, masculine history in the Phoenix Hall with a living, feminine tradition in the Boudoir, Japan deftly navigated the paradox of modernity in which non-Western nations found themselves—that in the effort to achieve modernization, it had lost its authenticity as a distinct culture and therefore was merely a poor imitator of a nation-state. If it was the 1893 Columbian Exhibition that would prove to be the event that sealed Japan's transformation in the eyes of the West, it was the representation of Japanese women at this fair that metaphorically reproduced Japan as the West's "other"— not in opposition to or outside of modernity, but as firmly located within it.

The Past Presented, or Japanese History Retold

More than mere entertainment, nineteenth-century international expositions promoted competition among imperialist powers that displayed the goods, technologies, and cultures of their respective imagined nations and colonies. The combined presentation of ancient heritage and technological advancement encouraged attendees to see Japan as belonging within the circle

Fig. 3.1. The Japanese Lady's Boudoir. Rinji Hakurankai Jimukyoku. Rinji hakurankai jimukyoku hôkoku zusetzu. [Illustrated Supplement to the Official Report of the Commission to the World's Columbian Exposition] (Tokyo: Ogawa, 1895. n.p.).

of legitimate modern nations. Yet the pavilion and its exhibits also illustrated an historic Japanese identity—one that both differed from that of China and demonstrated a long and unified history.[6] Such distinction mattered: not only did Japan wish to avoid the exclusionary policies the United States had imposed on Chinese immigration, it also competed with China for influence in Korea.[7]

Comprising three rooms, the Phoenix Hall displayed particular aspects of Japanese history while omitting others. The history espoused there carefully contrived to foreground Japanese cultural autonomy in the face of cross-cultural exchange. By explaining that the ability to assimilate lay within Japanese national character, commissioners found a "usable past."[8] Exhibits in the Phoenix Hall, with its three successive period-style rooms, told a story of political continuity. The temporal design of these three rooms—reflecting carefully selected eras in Japanese history—reinforced claims that Meiji rule was the culmination of an unbroken line of imperial succession by unifying them stylistically under one roof and replete with phoenix iconography of "just rule." Increasingly complex

LISA K. LANGLOIS

floor plans in each hall corresponded to the narrative of evolutionary progress (fig. 2), supported by the explanatory guide to the building by Okakura Kakuzô.[9] Japanese Commissioners endeavored to highlight the antiquity of Japanese history and the high level of its ancient cultural achievements in order to enhance the "national prestige" of Meiji Japan.[10] Thus for the first time in decades of Japanese participation in expositions, its national pavilion was modeled after a specific prototype: the Hôôdô, or "Phoenix Hall," of the Byôdôin temple of 1053.

Basing the pavilion on a well-known destination for European and American visitors to Japan facilitated the creation of a recognizable national identity. As Marilyn Ivy notes, discursive temporality is one feature of Japanese modernity (shared with other modernities) in which "tradition" serves as a background to progressive history in the narration of a unified "Japanese culture."[11] The possession of such a history had become a qualification for membership in the family of modern nations for the European polities and informed their national pavilions and exhibits as well.

Japan was not the only industrializing nation faced with the challenge of producing a past distinctive enough to demonstrate its historical trajectory along

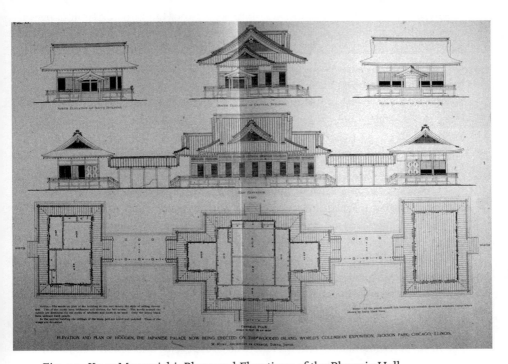

Fig. 3.2. Kuru Masamichi. Plans and Elevations of the Phoenix Hall. P. B. Wight, "Japanese Architecture at Chicago." *Inland Architect and News Record* 20, no. 5 (Dec. 1892): 49–50.

the lines of progress. The United States, often imagined as having no ancient roots at all, faced the same dilemma. Chicago-based fair organizers hoped to gain prestige for the United States through a contrived narrative of progress by displaying "the people who were in America 400 years ago, to form a background to the other departments of the Exposition in which will be illustrated the developments made during the last four centuries."[12] Tellingly, living tableaux of indigenous Americans inhabited the White City, not just the midway. Perhaps recognizing the tenuousness of this link to indigenous antiquity, American organizers deployed the opposite strategy as well: the selection of the neoclassical beaux arts style for the temporary steel-frame exhibition palaces, enveloped in an ephemeral plaster skin, attempted to link the American culture with that of Europe.[13]

Japanese planners wielded a comparable set of twinned strategies in the Phoenix Hall: with its rooms representing the ancient "Fujiwara epoch" (880–1150), intermediate "Ashikaga period" (1350–1550), and most historically recent "Tokugawa dynasty," (1603–1868, also referred to as the Edo period), Japanese designers provided a yardstick by which fairgoers could favorably compare the cultural sophistication of Japan's past with that of America's pre-Columbian, Columbian, and early modern periods. Japan successfully negotiated for exclusive use of the Wooded Isle by promising to make a gift of the Phoenix Hall, to be erected in permanent materials. Isolating the wooden hall from the ephemeral palaces of the White City situated Japan's past as different from—but as valid as—the European past. While both drew on "classical" styles for modern buildings, Japan's could only be viewed from the island—thus avoiding direct visual comparison between European and Japanese architectural traditions. Yet the three period-style rooms secured Japan's place in a Eurocentric world history anchored by the events of 1492. The Ashikaga rooms explicitly dated from the late fifteenth century and were complemented by rooms that antedated and followed Columbus's "discovery" of the New World.

Given the focus on Columbus's voyages at this exhibition, perhaps the "Columbian" comparison impressed American writers most.[14] Marietta Holley's popular fictional everywoman, "Samantha," upon exiting the Japanese island exhibit, dryly describes it to the reader of *Samantha at the World's Fair* (1893) this way: "In the other wing are Japan productions four hundred years old, showin' the state of the country when Columbus set out to discover their country."[15] Mocking the hubris that imagined Japan as in need of "discovery" by Westerners, Holley joins the chorus of the English-language press that accepted Japan's claims to its own venerable and verifiable past after experiencing Japanese representations of it at the fair. This level of comparison between Japan and Western markers of historical progress was not only expressed through sarcasm or fictionalized accounts of the fair. In the dedicatory speech opening the Phoenix Hall, exposition president Thomas Palmer favorably compared

LISA K. LANGLOIS

Japan's accomplishments at the time of Columbus to those of its European contemporaries—whom Palmer referred to as "nothing more than barbarians" in the same time period.[16] No yardstick, whether rhetorical, visual, or architectural in nature, would prove more useful to Japanese fair planners, however, than gender relations that mitigated the rapidity of Japan's modernization. An indelible impression left on visitors to the Japanese exhibits was created by Japanese women—through their embodied presence performing a premodern patriarchal past as well as through their notable absence in a contemporary Japan coded as masculine and modern.

Tradition, History, and the Invisible Japanese Modern Woman

Meiji officials recognized that Japan's international prestige and status as a legitimate, modern nation-state was linked to perceptions of Japanese women and their role in society. Criticism of the treatment of Japanese women appeared in periodicals, monographs, and travel diaries of the time. Moreover, the Board of Lady Managers, who invited Japanese participation in the Woman's Building, judged the progress of nations on the status of their women and explicitly ridiculed nations who refused to enter exhibits.[17] Board member Maud Elliot wrote in her guide to the Woman's Building, "That such [industrial reform] work is needed is evidenced by the pathetic answers from some of the countries where our invitation has been declined. . . . It seems incredible that the governments of these countries would be willing to make admissions which reflect so much upon themselves"[18] Japan faced a double-bind: refusing women's participation would condemn them to the "backwards" camp of non-Western peoples, while full participation in the fair—especially the Congress of Women—would attract more criticism at home and abroad of Japan's supposed abandonment of tradition.

Following more than two decades of women's participation in strikes, uprisings, and the People's Rights Movement, a backlash against women's political activity came, in part, in the 1890 law excluding women from public politics and refusing them admittance—even as observers—from the newly opened Imperial Diet.[19] According to Sharon Nolte and Sally Hastings, the Meiji state's configuration of Japanese women as public figures in the 1890 ban on women's participation in political parties implied that like civil servants, Japanese women had responsibilities to the nation which superseded their political interests.[20]

The Japanese Commission to the exposition and the Ministry of Education mounted exhibits of newly established female primary and normal schools in the Liberal Arts building. Complementing the literature supporting the Japanese

Lady's Boudoir, they addressed the fear that the world would judge Japan to be "uncivilized."[21] Exhibits provided the desired evidence of progress in the place of delegates to the World's Congress of Women. Materials promoted the New Japan as sharing economic, political, and social values with the industrialized nations of Europe and North America and portrayed a constitutional monarchy whose subjects, including women, were more like their Victorian counterparts than alien to them. Although sponsored by the empress and her court, the shapers of the Boudoir collaborated with their fellow exhibitors in supporting male supremacy. Japan, like many nation-states in the Woman's Building, was against female suffrage.[22] The Boudoir allowed a peek into the supposed private sphere of Japanese women, whose elegant and exotic surroundings threatened no one's sense of propriety or assumptions of Euro-American cultural superiority. A homogeneous "traditional" Japanese woman thus emerged in exposition books, architectural settings and their furnishings, dress, and visual representations in art.

Both the Phoenix Hall and the Japanese Lady's Boudoir incorporated vernacular styles, but it was within each exhibit's relationship to the past that Japan's anticolonial agenda was revealed. These venues allowed for parallel tactics in depicting Japan's rich cultural heritage. In the Phoenix Hall, men's achievements formed a narrative of active agency in shaping history. In contrast, the conflation of historic time in the Boudoir constructed Japanese women collectively as passive repositories of tradition. This strategy answered the criticism that in modernization, Japan had lost its authenticity. By linking the Meiji emperor with the cultural capital of Japanese antiquity and locating its ongoing tradition with Japanese women, diplomats could argue for equal treaties as a modern sovereign state.

This interpretation depends on the willingness to complicate understandings of the categories "modernity" and "tradition." Constructed as a pair of binary opposites in modernist discourse, "tradition" is often figured as the past in a linear model of chronological time.[23] The Japanese term most often translated as "tradition," *dentô*, does not appear in the primary source materials. Instead, the contrast and conflation of "ancient and modern" in the oft-repeated term *kokon* characterizes strategies for negotiating the conflicting domestic and international demands for a coherent "Japanese" identity. The tension between the discursive categories of "history" and "tradition" took tangible form in the settings and furnishings of both displays. The Phoenix Hall rhetorically constructed a masculinity that embodied dynamic change through biography, whereas the Boudoir purportedly spoke for all Japanese women, past and present. In the Phoenix Hall, history argued for the political legitimacy of the new Meiji government. Like the *History of the Empire of Japan*, Okakura Kakuzo's guide to the Phoenix Hall interpreted Japanese history to authorize the "restoration" of rule to the Emperor. Both texts stressed the continuity of the imperial line and the recent political reforms sanctioned by the emperor who, Okakura wrote, rode in a phoenix-adorned "state coach . . . on the occasion of the promulgation of the Meiji Constitution" in 1889.[24] The ubiquitous phoenix motif embodied the ideology of "just rule," which is stressed in Okakura's guidebook and the English-language press. Okakura informs readers that the phoenix appears "only when a just sovereign is on the throne."[25] Invoking the iconography of "just rule," phoenix-crest banners swathed the façade of the pavilion and Japanese exhibits in the White City, cloaking the Meiji government in legitimacy. One guidebook asserted that the phoenix "appears on everything Japanese on the grounds."[26]

Chicago's Phoenix Hall was designed by Kuru Masamichi, whose beaux arts training is apparent in his plans and elevations as published in the *Inland Architect and News Record* in December 1892 (fig. 2).[27] While Kuru's drawings recall the symmetrical organization of its eleventh-century namesake—a central pavilion flanked by two smaller outbuildings connected by corridors—it is modified in numerous ways. Most important, Kuru transformed the Uji building's small scale and elevated "wings" into functional exhibition spaces. The Uji temple was a suitable model for the Chicago pavilion because of its association with phoenix iconography and the fact that it allowed Kuru to present three distinct period styles within a single composition.

A broad, copper-sheet roof surmounted the stylistically unified exterior. Only wooden doors and shutters subtly marked the period of each building. The north pavilion, in the "Fujiwara" style, had vertical shutters reminiscent of shinden-style architecture of the period. The "Ashikaga" building had sliding wooden doors, like Yoshimitsu's fourteenth-century Kinkakuji, and the central hall had ceiling-to-floor paper-covered latticed screens, as seen in various Tokugawa-era temples. The interiors amplified this historical eclecticism. As Mishima Masahiro points out, competing plans for the interior of the pavilion sought to promote Meiji export art objects for domestic use. However, Okakura, as director of the Tokyo Fine Art School and Kuki Ryûichi, director of the Imperial Museum, ultimately organized the interior as a narrative history of Japanese art.[28] Phoenix references peppered the interiors and validated "New Japan" with its recently established Constitution and bicameral parliament.

While carved, painted, engraved, embroidered, and printed representations of phoenixes authenticated the Meiji regime throughout the fairgrounds, none were visible in the Japanese Lady's Boudoir, despite its patronage by the Meiji empress, whose position was long associated specifically with the symbol.[29] Instead, interior design choices and illustrated texts prepared for the fair collapsed time and rendered Japanese women bearers of a timeless tradition. As *Explanation of the Japanese Lady's Boudoir*[30] makes clear, the display intended to represent "a lady's private rooms . . . of the Tokugawa period" and "to show at the same time the manner of a Japanese lady's life at home."[31] This conflation of the past with the present was reinforced by the eclectic rooms and furnishings of the supposedly Tokugawa-style Boudoir, which had been loaned or donated by two members of the empress's circle.[32]

Carol Gluck argues convincingly that for Meiji Japanese, "Edo" (the period of Tokugawa family rule) stood for all premodern Japanese tradition in the Meiji era. "Newness was all," she notes, but points out that this newness "could only be grasped by juxtaposition to what was old." Gluck observes that even in the earliest years of the Meiji regime, "Japan's before-the-modern was imagined largely in terms of an Edo identified as Japanese 'tradition.' This grand conflation made it seem as if centuries of tradition had come to rest in the [Edo period]."[33] "Edo" contained pre-Meiji tradition as if it were a storehouse of all Japan's cultural bric-a-brac.[34] If women needed to guard Japan's premodern heritage, then the inner quarters of an Edo-period-style mansion—the stated model for the Boudoir—provided an ideal space for the protection of tradition from the onslaught of modernity.

This strategy also figures centrally in the book, *Japanese Women,* produced for the fair by the Japanese Woman's Commission that comprised court nobles and the wives of high-ranking officials. The book's authors claim to "present to the world's public . . . the true condition of Japanese women, ancient and modern."[35] Just as differences in historical past and present were elided, class differences among Japanese women were erased, producing a unidimensional image of "the" Japanese woman—one that was picked up by American report-ers who, in their ignorance of Japanese class markers as well as contemporary architecture, consistently referred to the Boudoir as a representation of a contem-porary house, typical of Japan.[36] While representations of women as guardians of tradition were unquestioningly accepted by an America press eager to exoticize Japan, similar representations of contemporary men would have undermined Japanese claims to social, industrial, military, and commercial equality with the imperialist nations at the fair. Instead, Japanese men were presented as both historic and contemporary—though not simultaneously so.

Okakura's Phoenix Hall guide contextualized Japanese masculinity within a trajectory of historical progress. In chronological order, Okakura explained that the "Fujiwara" wing "copied features of Uji's Phoenix Hall and apartments of the Imperial Palace at Kyoto." The "Ashikaga" wing purported to represent the library and tea room from Shogun Ashikaga Yoshimasa's 1479 Ginkakuji, or Silver Pavilion. Finally, the "Tokugawa" hall was billed as a "replica of a room in the old castle of Yedo,"[37] comprising four rooms: the audience hall in two levels, a library, and a room where food is arranged for presentation. Therefore, in terms of both their functions and patrons, these distinct rooms contrast with the dehistoricized spaces of the Boudoir.

Opposing gender logic imbued not only spatial orientations but also the furnishings within. Both exhibits' guidebooks included diagrams with labeled illustrations of their furnishings; many of the contents seem to be gender neutral, such as supplies associated with calligraphy. *Explanation of the Japanese Lady's Boudoir,* however, identifies writing desks and materials as for composing poetry, whereas in the Phoenix Hall, poetry was associated only with the earliest (Fujiwara era) exhibit. The dressing room and sitting room in the Boudoir had a remarkable array of makeup boxes and the paraphernalia for incense burning. Yet these were displayed only in the Fujiwara apartment. In short, the Japanese Boudoir contained items that corresponded to each of the period rooms in the Phoenix Hall, as though women continued practices from the ancient past, while men replaced old practices with new ones. Metonymically, the exhibits stood for feminine tradition in contrast with masculine history.

Dress was among the most important ways that Japanese women served as reminders of Japan's relationship to its illustrious but rapidly receding past. As with the furnishings that lay within Japanese exhibits, clothing, cosmetics, and tooth blackening in the Boudoir constructed women as guardians of the past and parallels the politics of personal adornment in 1890s Meiji society, which condoned European-style dress for men but condemned it for elite women—despite their need to act as hostesses to foreign dignitaries in Japan.[38] The emissary for the Board of Lady Managers in Chicago, Amédée Baillot de Guerville, vividly portrays Japanese noblewomen as hostesses in his account of his lantern show and meetings to secure Japanese participation in the Woman's Building.[39] His impression of the group of thirty women as "great ladies who spoke several foreign languages, discussed or postponed all questions, presenting a decision with rapidity and incomparable intelligence."[40] De Guerville's descriptions of sophisticated, well-heeled, polyglot Japanese ladies dining with gentlemen on the finest French food and wine served by boys in brocade britches ("Just like Paris!") echoes the notion that Japanese were the "Frenchmen of the Orient."[41] His emphatic surprise over Japan's success in reproducing elite European culture serves to invert the reader's expectation of a caricature of the Japanese as backwards and childlike.[42] More important, it stands in startling contrast to the "traditional" image of Japanese women presented in Chicago just one year later.

Japanese women had to be refashioned in kimono in order to mark the nation as authentic in ways that men could not. The *History of the Empire of Japan* describes the neotraditionalists' reaction to Meiji reforms as "rash denationalization and unpatriotic radicalism."[43] In December 1892 the Imperial Japanese Committee received a contract from exposition organizers that required all workers at the Japanese Bazaar on the midway to wear "native clothes." An American official argued that the midway intended to show the customs and lifestyles of indigenous cultures in "authentic" dress. The Japanese commissioner successfully argued that Western clothes "had . . . become Japan's national costume," exempting Japanese men from the general rule.[44] With ease the national costume for Japanese men became European; the kimono belonged to women and "backward" men.

Like the carpenters in Philadelphia for the Centennial Exposition of 1876, Ôkura Kihachirô's crew publicly assembled the Phoenix Hall as a kind of spectacle and were photographed and illustrated in an engraving in *Scientific American* (fig. 3). Unlike women's dress, men's clothing purported to reveal Japan's progress toward modernization. *Scientific American* deduces that "some have adopted modern garments, while others, who are more timid, retain a part of their national costume."[45] Having described them as "gradually becoming Europeanized," the author implies that, like a snapshot, this rendering of a moment lays an entire race before the empirical gaze of (scientific) Americans. Eliding differences of class and profession, the author misinterprets the wearing of coats bearing the name and crest of their employer as acts of "timidity." Unexamined are the presumably more "advanced" members of the Japanese Commission, who wore suits, top hats, and bowlers. It is little wonder that Japanese officials objected to the "authentic costume" clause in its contract. The Japanese officials clearly demarcated masculine modernity from both historical masculinity (visible only in books and in the Phoenix Hall) and traditional femininity.

Therefore it was imperative that Japanese women dress the part of the distinctly "Japanese" tradition, despite the fact that Japan might gain interna-

Fig. 3.3. "Japanese at the World's Columbian Exposition." *Scientific American* 68 (June 24, 1893): 392.

tional prestige by sending "modern" women such as had formed the Japanese Women's Commission to the fair. By instead portraying Japanese women as (re) producers of traditional culture, the imperial commission appeased foreign and domestic critics of Japan's appropriation of Western institutions and practices. "New Japan's" progressive policies could be showcased without the presence of actual women—in Japanese or Western dress—through didactic texts, graphs, and glass cases in the education section of the Liberal Arts Building and in the text *Japanese Women*. No Japanese woman addressed the Congress of Women or staffed the Boudoir. As the English-language press repeatedly pointed out (in this case, a contributor to the *Daily Inter Ocean*), "There is but one thing lacking in the Japanese exhibit. The house is there, the beautiful work of Japanese artists is there, but no pretty hostess in bright-colored kimono smiles a welcome to the visitor. Though the Japanese home is on exhibition, the Japanese woman is not."[46]

Nor were photographs of Japanese women displayed. Instead, line drawings for *Japanese Women* inscribed Japanese femininity. Eight monochrome prints complemented the eight chapters concerning the historical and contemporary Japanese women's involvement in politics, religion, literature, arts, domestic life, industry, education, and philanthropy from prehistoric times to the present. The conservative, anti-women's-suffrage tone of the book is neither surprising nor peculiar to Japanese authors. As Board of Lady Managers President Bertha Honoré Palmer quipped, "Those persons highest in authority [are] the most conservative" and the Japanese rhetoric of "good wives and wise mothers" was echoed by the hereditary elite of Europe.[47] However, its illustrations portraying these wives and mothers generalize and de-historicize Japan's women with the same strategies that are found in the Boudoir.

The illustrations for *Japanese Women* conflate ancient and modern architectural settings, furnishings, and clothing to create a Japanese everywoman. Although *Japanese Women* praises exemplary women, beginning with the mythological sun goddess (from whom the imperial family claims divine descent) and including, among others, real historical women such as the Empress Suiko and *Tale of Genji* author Murasaki Shikibu, the manner in which the women from the history are idealized implies, as Jayawardena finds in other examples, that women had recently lost the freedom and power they had in the past.[48] Thus we can interpret the inclusion of a litany of heroic women in the exposition literature as an effort to naturalize women's emancipation as a native, rather than foreign, practice.[49] Nevertheless, the inclusion of so many women from the past and present in the text makes their absence conspicuous in the book's illustrations. These accomplished philanthropists are just as invisible as the modern Japanese women of the Boudoir.[50]

The pronounced absence of portraits of exemplary women from a text rife with their biographies suggests a strategic creation of a "traditional" Japanese womanhood. Both the text and illustrations drew from the popular genre of didactic literature for women, filled with continental and Japanese representations of filial piety and historic, exemplary women. These illustrations also participated in the collapsing of historic time in its construction of Japanese femininity. Choices made in the characterization of the female figures through the pictures' compositions, settings, furnishings, women's attire, and their relationships with the written text portray Japanese women as timeless and enduring guarantors of the authenticity of modern Japan. For example, the untitled print by Murata Tanryô (1874–1940), facing the first page of text, depicts a woman seated on a large cushion leaning on an armrest. The reclining figure is depicted with shaved eyebrows and painted-on "moth" eyebrows high on her forehead, long unbound hair, and multiple layers of robes, which are consistent with pictures of Heian- (or Fujiwara-) era women. Nevertheless, the text on the facing page opens with discussions of contemporary women. "Japan, superficially, is now pretty well known to the world, but as regards her internal affairs she still remains quite a dark country to the Occident. Her women, for instance, are misunderstood to a great extent." The leitmotif of separate spheres has appeared, only now on a national level—the Boudoir is writ large. "We, therefore, publish this pamphlet to place them just as they are before the eyes of the world on this occasion of the World's Fair."[51] The authors of *Japanese Women* thus make a twofold claim of authenticity—both of the material in the book and of the eyewitness experience in which the reader is about to embark.

Owing to the juxtaposition of text and image, readers might (mis)understand the illustration as depicting Japanese women, as advertised in the text, "just as they are." The confusion of past and present is further complicated by the inclusion of historic anachronisms within the picture. A Heian-era court lady seated on a large cushion is out of place in a room with wall-to-wall mat flooring and painted sliding doors, both of which occurred in later periods.[52] When female figures appear in contemporary kimono, their images are unlabelled, and the text fails to identify or describe them.[53] These images purport to depict "daily life" but draw on visual and textual cues to encode layered meanings in their constructions of femininity. For example, Terazaki Kôgyô's untitled illustration facing the beginning of the chapter entitled "Japanese Women in Domestic Life" (fig. 4) depicts two figures seated before a decorative alcove. Both figures are dressed in kimono with hair up and secured by combs and pins. The older female holds a length of fabric, but she oversees the child's reading. The non-Japanese reader would likely be unable to determine whether the depicted costumes are contemporary or historical. The chapter opens with a juxtaposition of past and present that lends the image further ambiguity. "The customs of past centuries, to some

Fig. 3.4. Terazaki Kôgyô. Untitled illustration facing "Japanese Women in Domestic Life." Beikoku Daihakurankai Nippon Fujinkai. *Nihon no fujin.* Tokyo: Dai Nippon Kabushiki Kaisha, Meiji 28 [1896] and in Japanese Woman's Commission, *Japanese Women* (Chicago: McClurg, 1893, 74).

extent, still govern the lives of every Japanese woman. . . . When very young the child is carefully taught by its mother and grandmother to be graceful in manner, gentle in speech, polite and benevolent." The prose here supports the general argument that Japanese women remain in their sphere. "When she becomes a wife, a mother, or a grandmother these qualities continue to be imperative."[54] The reproduction of an authentic Japanese identity appears here in the metaphor of biological reproduction and matrilocal enforcement of normative femininity: in other words, tradition, unlike history, is continuously reenacted.

Kôgyô's image parallels this textual claim through the juxtaposition of two pair of mothers and daughters: one, the subjects of the domestic scene, and the other, the subjects depicted in miniature on a hanging scroll in the alcove. This compositional strategy invites a reading of the juxtaposition of a scene from "daily life" with the "painting" representing the reproduction of "customs" and comportment over time and across generations. That the depicted painting in the alcove illustrates the "Feudal period" and the foreground pair illustrates the "modern" is conveyed through the rendering of interior space. The minimally described architecture in the tiny image suggests the conventional tilting of the ground plane deployed in premodern Japanese painting. By contrast, Kôgyô's genre scene demonstrates an understanding of "modern" linear perspective— the spatial recession encodes the continuity of tradition over time.

Kôgyô's juxtaposition of past and present resembles the device used in both the English and Japanese versions of *Japanese Women* and the official Japanese report filed by the commission. Each of these sources uses a pair of oppositional terms to contrast and generalize the "ancient and modern." The preface to *Japanese Women* states, "The Commission desires and aims, in this work, to present to the world's public, however briefly, the true condition of the Japanese woman, ancient and modern." The key terms "ancient and modern" first appear in Japanese writing about the exposition as *kokon,* in a translation of the March 11, 1892, letter of invitation to participate in the Woman's Building from Bertha Honoré Palmer to the empress of Japan.

Like other emerging nations, Meiji Japan promoted the ability of the nation's women to be simultaneously "traditional" and "modern." The Japanese Lady's Boudoir and its supporting texts collapsed the historical and contemporary in its construction of femininity, alleviating the need for Japanese women to perform their identities at the exposition or risk criticism of transgression. The interiors of the Boudoir stood metonymically for all Japanese women within the beaux arts edifice of the Woman's Building. On the other hand, the masculinity of historic Japan was remote: safely contained within the wings of the Phoenix Hall on the Wooded Isle.

Conclusion

It is relatively easy to find examples of Japan's rapid appropriation of technology and social institutions that supported the country's industrialization in the late nineteenth century. More elusive is a comprehension of the complex waters of national identity Japanese officials negotiated in this formative period as they strove to establish treaty equity with Western powers. Once condemned as backward and as a cheap imitator of the modern West, Japan's savvy positioning of itself at the 1893 World's Columbian Exposition as a distinct and autonomously modernizing nation challenged an international ordering of nations that had located Japan perennially outside of history and, thus, also at odds with modernity. On the 1893 fairgrounds, Japan asserted compelling alternative narratives of its rise as a nation-state, successfully repositioning Japan as both rich in history and uniquely modern in particular and measurable ways. The key to maneuvering this paradox lay with presentations of patriarchal Japanese gender relations and, in particular, with presentations of Japanese women as "traditional" signs of an authentically unique Japanese heritage and culture. For European and American fairgoers and observers, the absence of "modern" Japanese women and the determinedly crafted presence of them as embodied signs of Japan's masculinist past produced a sense of Japan as different enough to comprise a nation in its own right—as sharing in a progressivist timeline with other modernizing nations. Japan's ability to enter into renegotiations in the 1890s, and to reframe international relations in its own terms at these occasions, followed from its success in establishing itself as a nation with an appropriately patriarchal past and masculinist present at the Columbian Exposition.

NOTES

1 My interest in the relationship between Japan's participation in the 1893 Columbian Exhibition and treaty renegotiation that took place in the 1890s was originally prompted by Neil Harris's suggestion of such a link in his essay, "All the World's a Melting Pot? Japan at the American Fairs, 1876–1904," in *Mutual Images: Essays in American-Japanese Relations,* ed. Akira Iriye, 46 (Cambridge: Harvard University Press, 1975). Quoted material appears on page 92 of the *Centennial Clippings,* Historical Society of Pennsylvania. Quoted by Harris, 36.

2 "A Japanese Temple," *World's Columbian Exposition Illustrated* 2 (June 1892): 74.

3 This Treaty of Kanagawa was signed one year after Commodore Perry's "Black Ships" came to Uraga, south of Tokyo. As Michael Auslin explains, Japan's contacts with Western states up to and including this treaty were "nonrevolutionary," but later treaties extracted progressively serious concessions that eroded Japanese sovereignty. Auslin, *Negotiating with Imperialism: The Unequal Treaties and the Culture of Japanese Diplomacy* (Cambridge: Harvard University Press, 2004), 12, 33. See also Louis Perez, *Japan Comes of Age: Mutsu Munemitsu and the Revision of the Unequal Treaties* (London: Associated University Presses, 1999), 47–63.

4 An earlier treaty with Mexico set precedent in 1888 by setting Mexican travelers under Japanese jurisdiction. Auslin, 199. Japan argued for the removal of extraterritoriality in books. Japan, trans. Captain Brinkley, *History of the Empire of Japan* (Tokyo: Dai Nippon Tosho Kabushiki Kwaisha, 1893), 398, 419–24; and Japan, *A History and Account of the Prisons of the Empire of Japan* (n.p.), 1893.

5 The term *kokon* literally combines "ancient" and "modern." Social class was conflated as *kisen.* Japan's attention to history at the fair illustrates Kumari Jayawardena's analysis of anticolonial strategies for the creation of new national identities in both the past and the present, naturalizing modernity as masculine, while situating women as both "modern" and "traditional," preserving their culture. Kumari Jayawardena, *Feminism and Nationalism in the Third World* (London: Zed, 1986), 15.

6 One organizer lamented that Westerners mistakenly thought Japan was a part of China. Mishima Masahiro, "1893 nen shikago bankokuhaku niokeru hôôden," *Nihon kenchiku gakkai* 429 (Nov. 1991): 154–55, citing the Imperial Japanese Commission, *Rinji hakurankai jimukyôku hôkoku* (1894) chap. 4, sect. 20.

7 Peter Duus, *The Abacus and the Sword: The Japanese Penetration of Korea, 1895–1910* (Berkeley: University of California Press, 1999), 29–56; W. G. Beasley, *Japanese Imperialism: 1894–1945* (Oxford: Clarendon, 1987), 42–54.

8 Henry Steele Commager, *The Search for a Usable Past* (New York: 1967). Kenneth Pyle borrows this turn of phrase in his study, *The New Generation in Meiji Japan: Problems of Cultural Identity* (Stanford: Stanford University Press, 1969), 55.

9 Okakura Kakuzô, *Illustrated Description of the Hô-ô-den or Phoenix Hall at the World's Columbian Exposition* (Tokyo: K. Ogawa, 1893).

10 Mishima, 155. See Ellen Conant's excellent overview of the Japanese participation in expositions in "Refractions of the Rising Sun: Japan's Participation in International Expositions, 1872–1910," in *Japan and Britain, an Aesthetic Dialogue*, ed. Tomoko Sato and Toshio Watanabe (London: Lund Humphries, 1991). Mishima notes this, as does Notoji Masako, in "Civilization Illuminating the World: The United States and Japan at the World's Columbian Exposition of 1893," *Journal of Human and Cultural Studies* (Musashi University) 20, no. 3/4 (1989): 269.

11 Marilyn Ivy, *Discourses of the Vanishing: Modernity, Phantasm, Japan* (Chicago: University of Chicago Press, 1995), 4–5.

12 Putnam, *World's Columbian Exhibition Plans and Classification, Dept. M.*, 8.

13 Stanley Appelbaum, *The Chicago World's Fair of 1893: A Photographic Record* (Mineola, N.Y.: Dover, 1980), 7, 13–14. Robert W. Rydell, *All the World's a Fair: Visions of Empire at American Expositions, 1876–1916* (Chicago: University of Chicago Press, 1984) 4, 39–40.

14 Henry Davenport Northrop, *Pictorial History of the World's Columbian Exposition* (Chicago: National, 1893), 239; Marrieta Holley, *Samantha at the World's Fair by Josiah Allen's Wife* (New York: Funk and Wagnalls, 1893), 403.

15 Holley, 403.

16 "Triumph for Japan," *Daily Inter Ocean* 22 (April 1, 1893): 5.

17 Maud Howe Elliot, *Art and Handicraft in the Woman's Building at the World's Columbian Exposition, Chicago, 1893* (Paris: Boussod, Valadon, 1893).

18 Ibid., 17–19.

19 Sharon Sievers, *Flowers in Salt: the Beginnings of Feminist Consciousness in Modern Japan* (Berkeley: Stanford University Press, 1983), 52–53. Sievers explains how women were added to an existing list of people who were banned from public meetings under article 5 of the Police Security Regulations and so could not observe proceedings in Japan's parliament. This ban was lifted, but women remained barred from joining political groups. Sharon Nolte and Sally Ann Hastings link the addition of women to those under article 5 as public servants whose roles as wives and mothers made them above politics. As they point out, other reasons included their presumed frailty and paradoxical potential to become dangerous. "Meiji Policy Towards Women, 1890–1910" in *Recreating Japanese Women, 1600–1945*, ed. Gail Lee Bernstein, 157 (Berkeley: University of California Press, 1991).

20 Nolte and Hastings, 157.

21 "In present-day Japan, the condition of women is such that Japan cannot be considered a civilized or cultured country," Iwamoto Zenji, in Jayawardena, *Feminism and Nationalism*, 230.

22 Tsuda Umeko, founder of Tsuda University and contributor to *Japanese Women*, denounced calls for female suffrage.

23 Jean-Paul Bourdier, "Reading Tradition," *Dwellings, Settlements, and Tradition* (Berkeley: International Center for the Study of Traditional Environments, 1989), 38.

24 Okakura, 13.

25 Ibid., 9.

26 Northrop, 585.

27 See Toshio Watanabe's "Japanese Imperial Architecture: From Thomas Roger Smith to Itô Chuta," in *Challenging the Past and Present: Metamorphosis of Nineteenth Century Japanese Art*, ed. Ellen P. Conant (Honolulu: University of Hawaii Press, 2006).

28 Mishima, 151–63. In her dissertation, *Art in Place: The Display of Japan at the Imperial Museums* (Harvard University, 2004), Alice Tseng argues that the Phoenix Hall represents one of two kinds of museum display, the other being that which is found in the National Museums. Also see Conant, "Japan 'Abroad' at the Chicago Exposition, 1893," in Conant, ed., *Challenging the Past and Present*, and Victoria Weston's *Japanese Painting and National Identity* (Ann Arbor: University of Michigan Press, 2004).

29 The absence of phoenix imagery supports an interpretation of ambiguity: phoenix imagery in noblewomen's apartments is documented in Princess Fushimi's sitting room in *Fujin gahô*. Jordan Sand, "Were Meiji Interiors Orientalist?" *Positions: East Asian Cultural Critique* 8, no. 3 (Winter 2000): 645.

30 "Round-about the Collecting World" (*Collector* 5, no. 1 [1893]: 3) suggests that the dealer, Takayanagi Tozo, organized the exhibit and authored or arranged the publishing of the *Explanation of the Japanese Lady's Boudoir*.

31 Japanese Ladies' Committee, *Explanation of the Japanese Lady's Boudoir* (Chicago: Mc-Clurg, 1893), 7.

32 Princess Mori, Marchioness Matsuda, and Marchioness Nabeshima each loaned or donated materials for the display.

33 Carol Gluck, "The Invention of Edo," in *Mirror of Modernity: Invented Traditions of Modern Japan*, ed. Stephen Vlastos, 262 (Berkeley: University of California Press, 1998). Gluck argues that the conflation of centuries of cultural practice as if typical of Edo creates an undifferentiated body of cultural material as a foil for proponents of reform. This strategy is seen in the Boudoir, but designers of the Phoenix Hall chose to highlight distinctions between past epochs to highlight the Japanese "progress," which could be compared to that of other nations.

34 Gluck notes that no matter how anti-Tokugawa their rhetoric, most Meiji writers found elements "from the past that they thought the future required" (266).

35 *Japanese Women* (n.p.)

36 See Elliot, 35; Ellen Henrotin: "Here is a Japanese woman's boudoir. It is exceedingly interesting as showing the surroundings of a Japanese woman in her home." "An Outsider's View of the Woman's Building," *Cosmopolitan* 15, no. 15 (September 1893): 565.

37 Okakura, 14, 20, 24.

38 Donald Shively, "The Japanization of the Middle Meiji," in *Tradition and Modernization in Japanese Culture*, ed. Shively, 82 (Princeton: Princeton University Press, 1971). Jayawardena, 233; also see Hastings, "The Empress's New Clothes and Japanese Women, 1868–1912," *The Historian* 55 (Summer 1993): 677–92.

39 Japan nearly abstained from participating in the Woman's Building. The Board of Lady Managers issued the invitation very late—March 11, 1892—when exposition funds had long since been appropriated. The empress emerged as patron of the exhibits and appointed Princess Yasu Mori as president of a Japanese Woman's Commission. A good (but often-overlooked) source is A. B. de Guerville, *Au Japon* (Paris: Lemerre, 1904), 119.

40 Ibid., 124–6.

41 Northrop, 247–48.

42 Ibid., 119–20. He describes the best French food and wine, Cuban cigars, and elegant garb.

43 *History of the Empire of Japan*, 410.

44 Notoji, 264. Christine Guth raises of fears that male kimono would be read as feminine: see Charles Longfellow and Okakura Kakuzô, "Cultural Cross-Dressing in the Colonial Context," *Positions: East Asian Cultures Critique* 8, no. 3 (Winter 2000): 622–25. See also Victoria Weston, *East Meets West: Isabella Stewart Gardner and Okakura Kakuzô* (Boston: Isabella Stewart Gardner Museum, 1992).

45 "Japanese at the World's Columbian Exposition" *Scientific American* 68 (June 24, 1893): 392.

46 *Daily Inter Ocean* 22 (May 5, 1893): 7.

47 Report to the Board of Lady Managers, second session, September 2, 1891. Quoting Princess Christian and Mme. Carnot of France on "good wives and mothers" (81).

48 Jayawardena argues that a strategy of colonial resistance was to "idealize the civilization of the distant past, speaking of the need to regain the lost freedom that women were said to have once possessed in their societies" (14).

49 Ibid.

50 Only one historic woman's image is used in the book, but she is not identified in the text, nor is the image captioned. Unless one reads the Japanese language version of this book, the picture of a woman repairing a paper-covered lattice door would be understood as a generic picture.

51 *Japanese Women* (n.p.).

52 In the Heian era, cushions were placed on one or more *tatami* mats on a highly polished wooden floor, and large, portable, painted screens would be placed in front of plaster walls or bays with hanging wooden doors. This type of matting, made up of rows of parallel mats, recalls the photograph of Princess Higashi-Fushimi's rooms from 1906 published in *Fujin gahô* (Sand, 645). This anachronism has a parallel in the Boudoir: *tatami* mats cover both floors in their entirety, and painted *fusuma* surround each room containing large cushions.

53 The placement of illustrations in the text resulted from editorial choices, as is suggested by the different positioning of illustrations in the Japanese-language version of this same book, *Nihon no fujin,* in 1896.

54 *Japanese Women*, 75.

CHAPTER 4

Manliness and the New American Empire at the 1915 Panama-Pacific Exposition

Sarah J. Moore

In April 1899, two months after the Senate ratified the treaty with Spain that concluded the Spanish-American War and established the Philippines as a colony of the United States, Theodore Roosevelt delivered a speech entitled "The Strenuous Life" in Chicago, in which he outlined the contours of America's new imperial physique. Defining the nation as one of "stern men with empire in their brains," the address exuberantly extolled imperialism as America's national destiny and as *the* force to expand the American economy, ensure military superiority and international trade, improve racial fitness, and invigorate the American man. "We cannot sit huddled within our own borders," Roosevelt admonished the audience. "We must build the isthmian canal and we must grasp the points of vantage which will enable us to have our say in deciding the destiny of the oceans of the East and West."[1] Sixteen years later, in the Court of the Universe at the Panama-Pacific International Exposition in San Francisco, Roosevelt was greeted by a massive audience who had gathered to celebrate Roosevelt Day. Exposition President Moore asked, "Who built the Panama Canal?" "Teddy," yelled the crowd.[2] Indeed, the crowd had no trouble linking the man—Theodore Roosevelt, former Rough Rider, president, and builder of the Panama Canal—with the exposition that heralded America's triumphant fitness to stand among the great nations of the world.

Designed to celebrate the rebuilding of San Francisco as the gateway between east and west, following the devastating 1906 earthquake and fire and the completion of the Panama Canal, the Panama-Pacific Exposition celebrated America's new empire with a heady sense of ownership over the Western hemisphere. Temporally situated between the Spanish-American War (and consequent establishment of a Pacific empire) and World War I, where the United States takes on a defining role in European and world affairs, the exposition provided evidence—visual, spatial, and ideological—of the efficacy and efficiency of America's transgressions of national borders. The link between San Francisco and the Panama Canal was not gratuitous; official chronicler of the Panama-Pacific Exposition, Frank Morton Todd, noted, "The Canal has given San Francisco a new position on the planet."[3] Each was a gateway between east and west; each provided a fluid boundary between nations and national bodies; and each was defined by the manly triumph of American hegemony. Within the 635-acre exposition fairgrounds, America's new empire was recreated in miniature and celebrated as a manifestation of the United States' imperial prowess and revitalized national manliness. Indeed, the physiognomy of America's newly minted imperial nationalism was inscribed on the male body—physically and ideologically—which was understood as vigorous, muscular, innately superior, powerful, and radiant.

The Panama-Pacific Exposition embraced the spirit of self-confident national bravura and buoyant optimism that had distinguished earlier American world's fairs. Like these other fairs, the 1915 exposition defined progress and civilization within the contours of the American national body. Moreover, it was imagined as providing a road map for future perfection with its overarching themes of progress and social harmony, much as the Panama Canal was understood, in the words of Theodore Roosevelt, as "the future highway of civilization."[4] This chapter examines three visual constructions of the Panama Canal in detail: Stirling Calder's *Fountain of Energy* in the main entrance to the fairgrounds; Pernham Nahl's official poster for the exposition, *Thirteenth Labor of Hercules;* and the gigantic miniature replica of the Panama Canal on the Zone. All three displays functioned pedagogically and embraced Social Darwinian logic, assuming an evolutionary trajectory of civilization. Paralleling Darwinian discourse that viewed civilization hierarchically, with white men at its apex, the fairground itself was a kind of ideological map in which progress was organized hierarchically and directionally. The cartographic design of the layout, approved by the exposition's organizers, functioned as a visual agent of regulation and social meaning, fixing nations and displays along spatial coordinates that assumed the authority and objectivity of the topographical map. Most significantly, each display was hinged on contemporary notions of manliness and utilized gender ideology to articulate contemporary ideas and assumptions about the American nation and its new empire.[5]

Fountain of Energy: Realizing the Centuries-Old Dream of Appropriating the Seas

The main entrance to the Panama-Pacific Exposition fairgrounds was on the city side at Scott Street. The south gardens, with some three thousand square feet of California's exotic flora, gave way to the *Fountain of Energy* and Tower of Jewels, the signature sculptural and architectural ensembles in the fairgrounds. The former represented the expansion of the American frontier in the Panama Canal Zone, while the latter symbolized the progress and abundant wealth of the host nation. Beyond the Tower of Jewels were the three principal courts of the fairgrounds. The courts were organized on an east-to-west orientation, paralleling the Panama Canal itself and metonymically standing for San Francisco's location, physically and ideologically, as the point of contact between the two. The Court of the Universe, designed by McKim, Mead, and White, stood in the center of the fairgrounds and was the largest of the principal courts.

Punctuated on the east and west by colossal triumphal arches of the rising sun and setting sun, respectively, the scale of the Court of the Universe was massive—712 feet long and 520 feet wide—and traced the trajectory of imperialism from the past to the triumphant present. Frank Morton Todd could scarcely contain his enthusiasm about the sheer grandeur of the Court of the Universe when he noted, "The Roman Colosseum could have been set down inside it . . . [and] the peristyle of St. Peter's could not approach it in interest."[6] He described the figures in the sculptural ensemble that topped the Arch of the Setting Sun, *Nations of the West,* in gendered terms—"rough and real . . . waste-conquering, desert-spanning" men—and located what he called the "thrusting heave of western ambition and progress" on the shores of the Pacific Ocean in San Francisco.[7]

The Court of Abundance, designed by Louis Christian Mullgardt, was located on the eastern-oriented Aisle of the Rising Sun and was punctuated at its easternmost edge by the Palace of Machinery. This building was the largest wood and steel structure in the world at the time—the entire personnel of the United States Army and Navy could have fit on the inside standing upright—and it was the site of the first indoor flight when pioneer aerialist and stunt man Lincoln J. Beachey flew through the building before it was completed. The western-oriented Aisle of the Setting Sun led to the Court of Four Sea-

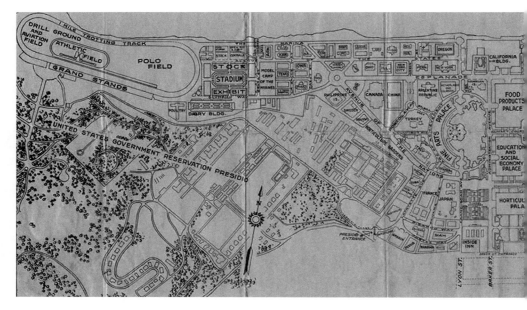

Fig. 4.1. Fairgrounds of Panama-Pacific International Exposition. Official Map of the Panama-Pacific International Exposition, San Francisco (San Francisco: Wahlgreen, 1915).

sons, designed by Henry Bacon, which was flanked on the westernmost edge by San Francisco architect Bernhard Maybeck's Palace of Fine Arts, the only building to be preserved at the close of the Fair in December. The *Column of Progress* punctuated the northernmost edge of the fairgrounds as they gave way to the Bay of San Francisco, which was traversed throughout the course of the Panama-Pacific Exposition by the so-called scintillator, a battery of search lights on a barge which beamed forty-eight lights in seven colors across the bay to illuminate the exposition's fairgrounds at night.[8]

A. Stirling Calder's *Fountain of Energy* had a place of honor in the main entrance to the fairgrounds and, as one contemporary observer noted, gave "the keynote of the Exposition a mood of triumphant rejoicing."[9] Calder served as the acting chief of sculpture at the Panama-Pacific Exposition and took full advantage of his sculpture's location to pay tribute to the completion of the Panama Canal, which the fair celebrated. The globe on which the equestrian statuary group stands suggests the sun's course—east to west—and the evolution of mankind to the pinnacle of civilization embodied at the exposition. *Energy,* a lean, nude male figure, also known as the *Lord of the Isthmian Way* and the *Victor of the Canal,* rides triumphantly on the Earth; his outstretched hands represent the severing of the lands that allowed for the waters of the Atlantic and the Pacific to pass. It embodied manliness, national determination, and, as Todd noted, "the qualities

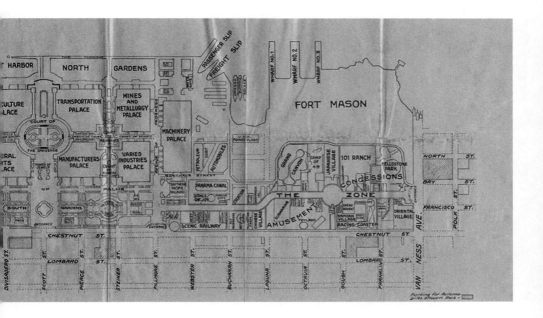

of force and dominance that had ripped a way across the continental divide for the commerce of the world."[10] Indeed, Calder's sculptural ensemble visualized Roosevelt's national admonition: "Let us therefore boldly face the life of strife, resolute to our duty well and manfully. . . . Above all, let us shrink from no strife, moral or physical, within or without the nation, provided we are certain that the strife is justified, for it is only through strife, through hard and dangerous endeavor, that we shall ultimately win the goal of true national greatness."[11] This triumphant superman, who stands atop a miniaturized globe, the topography of which has been refashioned by American technology and imperial desires, did not shy from his manly duty to his nation and to the world. Indeed, *Energy* "made the Isthmus of Panama look like a geographical nuisance no virile people could tolerate."[12] Calder's *Lord of the Isthmian Way* effectively takes on the role of chivalric rescuer, used so pervasively in imperial discourse, and visualized Roosevelt's assumption that the unquestioned superiority of Euro-American civilization justified any and all United States' imperial activities.

On top of the figure's shoulders stand fame and glory, "heralding the coming of the conqueror," in the words of the sculptor himself, and referencing imperial iconography.[13] In the basin of the fountain, at the cardinal points of the compass, are representations of the Atlantic, facing east, and the Pacific, facing west. In marked contrast to this heroic, manly ensemble is *Earth,* by Robert

Fig. 4.2. A. Stirling Calder, *Fountain of Energy*. Juliet James, *Sculpture of the Exposition* (San Francisco: H. S. Crocker, 1915).

Aitken, in the center of the Court of Ages to the east, in which a slumbering female form embodies the assumption of the New World as a female figure in profitless slumber who awaits arousal and implantation of the seeds of civilization by the likes, one assumes, of the *Lord of the Isthmian Way*.[14] As such, this sculptural ensemble traces the history of the manly American empire: European colonist becomes intrepid pioneer becomes modern day imperialist hero with dominion over the earth.

Thirteenth Labor of Hercules: A Manly Nation Builds the Panama Canal

The parallels between Calder's *Victor of the Canal* and the official poster for the Panama-Pacific Exposition, Perham Nahl's *Thirteenth Labor of Hercules,* are striking. In the latter, a nude, hypermuscular male is thrusting apart the continental barrier at Panama—the pastoral Culebra Cut—to allow the seas to meet in an embrace of historic proportions and imperial fantasies. That the completion of the Panama Canal realized the fantasy of explorers over four centuries earlier to find a navigable passage from east to west was not lost on contemporary viewers. California State Commissioner Chester Rowell, for example, declared the Canal "celebrat[ed] the finish of the journey of Columbus."[15] Below Hercules' feet, in the misty distance, rise the domes and pinnacles of the fairgrounds themselves. Although many previous world's fairs in the United

States employed a similar visual device for their publicity images—a representative figure of America gestures from above to a bird's-eye view of the fairgrounds below[16]—Nahl's heroic nude figure departs from the more typical allegorical representative of the nation in the guise of a colossal female figure: Columbia, Liberty, or Republic.[17] This male Gargantua is both technological engineer and preindustrial laboring giant: a national superman carrying out the thirteenth, and by all contemporary accounts, most important modern labor, whose physical strength and vigorous masculinity embody the bravura, extreme confidence, and technological accomplishment of the United States within an international and imperial context. Geologist and historian Vaughan Cornish described the Panama Canal as one of the wonders of the world when he declared: "To go to Culebra is as if one were privileged to watch the building of the Pyramids."[18]

Nahl may well have had in mind another American laborer cum engineer in his creation of Hercules: that of Edwin Blashfield in his collar decoration for

Fig. 4.3. Perham Nahl, *Thirteenth Labor of Hercules.* John Barry, *The City of Domes* (San Francisco: J. J. Newbegin, 1915).

the Library of Congress in Washington, D.C., in 1896. Blashfield's *America* is the twelfth and final figure in *The Evolution of Civilization,* an elaborate allegory of the American Renaissance ideal of the United States as the culmination of history and the heir of the sum total of human knowledge, achievements, and culture. Paralleling the mapping of civilization's march from east to west in the Court of Honor at the World's Columbian Exposition of 1893, in which the artist participated as a muralist, Blashfield's figures assume an evolutionary logic and directional flow of civilization: the first figure, *Egypt,* is associated with the East; *America,* the final figure, is aligned with the West. With science as its contribution, *America* is a brawny and muscular laborer who sits with a dynamo between his legs and holds a book in one hand. As such, *America* is both manly laborer and intellectual engineer who can harness the potential of technology, represented by the dynamo, and as such can enact the progress of civilization.[19] The connection between American technological prowess and the Panama Canal was noted by others; the locks of the Panama Canal, for example, were compared by more than one contemporary observer to the dynamo, "as one of the crowning achievements of the western mind."[20]

Hercules embodies the manly will, inspired by imperial fantasies and fueled by Social Darwinian presumptions, of the United States to complete the Panama Canal, and the history of the national body as pioneer and farmer who wrestled a nation out of the wilderness. As a contemporary chronicler of the Panama Canal noted, "Now that the government of a great nation has put their hands to the plow the furrow will be driven through."[21] There are no traces here of the dreaded overcivilized neurasthenic whose lack of vitality, as Roosevelt and others warned, threatened not only the viability of the American nation but the entire Anglo-Saxon race.[22] The gigantic male body metaphorically refers to the massive machinery and technology that was used in the actual building of the Panama Canal. At the same time, it also suggested that there was an historical inevitability to American progress attributable to a national prerogative to confront the wilderness and pursue an ever-receding frontier. The natural landscape is overwhelmed by the power and size of this American giant. A photograph of Theodore Roosevelt—notably not on horseback as was the pictorial tradition in imperial iconography but instead at the controls of a colossal Bucyrus shovel at Pedro Miguel in the construction zone—posits the conflation of body, machine technology, and national manhood in what historian Bill Brown has called "an imperial vortex."[23] Roosevelt is rendered gigantic—natural man becomes superman as continental nation becomes extracontinental nation—much like the body of Hercules, although not by sheer muscularity but through the prosthetic of the dispassionate machine.[24]

Brown defines Nahl's figure of Hercules as "the vision of an imperialist American body" which will remasculinize and, as such, recuperate the nation.[25]

Fig. 4.4. Theodore
Roosevelt in the
Panama Canal
Construction Zone.
New York Times,
Pictorial Section, part 1
(December 2, 1906).

Hercules' confrontation of the wilderness at Culebra regenerates, in Roosevelt's words, "the vigorous manliness for the lack of which in a nation, as in an individual, the possession of no other qualities can possibly atone."[26] The supernatural man and Panamanian geography converge into a national body whose corporeal coherence and fitness naturalize United States' imperial practices and technological triumph. Indeed, this Hercules who labors in Central America embodies United States' development from adolescence to manhood in imperial prowess, looking back to the Spanish-American War of 1898, which itself functioned as a political rationale for the completion of the Panama Canal, and to the 1904 Louisiana Purchase Exposition, in which the imperial trophies of that first transcontinental excursion were exhibited to the world.[27] Not coincidentally, 1904 was the year in which President Theodore Roosevelt created the commission to oversee the construction of the Isthmian passageway and in which San Francisco businessmen and financial tycoons proposed a world's fair in San Francisco to celebrate the engineering triumph in Central America. The Panama-Pacific Exposition's Board of Directors, which included Charles C. Moore, president of one of the nation's largest hydroelectrical engineering firms, and William H. Crocker, son of one of the builders of the transcontinental railroad and vice-president of Pacific Telephone and Telegraph, sought, as historian Robert Rydell notes, to "preserve the people's faith in the idea of progress—with all its interlaced connotations of technological advance, material growth, racism, and imperialism—and to reshape that faith with particular reference to the challenges posed by domestic and international turmoil."[28]

Indeed, Nahl's Hercules embodies the ultimate solution to the anxiety provoked by Frederick Jackson Turner's announcement in 1893, not coincidentally at the World's Columbian Exposition in Chicago, of the closing of the frontier. The apparent foreclosure of the American wilderness, where men were regenerated and the American nation was formed, was overturned with United States' embarkation upon a geopolitical shift from continental expansion to overseas empire with the Spanish-American War in 1898. The promise of imperial expansion offered, as historian Amy Kaplan argues, "a new frontier, where the essential American man could be reconstituted."[29] Turner, himself, proposed overseas expansion, including the building of an isthmian canal, as a solution to "the problem of the west," as he called it, invoking Bishop Berkeley's often-repeated declaration—"Westward the course of empire takes its way"—of the 1720s as a foundational staple of American self-conception by this time. Turner's thesis looked backward—"For nearly three-hundred years the dominant fact in American life has been expansion"—while bemoaning a contemporary state wherein westward expansion, which Turner and others assumed to be the natural and inevitable movement of the national body, had come to a fateful close with the settlement of the Pacific Coast. Nonetheless, Turner remained optimistic that the West represented not one particular place or coordinate on a map but rather a national mindset premised on progress and the manly triumph of civilization over wilderness. Just as, in Turner's words, "Decade after decade, West after West, this rebirth of the American society has gone on,"[30] Nahl's heroic nude Hercules posits, with supreme confidence, the coordinates of American masculinity, nationhood, and progress along the imperial frontier.

Nahl's Hercules can also be understood as the modern hero/engineer whose prowess is evidenced by his re-creation of the natural world: the ability to make machinery serve human needs; to redeem and surmount the inefficient forces of nature; in short, to wear the mantle of civilization and win wilderness over to order. As historian Cecilia Tichi observes, "In controlling and utilizing the forces of nature, the engineer makes the continent itself his studio as well as the medium in which he works. He is, moreover, an instrument of (and at the same time the embodiment of) national destiny."[31] Indeed, this heroic superman embodied both the history of United States' taming of the frontier and its imperialist future, and offered visual evidence of the inevitability of American progress.

As with the Panama-Pacific Exposition itself, Nahl's Hercules links gender and imperialism and posits both as constitutive of nationalist ideology. Moreover, as the fair defines America's progress and civilization as hierarchical, evolutionary, and gendered male, so Hercules pushes back the spectacle of barbarism and primitivism that defined the canal zone prior to the canal—the Panamanian Joy Zone, if you will—and reveals the accomplishments of the nation as embodied in the official fairgrounds. Finally, in the canal's realization of Columbus's imperial fantasy of a passageway from east to west, Hercules underscores the evolutionary and historical nature of America's technological triumph and rightful, if newly won, place at the imperial table.

American Pioneer and The End of the Trail: Naturalizing Progress and Territorial Expansion

The sheer national will and manly might to overcome the powers of nature and subdue the continent were evoked in numerous pronouncements and public addresses regarding the Panama-Pacific Exposition. One contemporary observer, for example referred to America's accomplishment with the Panama Canal as a "correct[ion] of the oversight of nature in omitting to provide a channel into the Pacific."[32] The intrepid pioneer, who wrought civilization and progress from nature's profitless slumber, was imagined as the national patriarch who articulated the model for manly progress for the nation that began with Europeans' first encounters in the New World and ended with America's ascendancy as an imperial nation, as made manifest by the Panama Canal and celebrated at the Panama-Pacific Exposition. United States' Secretary of the Interior Franklin Lane, for example, traced America's triumphant accomplishment in Panama to that of the pioneers: "Theirs be the glory today for they have slashed the continent in two, they have cut the land that God made as if with a knife."[33] Indeed, images of and allusions to the archetype of the American pioneer were prevalent at the exposition and provide further evidence of the masculinist and imperialist preoccupations of the fair. Moreover, they provide historical evidence for the inevitable evolution of the new manly American empire.

Among the most prominent sculptural evocations of this theme was created by Solon Borglum. His work, American Pioneer, took the form of an equestrian statue, a visual staple of imperial iconography, more than two-and-a-half times life size. A man sits at ease atop a magnificent horse whose elaborate tack seems more at home in Renaissance pageantry than in the American frontier. The pioneer holds a gun aloft in one hand and rests his other hand on his chin, as if to contemplate his defining role in national destiny. Borglum's statue rehearsed the narrative of the "advance of civilization in the new American Eden"[34] depicted in countless visual images of the nineteenth century, with a gun, a plow, and an axe as the tools with which he fashioned the wilderness into the American nation.

This pioneer expresses no nostalgia for America's wilderness past or concern for the "ravages of the axe," as did many of the artists of those nineteenth-century images.[35] Unquestionably linking American progress from its historical roots in the pioneer to its modern manifestation as manly imperialist, one contemporary observer noted: "The greatest adventure is before us, the gigantic adventures of an advancing democracy—strong, virile, and kindly—and in that advance we shall be true to the indestructible spirit of the American pioneer."[36] Roosevelt himself was quick to draw an historical trajectory from that of the intrepid pioneer of the nineteenth century, to the Spanish-American War, and to the building of the Panama Canal. Casting westward expansion in gendered terms and as a prelude to imperialist activities, Roosevelt defined America's triumph in the Panama Canal as a providential expression of the United States' national will and manly desire to "struggle for a place among the men that shape the destiny of mankind."[37]

Standing opposite Borglum's *American Pioneer* in the Court of Palms was the equally massive equestrian statue, *The End of the Trail*, by James Earle Frasier. A bare-chested Native American man sits bareback on a bridleless horse. Both rider and horse slump forward in utter exhaustion. The overarching didacticism of the fair's sculptural grouping, buttressed by their placement within the fairgrounds—the ideological mapping of the march of civilization, as it were—was made patently obvious in this sculptural counterpoint, as were the racial assumptions of Social Darwinism. In contrast to the triumph of progress of Euro-Americans in Borglum's *American Pioneer*, Frasier's vanquished Native American, enervated and exhausted, has reached the end of his trail, and by extension, the extinction of his race. A contemporary guidebook described it: "But alas! . . . His trail is now lost and on the edge of the continent he finds himself almost annihilated."[38] The artist's language evokes a similar notion of the noble savage doomed to extinction when he said: "[I] sought to express the utter despair of this conquered people, a weaker race . . . steadily pushed to the wall by a stronger one."[39]

Such racial discourse naturalized Euro-American superiority over Native American and the inevitability of the latter's demise and was designed, as cultural historian Stuart Hall has noted, "to *fix* difference, and thus secure it forever."[40] Frasier's *The End of the Trail* buttressed the logic of manly empire building and Social Darwinism by providing a history lesson in American colonial encounters and their foundation on contemporary notions of civilization and progress in contrast to primitivism. In fact, the United States' national agenda of the nineteenth century to subdue and civilize the wilderness, which included the Native American, was understood as a template for and dress rehearsal of subsequent imperial endeavors outside the continental boundaries of the United States that began with the Spanish-American War in 1898.[41] Moreover, Frasier's sculptural embodiment of the concept of racial progress permeated the Panama-Pacific Exposition as a whole and functioned as an official expression of what Rydell has argued is among the central prerogatives of host nations at world's fairs: the display of their colonial accomplishments and possessions.

The one arena in which Native American cultures were shown flourishing was in a faux Hopi Village, poignantly called "Life of the Vanishing Race" in official guidebooks, on the roof of the Grand Canyon display in the Zone. The Grand Canyon of Arizona display, put on by the Atchison, Topeka and Santa Fe Railroad, featured a nearly six-acre model of the Grand Canyon with a simulated Indian village on top of the building. The miniaturized recreation of the new world's arguably most sublime natural wonder was constructed over a period of three years at a cost of $300,000 and highlighted seven principal sites of the canyon, all of which were viewed from specially designed observation parlor cars, moved by electricity on an elevated trestle along the simulated rim of the canyon.[42] The entire journey took thirty minutes. Every attempt at accuracy was made, including all the foreground material being brought in from the canyon itself—rocks, old trees, and cacti—while the background featured painted set pieces carefully constructed to reproduce the perspective and topography of the great chasm. Well-known scenic artist, Walter W. Burridge, was hired to paint the scenes and spent two months doing so on site.[43]

Atop the building that housed the gigantic miniature of the Grand Canyon was a Pueblo (Hopi) Village that, much like the so-called living ethnological displays that were standard features in previous world's fairs, was designed to provide an accurate accounting of the life of Pueblo Indians. In fact, twenty families were brought to live in the faux pueblo for the duration of the fair and such so-called traditional items as blankets and jewelry were available for sale, just as they were along the train routes and in the hotels managed by the Fred Harvey Company for the Santa Fe Railroad that had made the Grand Canyon a tourist destination. The official brochure underscores the didactic nature of the spectacle: "[Here] the daily life and the character of the Pueblo Indians are shown accurately. These wards of the Nation, these vanishing tribes of men, are living here, engaged in the occupations of their daily life, in the same environment that surrounds them on the reservation."[44] Moreover, it posits internal colonialism, and by extension current imperial activities, as a philanthropic practice: a cultural benefaction, as it were. Much as Borglum's *American Pioneer* and Frasier's *The End of the Trail* visualized current assumptions about the heroic manliness of the former in contrast to the emasculated, vanishing Native American, the Pueblo village of the Grand Canyon display reiterates the masculinist and imperialist discourse of westward expansion in the nineteenth century. The Native Americans' embeddedness in the natural (read: feminine) world is considered evidence of the inevitability of their demise and their inferior position on the evolutionary trajectory of civilization.

As anthropologist Stephen Becker has observed, the Santa Fe Railroad embarked upon an "Indian Campaign," as they called it, beginning around 1900 in order to promote tourism to the Southwest, including collecting paintings of the American west for the decoration of railway stations and promotional brochures. The creation of the Grand Canyon and the Pueblo exhibits at the Panama-Pacific Exposition represented the railroad's most self-conscious construction of an "authentic" American West—both its nature and its culture—that existed solely within and was defined by the constructs of the tourist industry. Indeed, both the natural wonder and the Native Americans were civilized, as it were, through the technological resources of the exhibition's organizers, and by extension, the railroad itself. As the exhibition brochure noted, "All resources of modern science and electrical effects have been exploited, and the best talent of the world was engaged in the work of reproduction."[45] As such, the technological know-how of the Grand Canyon display paralleled, in miniature, the national will, technological prowess, and masculine desire to tame the western frontier. Moreover, much as the Panama-Pacific Exposition celebrated the completion of the Panama Canal as a national triumph of United States' manly will and technological know-how over the savage (read: uncivilized) landscape of the canal zone, so the Grand Canyon display offered a gendered reading of the landscape that was rendered useful, even profitable, through its transformation from feminine nature to masculine natural resource.

A Gigantic Miniature: Paradoxes of the *Panama Canal*

Given the Panama-Pacific Exposition's dedication to the building of the Panama Canal, it is no wonder that references to and images of the "greatest marine achievement since the discovery of America," in the words of Exposition chronicler Frank Morton Todd,[46] would abound throughout the fairgrounds. Among the most astonishing, in scale and ambition, was the gigantic yet miniature replica of this engineering feat, the *Panama Canal*, located on the Zone. The sixty-five-acre amusement section of the fair, known as the Zone, or the Joy Zone, extended to the east of the main fairgrounds and featured over a mile of booths, entertainments, and pavilions, including twenty-five theaters and the aeroscope (the exposition's response to the Ferris wheel of the World's Columbian Exposition in Chicago, 1893) which featured a two-story booth at the end of a two-hundred-foot steel arm that was lifted high above the fairgrounds for a panoramic view. The Zone displays were designed to be sensational, and yet the spirit of didacticism that defined the main fairgrounds infused many of the attractions on the Zone as well, perhaps none more so than that of the *Panama Canal*. Located near the Fillmore Street entrance to the fair at its eastern edge and directly adjoining the Machinery Palace, the physical space of the exhibit mediated between the official fairgrounds and the Zone. The pedagogical motivation of this display was formally recognized by its receipt of a grand prize under the Liberal Arts Section, the only Zone exhibit to be so awarded. The quasi-official status of the *Panama Canal* display was also evidenced in the imitation travertine marble exterior of the building itself, a veneer otherwise reserved to the exposition palaces of the main fair.

The model covered almost five acres—"the largest reproduction of any subject ever created," noted a contemporary guide book[47]—and represented an extraordinary attempt to reproduce accurately a great expanse of territory. Every minute detail was worked out with engineering accuracy from plans and drawings furnished by the United States Government through the courtesy of the Isthmian Canal Commission and Major General Geo. W. Goethals, governor of the Canal Zone. The thoroughness and faithful accuracy of the working reproduction of the Panama Canal and Canal Zone were attested by Major F. C.

Fig. 4.5. Model of Locks at Panama Canal Exhibit. *The Panama Canal at San Francisco 1915* (San Francisco: Panama Canal Exhibition Co., 1915).

Boggs, chief of the Washington office of the Panama Canal, who, following his inspection of the display in February 1915, reported: "This is to advise you that I have completed the checking and examination of your reproduction of the Panama Canal . . . and I find that it is so accurate that it will in half an hour import to anyone a more complete knowledge of the Canal than would a visit of several days to the waterway itself."[48] As such, the miniaturized replica was endowed with a pedagogical prowess unachievable by the actual site itself. Indeed, the *Panama Canal* display could be understood as a miniaturized version of the Panama-Pacific Exposition itself that assumed the imperialist authority to recreate the world as a manifestation of America's manly power and progress.

The astonishing ambition, scale, and technological advancements that marked the construction of the Panama Canal were mirrored in the model that was built over a period of fifteen months at a cost of approximately $250,000; the engineering marvel was conceived and built by the Chicago firm L. E. Myers Co., Builders and Operators of Public Utilities. The expenditure was more than repaid, however, with this concession being among the most popular on the Zone; the display took in over $338,000 from ticket sales, each of which were fifty cents. More than two million feet of lumber and 217 tons of cement and plaster were used in the construction of the building and the canal. Within the building a large oval amphitheater, 1,440 feet in length, surrounded the model, which was depressed some twenty feet below the spectators so as to provide a bird's-eye view, not only of the *Canal* but the territory within and adjacent to the *Canal Zone*. Panoramic paintings along the vertical walls surrounding the territory replicated in miniature were designed for their topographical accuracy and to give the spectator, as the contemporary guide noted, "a boundless horizon, miles in extent." The building was open to the sky in the center so as to cast natural light on the scene, giving a "remarkable illusion," as Todd noted.[49]

The working model of the *Canal* had an ocean at each end and featured boats, trains, and lighthouses in operation; the ships were timed to pass through the miniature locks at the same pace relative to what it would take a ship passing through the real canal. To facilitate the inspection of the working model, the amphitheater revolved and was divided into 144 cars, elegantly appointed and with two tiers of comfortable seats; twelve hundred passengers in all could be accommodated on what was a twenty-three-minute tour around the entire display. In order that no detail of the marvel would escape the spectators, a system was invented by which a lecture was delivered through headphones from a novel combination of phonographs and telephones. The lecture was broken down into forty-eight sections, corresponding to the location on the tour, and were switched on an off by rail contact under each respective car. The expense and detail of the elaborate display underscore its self-conscious pedagogical function to visualize, before the eyes of dazzled viewers, the national will of the manly United States to enact the progress of civilization. The viewers, in effect, become the national body as they cast an imperial gaze over the landscape.

The gigantic miniature of the Panama Canal offers an ideologically saturated view to the disembodied tourist who is privileged by modern technology to experience the entire scene at once. The sublimity of the landscape itself is dwarfed, miniaturized in effect, by the technological sublime that transforms and civilizes the anomalies of nature. Borrowing cultural historian Susan Stewart's conception of the miniature and the gigantic, the American national body is both the tourist on the car of the *Panama Canal* display—the miniature for whom historical events are brought to life, as if by magic, not by labor—and the invisible technological force and manly will—the gigantic "as the abstract authority of the state and the collective public"[50]—that brought forth the "real wonder," as Todd noted, in which time and space were diminished.[51] Contemporary literature abounded with references to the Canal having compressed the globe itself; distances between the East and the West were cut by more than half, as was the time for the journey. Moreover, the commercial potential was effectively doubled as a ship could go between ports far more rapidly and expeditiously, and the military might of the American nation was restored.[52] As such, the technological accomplishments of the Panama Canal redefine not only the site itself but the entire world, effectively miniaturizing the globe under the manly gaze of American civilization.

Conclusion

> It is the ambition of the PPIE [Panama-Pacific International Exposition] management to produce in San Francisco a microcosm so nearly complete that if all the world were destroyed except the 635 acres of land within the Exposition gates, the material basis of the life of today could have been reproduced from the exemplifications of the arts, inventions and industries there exhibited.
> —FRANK MORTON TODD, *THE STORY OF THE EXPOSITION* (1921)

The pedagogical intention of the Panama-Pacific Exposition is clearly articulated in Frank Morton Todd's history of the exposition, in which he outlines the prerogative of the exposition to reproduce the world in a gigantic miniature. This was a world whose topography, physically and ideologically, Todd tells us, had been transformed by contemporary imperial ventures to reflect a newly masculinized American body politic. Todd underscores the fair's emphasis on visuality, calling it "a vast and illuminated book" within which were written broad narratives extolling American progress, manliness, and civilization.

Indeed, visual reconstructions of the Panama Canal at the Panama-Pacific

Exposition, such as those analyzed in this chapter, provide a dense surface of social and cultural inscription and offer evidence—material, intellectual, and ideological—of progress, civilization, and manliness as they were refracted through the lens of Social Darwinism. Foundational as it was to ideas about the reproduction of the nation, of masculinity, and of whiteness, gender's imprint on the physical, social, cultural, and political terrain of the exposition is unmistakable. Manliness and its mechanical prosthetic, technology, became the arenas through which the United States refashioned its national body and confidently assumed its new role as imperialist on the world stage. Much as the globe had ostensibly shrunk with the completion of the Panama Canal, the Panama-Pacific International Exposition compressed the world into a compelling and legible miniature in which to celebrate the new national body: one that was invigorated, imperial, manly, and indelibly technological. At this fair, white American men mobilized technology (along with the semi-coerced labor of countless Panamanian men) in ways that served to transform the incoherent and unproductive landscape (read: female) of the Canal Zone into a legible site of coherence, productivity, and discipline (read: male). So, too, was the gendered and imperialist discourse of civilization mobilized to enunciate the national body of the new American empire as white, male, immensely powerful, and extracontinental in its reach—equal to that of Hercules performing his thirteenth labor.

NOTES

1 "The Strenuous Life" was delivered before the Hamilton Club, Chicago, April 10, 1899. See Theodore Roosevelt, *The Strenuous Life: Essays and Addresses* (New York: Century, 1902), 7 and 9, respectively.

2 Roosevelt Day was held on July 20, 1915. The most complete contemporary record of the Panama-Pacific Exposition is compiled in five volumes by Frank Morton Todd, *The Story of the Exposition: Being the Official History of the International Celebration Held at San Francisco in 1915 to Commemorate the Discovery of the Pacific Ocean and the Construction of the Panama Canal* (New York: Putnam, 1921); this account is in vol. 3, p. 94.

3 Todd, 1:31. See also Kristin L. Hoganson, *Fighting for Manhood: How Gender Politics Provoked the Spanish-American and Philippine-American Wars* (New Haven, Conn.: Yale University Press, 1998).

4 Roosevelt, cited in Matthew Frye Jacobson, *Barbarian Virtues: The United States Encounters Foreign Peoples at Home and Abroad, 1876–1917* (New York: Hill and Wang, 2000), 45.

5 For an important distinction between manliness and masculinity, see Gail Bederman, *Manliness and Civilization: A Cultural History of Gender and Race in the United States, 1880–1917* (Chicago: University of Chicago Press, 1995).

6 Todd, 2:299. For information about the architecture of the Panama-Pacific Exposition, see also Gray Bechlin, "Sailing to Byzantium: The Architecture of the Fair," in *The Anthology of World's Fairs: San Francisco's Panama-Pacific International Exposition of 1915*, ed. Burton Benedict, 94–113 (London: Lowie Museum of Anthropology/Scholar Press, 1983).

7   Todd, 2:302.

8   For information on the lighting effects of the Panama-Pacific Exposition, see Todd, "And There was Light," 2:342–49.

9   A. Stirling Calder, *The Sculpture and Mural Decorations of the Exposition: A Pictorial Survey of the Arts of the Panama-Pacific International Exposition* (San Francisco: Elder, 1915), 14.

10 Todd, 2:310.

11 Roosevelt, "Strenuous Life," 21.

12 Todd, 1:14.

13 Calder, 16.

14 Elizabeth N. Armstrong notes that the Court of Ages focused on Darwinian themes including large friezes with such titles as "Natural Selection" and "Survival of the Fittest." See "Hercules and the Muses: Public Art at the Fair," in Benedict, 117–20.

15 California State Commissioner Chester H. Rowell, cited in Todd, 3:131.

16 Albert Boime uses the term "magisterial gaze" and notes its resonance with countless images of manifest destiny in the nineteenth century. See Albert Boime, *The Magisterial Gaze: American Landscape Painting 1830–1865* (Washington, D.C.: Smithsonian Institution Press, 1991).

17 For a discussion of these allegorical female figures, see Martha Banta, *Imaging American Women: Idea and Ideals in Cultural History* (New York: Columbia University Press, 1987), 499–552.

18 Vaughan Cornish, *The Panama Canal and its Makers* (London: Unwin, 1909), 89.

19 See Sarah J. Moore, "Our National Monument of Art: Constructing and Debating the National Body at the Library of Congress," *Library Quarterly* (forthcoming, fall 2011). See also Herbert Small, comp., *Handbook of the New Library of Congress in Washington* (Boston: Curtis and Cameron, 1897).

20 Todd, 1:21.

21 Cornish, 18–19.

22 For a discussion of the social implications of neurasthenia, see T. J. Jackson Lears, *No Place of Grace: Antimodernism and the Transformation of American Culture, 1880–1920* (New York: Pantheon, 1981).

23 Bill Brown, "Science Fiction, the World's Fair, and the Prosthetics of Empire, 1910–1915," in *Cultures of United States Imperialism,* ed. Amy Kaplan and Donald Peace, 141 (Durham, N.C.: Duke University Press, 1993).

24 See Brown; see also Mark Seltzer, *Bodies and Machines* (New York: Routledge, 1992).

25 Brown, 135–37.

26 Cited in Seltzer, 149.

27 See, respectively, Todd, 1:14–15, and Robert W. Rydell, "The Culture of Imperial Abundance: World's Fairs and the Making of American Culture," in *Consuming Visions: The Accumulation and Display of Goods in America, 1880–1920,* ed. Simon J. Bronner, 191–216 (New York: Norton, 1989). See also Brown, 140–42.

28 Robert W. Rydell, "World of Tomorrow," in *All the World's a Fair: Visions of Empire at American International Expositions, 1876–1917,* 219 (Chicago: University of Chicago Press, 1984).

29 Amy Kaplan, *The Anarchy of Empire in the Making of U.S. Culture* (Cambridge, Mass.: Harvard University Press, 2002), 99. See also Seltzer, 150, and Ronald Takaki, *Iron Cages: Race and Culture in Nineteenth-Century America* (New York: Knopf, 1979), 253–79, who describes America's pursuit of the imperialist frontier as a "masculine thrust."

30 Frederick Jackson Turner, "The Problem of the West," *Atlantic Monthly* 78 (September 1896): 296.

31 Cecilia Tichi, *Shifting Gears: Technology, Literature, Culture in Modernist America* (Chapel Hill: University of North Carolina Press, 1987), 120.

32 Todd, 1:7.

33 Franklin K. Lane, cited in Armstrong, 115.

34 Armstrong, 121.

35 The phrase "ravages of the axe" was used by American landscape painter Thomas Cole in the late 1830s. For a discussion of art of this period in light of contemporary concerns about the rapid encroachment of civilization upon the American wilderness, see Nicolai Cikovsky Jr., "The Ravages of the Axe: Meaning of the Tree Stump in Nineteenth-Century American Art," *The Art Bulletin* 61 (December 1979): 611–26.

36 Todd, 2:270.

37 Roosevelt, "Strenuous Life," 16.

38 J. James, *Sculpture of the Exposition Palaces and Courts* (San Francisco: Crocker, 1915), 34.

39 Armstrong, 121.

40 Stuart Hall, "The Spectacle of the Other," cited in Elisabeth Nicole Arruda, "The Mother of Tomorrow: American Eugenics and the Panama-Pacific Exposition," (master's thesis, San Francisco State University, 2004), 108.

41 For a discussion of the Spanish-American War and its impact on the 1901 Pan-American Exposition in Buffalo, see Sarah J. Moore, "Mapping Empire in Omaha and Buffalo: World's Fairs and the Spanish-American War," in *The Legacy of the Mexican and the Spanish-American Wars: Legal, Literary, and Historical Perspectives,* ed. Cornelia Candelaria and Gary Keller, 111–26 (Tempe, Ariz.: Bilingual, 2000).

42 "The Grand Canyon of Arizona at the Panama-Pacific International Exposition," *Santa Fe Magazine* (July 1914): 49–50.

43 Burridge painted sets for the New York and Chicago productions of L. Frank Baum's *The Wizard of Oz*. See Mark Evan Schwartz, *Oz Before the Rainbow: L. Frank Baum's The Wonderful Wizard of Oz on Stage* (Baltimore: Johns Hopkins University Press, 2000), 110–14.

44 "Grand Canyon," 49.

45 Stephen Becker and Pamela Young Lee, "Ethnography on Display: The Panama-Pacific International Exposition," in *Theodore Wores in the Southwest,* ed. Stephen Becker, 41 (San Francisco: California Historical Society, 2006).

46 Todd, 2:53.

47 *The Panama Canal at San Francisco 1915* (San Francisco: Panama Canal Exhibition Co., 1915), n.p.

48 Ibid.

49 For details about the Panama Canal exhibit on the Zone, see *Panama Canal*, and Todd, 2:150–51.

50 Susan Stewart, *On Longing: Narratives of the Miniature, the Gigantic, the Souvenir, the Collection* (Durham, N.C.: Duke University Press, 1993), xii.

51 Todd, 1:29.

52 See, for example, Todd, 1:29–33; *Panama Canal,* 1915; and Cornish.

PART II
Women in Action

Never before has the name Mormon met with a
general respectful courtesy. . . . Everywhere, in
cars, in hotels, in any and all of the buildings and
resorts in the Fair if one dropped a word about
Utah, there was immediate and what was more
remarkable, kindly attention. What could have
wrought this marvelous change?
—Susa Young Gates (editor), *The Young Woman's
Journal*, 1894

CHAPTER 5

Mormon Women, Suffrage, and Citizenship at the 1893 Chicago World's Fair

Andrea G. Radke-Moss

On Saturday, May 20, 1893, while representing Utah Territory at the
World's Congress of Representative Women, Mormon leader Emmeline B.
Wells was invited to preside over the proceedings for one day. Considering
how nineteenth-century Americans looked down upon the polygamous and
culturally isolated Mormon women as objects of pity and even contempt, Wells
appreciated the significance of the invitation as "an honor never before accorded
to a Mormon woman." Indeed, the presence of women of the Church of Jesus
Christ of Latter-day Saints (Mormons, or LDS) at the Congress was in itself
a great achievement. However, Wells lamented, "If one of our brethren had
such a distinguished honor conferred upon them, it would have been heralded
the country over and thought a great achievement."[1] This comment highlights
the central irony of the Chicago World's Columbian Exposition of 1893 for the
women who benefited from the unprecedented attention to women's rights and
contributions that the fair offered, but who still found themselves excluded from
the masculine achievements of the White City.[2] Indeed, it was just this gender
segregation that permitted Mormon women's presence at the fair to outshine

Mormon men's that summer. Taking advantage of an invitation to participate in the World's Congress of Representative Women, Mormon women attempted to fashion a new image for themselves as liberated representatives of a rapidly Americanizing church. The World's Congress, held in conjunction with the fair, proffered Mormon women an unparalleled public opportunity to assert their identity as modern women who were moral, progressive, patriotic, and stood on the cutting edge of suffrage activism.

The Chicago World's Fair of 1893 marked a major crossroads for Mormon women, poised exactly midpoint between the passage of the 1890 Manifesto that ended polygamy for the Utah-based church, and the achievement of Utah statehood in 1896. Since the 1860s, federal antipolygamy legislation had fed persecution and misunderstanding of the Mormons and had also resulted in numerous failed attempts by Utah to achieve statehood. The Manifesto signaled the Church's decision to eschew polygamous practice in favor of more acceptable monogamous marriages. Utah's statehood was the ultimate reward for accepting federal authority, but it also represented a major step for Utah's Mormon majority to prove their assimilation within American society. Significantly, statehood also came with full suffrage rights for women, a move that surprised many who had viewed Mormon women as subjugated and degraded.[3]

The challenge that lay before Mormon women during the exposition was to shift the popular view of themselves away from an association with backwardness that had clung to Mormons since the founding of their religion in 1830, and especially since they began the open practice of polygamy in 1852. As the World's Fair opened, Mormon women were perceived at best as oddly religious, and at worst as freakish curiosities who lived in harem-style marriages. In 1893, through a concerted de-emphasis on the peculiarity of polygamy and religious isolation, Mormon women sought to shed their lingering stereotype of "oppressed" plural wives while also showing themselves as progressive women who would soon lead the way in a major state women's suffrage victory. The high profile and public organizing experience that LDS women achieved through the Congress of Women and other fair efforts helped them to focus their energy toward later successful efforts to expect and demand suffrage as a facet of statehood when it came three years later.[4]

Choosing an Experienced Leadership

It should be no surprise that the women chosen to direct Utah's participation in the World's Congress were those who already held other important leadership positions, especially through the Relief Society and the Young Ladies Mutual Improvement Association (YLMIA), the Church's two organizations for adult and adolescent women. Further, many of these women also brought with them previous experience in organized suffrage activism, political involvement, and charitable work. In June 1892, Governor Arthur L. Thomas appointed Emily S. Richards as President of Utah's Board of Lady Managers for the fair. Richards represented Utah well. She had served in the Relief Society with other high-ranking Mormon women and, as the wife of nonpolygamist church attorney Franklin S. Richards, she was a politic choice to speak for the territory's women in 1893. Free of the taint adhering to a plural-wife status, she could better speak on broader women's issues without drawing unwanted attention to her personal life. For the same reason, Richards had been chosen as Utah's first delegate to the National Council of Women (NCW) meeting in Washington, D.C., in 1888.[5] Her performance was a great success, portraying a positive view of Mormons, and she brought that experience of powerful self-representation to her preparations for the Chicago exposition in 1893.[6] Richards's vice-president was Jane S. Richards, who was Emily's mother-in-law and the wife of apostle Franklin D. Richards. That so many of Utah's women leaders were married to high-ranking church officials guaranteed important institutional connections, especially as they sought and gained support for suffrage.[7]

Not all of Utah's fair leadership came from among Mormon circles. Governor Thomas appointed Margaret Salisbury as the chair of Utah's Lady Commissioners and Alice J. Whalen as her assistant—both noteworthy as non-LDS women.[8] This leadership displayed a united front of Mormon and non-Mormon women, which was especially important in light of the history of religious tensions in Utah.[9] Other women worked tirelessly in World's Fair work. Zina D. H. Young was one of Brigham Young's surviving widows, a staunch suffrage activist and the Relief Society president for the church.[10] Emmeline B. Wells was Young's Relief Society secretary and the widow of apostle Daniel H. Wells. She served as the chair of the Salt Lake County Board of Lady Managers and as a Utah Lady Commissioner. A staunch advocate of woman's suffrage and journalism, Wells enthusiastically promoted women's participation in the World's Congress by publishing reports of the exposition in her pro-suffrage newspaper, *Woman's Exponent*. This paper served as a medium of interconnection among Mormon women by keeping them informed of Relief Society news, local and national suffrage activities, and other club work.[11]

Utah women's preparation for World's Fair leadership was a natural extension of their previous experiences in other progressive work. Every member of the board was also involved in suffrage activism, journalism, public welfare, or the Church's women's organizations. In fact, a sampling of Utah's most elite female leadership shows the interconnections between their positions on fair organizing committees and their past contributions to reform. Many women had cut their teeth on suffrage activism through local Relief Societies, and women's leadership often overlapped with participation in other categories of organizational club work. Not only were these women experienced organizers and speakers, but they were also contemporary with their national sisters in many areas of progressive action. For example, in 1891, Wells had founded the Utah Women's Press Club (UWPC) for the progress of women in literature and journalism. Wells intended the club to act as another vehicle for organizing world's fair work, especially because she planned to attend a conference of press women during the congresses in May.[12]

Perhaps the best example of Utah women's efforts toward reform was the Salt Lake Deseret Hospital. Founded in 1882 as an institution where "the sick and afflicted can receive equal care and attention, regardless of race or denomination," the hospital was the first truly significant charitable project administered almost entirely by Utah women.[13] Most of its financial support came from the Relief Society and the YLMIA, which showed the intersections of women's religious and public welfare work.[14] Much like the UWPC, the hospital's board of directors included many women who would later stand for Utah's women at the World's Congress, where they consciously chose to highlight these activities as examples of their progressive spirit.

Figure 5.1. Deseret Hospital Board of Directors, 1882. *Front row, left to right:* Jane S. Richards, Emmeline B. Wells. *Middle row:* Phoebe Woodruff, Isabelle M. Horne, Eliza R. Snow, Zina D. H. Young, Marinda N. Hyde. *Back row:* Dr. Ellis R. Shipp, Bathsheba W. Smith, Elizabeth Howard, Dr. Romania B. Pratt Penrose. Used by permission, Utah State Historical Society.

Utah women's desires to overcome unfair prejudice fed a subtle undercurrent of all their fair efforts but were felt most keenly in their preparations for the World's Congress. In April 1893, Susa Young Gates reviewed the negative stereotypes that had long followed Mormon women: "We, the women of Utah, have been considered slaves and fools, have been looked upon as without mind or intelligence. That we are true to our husbands and families has been accounted to us as a sure mark of vile inferiority of intellect."[15] In spite of these negative images, Gates celebrated the great possibilities for Mormons to improve their image, especially through interactions with national women's leaders at the congress: "And now we are met by these wide-minded, deep-thoughted women in Chicago as equals, as women with at least mind enough to speak for ourselves." Gates also recognized a spiritual mandate for Mormon women to represent their religion in a public forum. Because of that religious connection, she saw LDS women's presence at the fair as a fulfillment of divine prophecy for the advancement of women. "I heard President Joseph F. Smith say about five years ago that the time was close at hand when the women of this Church would be required to stand in public places and give a reason for the hope within them. The prediction begins to be fulfilled."[16]

With this sense of providential calling that women's work at the exposition would lead Mormon women to greater rights, Gates called for young women all over Utah to "daily remember in our earnest prayers our beloved leader, Sister Elmina S. Taylor, that wisdom and great power may be given her." Indeed, Taylor and her YLMIA presidency went to Chicago as "mouthpieces"—worthy of the divine help of heaven through fasting and prayer. The unification of secular and sacred for Mormon women shows how the fair also became a venue for negotiations of faithful purpose and righteous devotion, ultimately leading to the achievement of women's equal rights, or for Gates, the "unlatching of a door that shall soon be flung wide between the women of this gospel and the women of the world?"[17]

One of the first tasks for recruiting Mormon women's support for the exposition and the World's Congress was to highlight an increasing sense of belonging to the national American culture. For a people who had just a few years earlier endured persecution by the federal government through antipolygamy legislation, a reemphasis on patriotism was necessary for a new public image. Mormons sought to unify themselves with the nation, especially by sharing the meaning of common cultural and patriotic symbols. In front of a Chicago audience, Chairman R. C. Chambers of Utah's Board of Commissioners contrasted Mormons' newfound emphasis on patriotism with past accusations of their disloyalty and separation: "The people of Utah . . . love the Union and the Union's flag, and, no matter what may have been said of them in the past, to-day they are marching in harmony with the men and women of this great Nation."[18]

Utah's women leaders also pursued this renewed rhetoric of patriotic devotion, usually by emphasizing associations with Columbus and Queen Isabella as inspired leaders. Wells called for women to organize "Queen Isabella Circles" and "Columbian Clubs," in affiliation with Relief Societies.[19] That Isabella received so much acclaim showed a significant women-centered take on Columbus's discovery, that his voyage was sponsored by a female monarch. Wells asked, "Who is there among the patriotic women of America whose heart does not bound with enthusiasm at the name of Isabella of Castile?"[20] Mormon leaders consciously applied these symbols toward a greater association with American providence and patriotism, especially in light of invitations for women to participate in the World's Congress.

World's Congress of Representative Women

Mormon women began preparing for the World's Congress of Representative Women as early as 1891. With the intent of demonstrating the articulate nature of Mormon women, Emmeline Wells's strategies for her own Salt Lake Columbian Club included teaching women "facts and current events," especially to "help some of us to be come [sic] better speakers and more intelligent on all general subjects."[21] Employing their experience in public speaking and organizing, women participated throughout the congress both as speakers and as panel discussants. Zina Young joined with six panelists in a discussion entitled "Charity, Philanthropy, and Religion," and she successfully held her own with "fourteen women ministers of different denominations, conversing freely with them."[22]

The most anticipated day for Utah was Friday, May 19, at a morning session for the National Woman's Relief Society.[23] On this important day when Mormon women would present themselves to the world, Wells admitted to some jitters: "This was the morning of our own meeting and of course it was natural that we should feel the greatest anxiety." However, the women were well prepared and came with the support of some high-ranking church leaders. In spite of the nerves, the women performed excellently, and they later attended a gathering in their honor. Wells, Young, and Salisbury enjoyed many receptions with national women's leaders and newspaper reporters; these associations added further to the public attention Mormon women received.[24]

The speeches remained consistent to Utah women's intended messages, that Mormons were patriotic, moral, and progressive. Zina Card's speech emphasized that Utah children "are taught lessons of patriotism and purity." Then, perhaps to invoke audience sympathy for the church as a persecuted group, Isabella Horne spoke of the many hardships Mormons had to endure on their

1847 exodus from Illinois to Utah. Nellie Little reemphasized this image of persecution by recounting the federal army's 1857 invasion of Utah to "quell an insurrection," but she added that the Mormons were "listening to a reading of the Declaration of Independence" at the time.[25]

Two of Utah's female medical doctors spoke, including Ellis R. Shipp, who discussed Utah women's great successes in medicine; Shipp later gave another talk, "Medical Education of Women in Great Britain and Ireland," which made it into the final publication of the World's Congress. Dr. Martha Hughes Cannon spoke on the types of women "who represent the Mormon faith."[26] Utah women "are of distinct New England type of character . . . [who] did not forget the principles for which so much had been sacrificed to establish religious toleration on the free soil of America." Cannon reminded the audience that these women often "proved their patriotism and loyalty by rallying around their husbands and sons while they raised the Stars and Stripes."[27] These repeated references to Utah's patriotism added to Mormon women's message of their loyal integration within the national community.

Electa Bullock concluded the meeting with a talk that celebrated the industrial successes of women. Directing her speech outside of Mormon circles to include all men and women, Bullock warned against taking away women's influence from government, industry, and education. If women were confined only "to the narrow sphere of house-wife and maid-servant, [then] the wheels of progress would turn backward."[28] By demanding an inventory of legal and professional equality for women, Bullock transcended her status as a so-called degraded Mormon woman, and successfully stood out as a bold spokesperson for all women's rights.

Emmeline Wells gave perhaps the most important talk of the morning, which discussed how Utah women developed their literary and journalistic talents as a strategy for responding to the hardships of frontier life. As president of the Utah Women's Press Club, Wells used her speech to promote the *Woman's Exponent* and the *Young Woman's Journal*, both on display at the fair.[29] She also published a special edition of the *Exponent* and encouraged her readers that "[d]uring the Columbian Exposition, thousands of copies should be given away." Showing off the paper would help in defending Mormon women, for, as she said, "It is still very generally believed that women in this Church are ignorant and in subjection, [so] one copy of the *Exponent* . . . is tangible proof to the contrary." In fact, she suggested with some surety, the *Exponent* "enters where no Mormon Elder would be permitted."[30]

Fairgoers could access other publications by Utah women, including Wells's compilation, *Songs and Flowers of the Wasatch*, and the *World's Fair Ecclesiastical History of Utah*, edited by Sarah Kimball.[31] Wells also promoted her pamphlet, *Charities and Philanthropies and Woman's Work in Utah*, which celebrated Utah women's longstanding commitment to public welfare and charity. By emphasizing the Deseret Hospital and the Relief Society's efforts in wheat cultivation, Wells consciously fashioned an image that was repeated throughout the fair, that Mormon women were examples of Christian charity and progressive club work.

Following the successful morning program, the Young Ladies' Mutual Improvement Association held its own proceedings Friday night, again to much acclaim. The participants "compared favorably with the women of the East, and were real artists."[32] Emily Richards earned even more attention by having her speech printed in the official publication of the congress. She firmly outlined a history of women's rights in Utah, from the earliest granting of the franchise (and the unfair removal of that right by the federal government's antipolygamy legislation) to married women's rights to own property and obtain divorces on equal terms with men. She also emphasized Utah's progressive dower and custody laws, along with other rights women enjoyed: "All our educational institutions are open to [women]. They are encouraged to practice law, medicine, and all the other professions. They are at liberty to preach the gospel, speak at public gatherings, visit the sick and officiate at funerals."[33] These advancements came not in spite of men's oppression but because of their support, for, she said, "The efforts and achievements of our women are appreciated by the men, who give them every encouragement and assistance in their various enterprises."[34] Richards's talk represents Utah women's two chief aims—to defend themselves against unfair stereotyping and to show the strong connections between fair participation and women's broader hopes for legal and political rights.

The Congress of Women presented Utah women with a unique opportunity, one that had no parallel among Utah's male leadership. There was no official venue for LDS men to single out their successes. Utah Day—held later on September 9—provided the only significant occasion for male leaders to speak to a national audience. President Wilford Woodruff's speech was brief and lackluster due to his illness during the fair, and both he and Cannon generally stuck to stories of Mormons' past persecutions and trials, rather than looking ahead to commonalities and national progress, as Utah's women had done.[35] The World's Congress of Women may have provided the perfect venue for Utah's women to leave a mark on the fair, but it was Utah women's preparation and organizing skills that permitted them to make the most of it.

Woman's Suffrage and the World's Fair

Utah women interpreted the potential benefits of the fair for changing the perceptions of Mormon women, but also for achieving woman's suffrage for all. In fact, Wells noted that "really the woman suffrage question was one of the most popular themes of discussion presented" at the World's Congress.[36] Utah's world's fair leadership saw little or no difference between women's work at the exposition and their orchestrated campaign for attaining the vote.

Perhaps the strongest indicator of Mormon women's prosuffrage attitudes was that so many Lady Managers were suffrage leaders at home and nationally, especially through their beneficial associations with the National Council of Women and International Council of Women (ICW). Wells had the special privilege of being Utah's editor-activist for suffrage, and she often corresponded with national suffrage leaders.[37] She added her voice to Utah's suffragists who also spoke in Chicago, including Sarah Kimball, Electa Bullock, and Emily Richards. In preparation for the congress, these leaders used special meetings of Utah's Woman's Suffrage Association (WSA) and the UWPC for endorsing suffrage ideologies. And county world's fair organizations and Relief Societies worked in tandem toward suffrage goals, by holding joint discussions of the suffrage question and by sharing organizational and ideological experience.[38]

Utah's women leaders saw a direct correlation between overcoming past prejudice against Mormon women and the ultimate achievement of woman suffrage. Regarding the 1892 presidential election, Wells insisted that "the women of this Territory should have had the same privilege in this Presidential election . . . as the women of Wyoming." Wells made a clear connection between the world's fair and suffrage goals, since "the Columbian Exposition will do more to bring about the enfranchisement of women than all other causes put together."[39] Emily Richards recognized the same correlation and wanted to "see every woman come here as intelligent beings ready to receive the ballot, that we should prepare ourselves to join hands with the women of the world and be honorably noted as women of Utah." With that in mind, she "urged all to go to the World's Fair that could."[40]

Much of the success of these suffrage leaders came because they did not put themselves at odds with Utah's male politicians. Utah women earned the support of men who saw a definite connection between woman's suffrage and their hope that statehood would bring political equality for all. One ex-mayor of Provo hoped that statehood would bring suffrage, and for that purpose he encouraged women toward "taking an interest in the World's Fair."[41] In the months before the exposition, LDS church leaders gave public statements in support of suffrage, with an appeal for women to continue their organizational efforts. Because so many prosuffrage LDS leaders were the husbands and fathers of Utah's suffragists, these women therefore exerted even greater influence toward legalizing the vote.[42]

Utah's suffrage victory directly stemmed in part from the experiences Utah women had gained at the World's Fair. The improved harmony between Mormon and non-Mormon women after the 1890 Manifesto was further reinforced through their unified efforts in preparation for the World's Congress of Women. Utah women also enjoyed the support of the NCW, ICW, and National American Woman's Suffrage Association, whose associations brought Mormon women greater public respect for their charitable work, journalism, and political action. Most important, the fair's positive exposure helped to foster support for women's rights among Utah's male leaders, national women's groups, the press, and Utah women themselves.[43] Because Utah's women had already enjoyed the right to vote between 1870 and 1882, suffrage support came more easily in 1896, especially in the wake of a stunningly successful showing by Utah women at the Chicago World's Fair.

Outsiders' Responses

Utah women received the public attention that they had expected at the fair. Many visitors attended the congresses and Utah's exhibits out of curiosity more than anything else. The *Deseret News* reported: "People come in to see what Utah had. They don't expect much. In fact, many of them come in more

Figure 5.2. Columbian Exposition, Chicago, 1893. Distinguished Mormon visitors to the Utah Building. Used by permission, Utah State Historical Society.

ANDREA G. RADKE-MOSS

to 'see a Mormon' than anything else, but they go away praising our display and congratulating Utah people on their enterprise."[44] Mormon women also benefited from many complimentary remarks made by sympathetic spectators, including Elizabeth Lisle Saxon, who had visited Utah in years past, and reported her observations at the World's Congress. As a non-Mormon speaking positively about Mormons, she gave "perhaps the most important impression effected during the morning session." She "paid high compliments to the purity and intelligence of the Mormon women and declared the prevailing opinion and prejudice regarding the social life of women in Utah to be totally unmerited."[45] Utah's women met many notable leaders during the Congress, including May Wright Sewall, Anna Howard Shaw, Rachel Foster Avery, Isabella Beecher Hooker, and other authors, activists, reporters, and national club presidents. Bertha Palmer herself received Wells, Young, and Richards at a reception in her home.[46] Because Utah women achieved such a presence—especially through the World's Congress of Women—they earned the most attention, not always accurately, but often positively.

The public relations campaign seemed to work desired results among the press. The *Chicago Daily Tribune* attended the session on May 19 and then published a positive report of the speeches, which Wells reprinted in the June 15 *Exponent* for Utah readers. Etta Gilchrist, an Ohio reporter and friend of Wells and Young, who had previously "written a book against [the Mormons'] institutions," attended the May 19 meeting and was moved to reverse some of her past opinions. She recounted that "Mrs. Wells called me to the platform and I went and sat by Brigham Young's wife [Zina Young] and took by the hand each of those women with whom my sympathy had been so long." In a moment, her sympathy turned to admiration: "Truly their forbearance and kindness is saint-like. This one meeting was to me worth coming to Chicago for."[47]

Some reactions bordered on shallow, as when one Chicago newspaper remarked, "All of the Mormon delegates are fine looking women. It is said that Utah will rival Kentucky in its pretty women."[48] The favorable responses continued with more substance, although at times with some dramatic exaggeration. On June 18, Augusta Prescott of the Chicago *Inter Ocean* declared to her readers: "MORMON WOMEN Who Will Take Part in the Fair Congresses ARE NOT POLYGAMISTS," and highlighted Emily Richards and Electa Bullock as examples of progressive Utah women."[49]

Prescott met with May Wright Sewall, president of the World's Congress and also a friend of Wells, and asked her to tell her "something new and interesting about the work which is going on in Chicago for the benefit of women." Of all of the hundreds of women speakers and topics that she could have mentioned, Sewall chose to single out Mormon women's presence at the fair: "Have you heard that we are to have Mormon women to take part in all our congresses this summer?" Then, perhaps disappointing the taste for the exotic, Sewall added, "And do you know that these Mormon women represent some of the finest women clubs and women organizations that are to be found in America?" Here Sewall reinforced the exact message that her Mormon friends had intended for the fair. Not completely convinced, Prescott pressed Sewall further, inquiring, "Do you allow polygamists to address your meetings? And do you countenance polygamy in any of its forms, even though its representatives be pretty women and even club women and woman suffragists?"

"Why, no," said Mrs. Sewall. "We do not countenance polygamy. We were spared the trouble of deciding whether we would allow it to be represented at our congresses by the fact that none of the women who come to Chicago from Utah were of that belief."[50]

It seems unlikely that Sewall was not aware of the continuing polygamist sympathies of many of her Mormon friends. Perhaps the statement that "none of the women . . . were of that belief" indicated the church's 1890 Manifesto renouncing polygamy, which allowed her an ambiguous but technically accurate defense of Utah women. But it also indicates the power to which Mormon women could affect such a publicity miracle, when some of them still did believe in plural marriage. Upon further investigation, Prescott discovered more complexities of polygamy, that while some still kept their plural marriages, "there are many who belong to the Mormon church who have never liked the idea of taking several wives." Prescott described Mormon women as overwhelmingly relieved at the laws abolishing plural marriage, and she argued that they had only progressed and thrived since the abolition of polygamy. Her impressions of Utah women prior to the Manifesto employ the exotic associations of Turkish harems: "Young girls were given no advantages at all. They were kept in great ignorance. They were scarcely sent to school [and] girls were taught nothing at all. . . . They were as ignorant as Turkish women or Japanese girls waiting for a sweetheart. But they had to work from morning until night, scrubbing, sweeping, baking and sewing."[51]

So while the reporter recognized the progress of Mormon women as portrayed at the fair, she attributed it entirely to their being free of the oppression of polygamy. It is interesting that she failed to notice how such grand advancements among the women delegates could have been accomplished in a mere three years. Nor did she mention the extent of Utah women's suffrage activism, charitable work, education, and journalism *prior to* 1890. But still she admitted, "All of the Mormon delegates are fine looking women. . . . They are becoming intelligent. And intelligence makes beauty." She seems particularly smitten with Emily Richards, "an ardent woman's suffragist [who] is interested in many forms of club and charitable work," and also with Mary Romney, who is "determined never, no never, to be a polygamist."[52]

How did Mormon women perceive their own public-relations success at the Chicago World's Fair? Susa Young Gates reported in December 1893 that "Henry Ward Beecher's sister . . . said that if half she had heard was true, she wanted to come to Utah and remain. . . . This is a new day, a new era for Utah!"[53] Wells also noted those comments by Isabella Beecher Hooker, who "spoke up for our people and mentioned what Mrs. Salisbury had said about our women."[54] These compliments did not go unnoticed by Wells, who declared, "Great results are expected from the Woman's Congress."[55] Gates also reported with optimism that "never before has the name Mormon met with a general respectful courtesy. . . . Everywhere, in cars, in hotels, in any and all of the buildings and resorts in the Fair if one dropped a word about Utah, there was immediate and what was more remarkable, kindly attention. What could have wrought this marvelous change?"[56] Much of the credit must go to Utah's women—Mormon or not—who actively used the Chicago World's Fair of 1893 as a venue for reinventing their public image. Working autonomously and demonstrating real innovation and imagination in their organizational strategies, Utah women completed their fair work almost entirely without the assistance, monetary support, or instruction of male church leaders.

Indeed, Mormon male leaders failed to enact a concerted public relations effort at the fair. In part, their integration into the main space of the fair worked, ironically, against their efforts. Most of Utah's masculine pursuits were not highlighted as successes unique to Mormon men but were couched within the Utah Board of Commissioners' larger, nonsectarian exhibits on mining, industry, and agriculture. However, Mormon men's relatively unspectacular impact on the fair was largely a matter of their own failures relative to their female counterparts. Mormon men did not benefit from associations with any national organizations or "cause," as Utah women enjoyed with national suffrage organizations. Utah women had spent the 1880s networking with notable women's leaders, while men had spent that same time in hiding from prosecution or trying to recoup their financial and political losses during the time of federal antipolygamy action. In fact, the First Presidency had requested access to the World's Parliament of Religions in 1893 but had been soundly rejected. Still, in a "remarkable incident," Emily Richards was invited to appear "before the woman's branch of the Parliament of Religions," where she spoke on the "Women of Mormondom."[57] Annie Wells Cannon noted the significance of this event, "for though the Parliament of Religions had refused admission to the male representatives of the Church, yet this gracious lady found opportunity for a hearing through the auxiliary." Richards's experience shone through, for her speech was "carefully prepared, and . . . she gave a fine and sincere talk which carried its truths to the hearts of her audience."[58]

Utah's Mormon women consciously and successfully planned and carried out a public-relations miracle, whereby they gained power over their own message and recreated a new image. Emmeline Wells had drawn a hasty and cynical conclusion about the fact that her appearance at the World's Congress did not receive the same attention as if she had been a man. Contrary to that image, Emily Richards's singular performance at an event where Mormon men were not welcome showed how Mormon women surpassed all expectations in 1890s America for their gender and their religion. These female leaders took advantage of the opportunities that the fair and the congress afforded for women and added to those their own experiences as women of thought, substance, and action.

Perhaps at no other event than the Chicago World's Columbian Exposition of 1893 could the gendered forces of organization, publicity, energy, and talent have merged to favor Utah's LDS and non-LDS women. In 1893, Mormon women went from oppressed and silenced plural wives to patriotic, intelligent, and moral women of political success and progressive benevolence. They had met America and the world, and they were now ready to meet the twentieth century.

NOTES

1 Emmeline B. Wells, Typescript Diary, May 20, 1893, vol. 16 (1893), 22 (L. Tom Perry Special Collections, Lee Library, Brigham Young University, Provo, Utah).

2 Gail Bederman, *Manliness and Civilization: A Cultural History of Gender and Race in the United States, 1880–1917* (Chicago: University of Chicago Press, 1996).

3 By 1896, Utah was one of only four states that had granted full suffrage to women—Wyoming (1890), Colorado (1893), and Idaho (1896)—while a national constitutional amendment was still a generation away. On Utah's battle for woman suffrage, see Lola Van Wagenen, *Sister-Wives and Suffragists: Polygamy and the Politics of Woman Suffrage, 1870–1896* (Provo: Joseph Fielding Smith Institute for Latter-day Saint History and BYU Studies, 2003).

4 See Richard Van Wagoner, *Mormon Polygamy: A History* (Salt Lake City: Signature, 1986).

5 Jean Bickmore White, "Women's Suffrage in Utah," *Utah History Encyclopedia*, found at http://www.media.utah.edu/UHE/w/WOMANSUFFERAGE.html (accessed August 10, 2007). See also Van Wagenen, 130–31.

6 Annie Wells Cannon, "Emily Sophia Tanner Richards," in "In Memoriam: Emily Sophia Tanner Richards, 1929," 20 (Archives of the Church of Jesus Christ of Latter-day Saints, Salt Lake City, Utah). See also Van Wagenen, 131.

7 *Woman's Exponent*, March 1, 1892, 126; and October 1, 1892, 52.

8 Carol Cornwall Madsen, *An Advocate for Women: The Public Life of Emmeline B. Wells, 1870–1920* (Provo: Brigham Young University Press, 2006), 387.

9 On the tensions between Mormon and non-Mormon women throughout Utah's suffrage activism, see Van Wagenen.

10 A spiritual and charitable organization for Mormon women, the Relief Society was headquartered in Salt Lake City as the umbrella organization for smaller stake and ward Relief Societies throughout the territory. In Mormon lexicon, a stake is an organizational unit made up of small congregations called wards or smaller units called branches. Each stake consisted of anywhere from ten to thirty wards or branches, each with its own Relief Society. See Janath R. Cannon, Jill Mulvay Derr, and Maureen Ur-

senbach Beecher, *Women of Covenant: A History of Relief Society* (Salt Lake City: Deseret, 1991).

11 *Woman's Exponent,* May 1, 1892, 159; on Wells and the *Exponent,* see Madsen.

12 *Woman's Exponent,* March 15, 1892, 136. See Linda Thatcher and John R. Sillito, "'Sisterhood and Sociability': The Utah Women's Press Club, 1891–1928," *Utah Historical Quarterly* 53 (1985): 144–56.

13 Quoted in Martha Sonntag Bradley and Mary Brown Firmage Woodward, *4 Zinas: A Story of Mothers and Daughters on the Mormon Frontier* (Salt Lake City: Signature, 2000), 235.

14 *Woman's Exponent,* February 15, 1893, 127.

15 Susa Young Gates, ed., *Young Woman's Journal* (April 1893), 326.

16 Ibid. Joseph F. Smith was a counselor to numerous church presidents, including Wilford Woodruff during the fair, and Smith himself was president from 1901 to 1918.

17 Gates, 326–27.

18 E. A. McDaniel, *Utah at the World's Columbian Exposition* (Salt Lake City: Lithographing, 1894), 51. On the transition of the LDS Church from isolation and polygamy to patriotism and assimilation, see Thomas G. Alexander, *Mormonism in Transition* (Urbana: University of Illinois Press, 1986).

19 *Woman's Exponent,* June 15, 1891, 186.

20 *Woman's Exponent,* November 1, 1892, 65.

21 Wells, Transcript Diary, July 26, 1892, vol. 15 (1892), 68.

22 Bradley and Woodward, 356.

23 *Woman's Exponent,* April 15 and May 1, 1893, 157.

24 Wells, Typescript Diary, May 19, 1893, vol. 16 (1893), 21.

25 *Woman's Exponent,* June 15, 1893, 177.

26 *Deseret Evening News,* May 27, 1893, quoted in "The World's Fair: Utah at the Fair," *Lesson for September 1993: A Century Ago,* comp. Beatrice B. Malouf, 19 (Salt Lake: Daughters of the Utah Pioneers, 1993).

27 *Woman's Exponent,* June 15, 1893, 179.

28 Electa Wood Bullock, "Industrial Women," in *The Congress of Women: Held in the Woman's Building, World's Columbian Exposition, Chicago, U.S.A., 1893,* ed. Mary Kavanaugh Oldham Eagle, 510–11 (Chicago: Monarch, 1894).

29 *Woman's Exponent,* June 15, 1893, 178.

30 *Woman's Exponent,* July 1 and 15, 1893, 188.

31 Madsen, 387–88.

32 *Woman's Exponent,* June 15, 1893, 179.

33 Emily S. Richards, "The Legal and Political Status of Woman in Utah," in *The World's Congress of Representative Women,* ed. May Wright Sewall, 913 (New York: Rand McNally, 1894).

34 Ibid.

35 McDaniel, 54–57. The World's Fair was significant for bringing national, positive attention to Utah's legendary Mormon Tabernacle Choir—a topic too large for discussion here.

36 *Woman's Exponent,* June 1, 1893, 172.

37 *Woman's Exponent,* May 1, 1892, 158.

38 Sarah M. Kimball, "The Woman Suffrage Association of Utah," quoted in Malouf, 42; and "Constitution of San Pete County World's Fair Association," p. 11, Mss 566, L. Tom Perry Special Collections and Archives, Lee Library, Brigham Young University, Provo, Utah.

39 *Woman's Exponent*, November 15, 1892, 76. Utah's Mormon women had enjoyed the vote between 1870 and 1882, when it was revoked by a federal law that disfranchised polygamists. The 1887 Edmunds-Tucker Act revoked suffrage for *all* Utah women. By 1893, Utah women maintained a hope that suffrage would return with statehood. See Van Wagenen.

40 *Woman's Exponent*, October 15, 1892, 61.

41 Ibid., 61–62.

42 *Woman's Exponent*, March 15, 1892, 133. The Church's first presidency and many apostles all favored woman's suffrage. See Madsen, 280–88.

43 On Utah's statehood and suffrage, see Van Wagenen.

44 *Deseret Evening News*, June 2, 1893, quoted in Malouf, 21–22.

45 *Deseret Evening News*, May 27, 1893, quoted in Malouf, 21–22.

46 Wells, Transcript Diary, May 22, 1893, vol. 16 (1893), 23.

47 *Woman's Exponent*, June 15, 1893, 178–79.

48 Cannon, 24.

49 *The Chicago Inter Ocean*, June 18, 1893, in Charles E. Johnson Collection, P0011, Box 11, Newspaper Clippings, Utah State University Archives and Special Collections.

50 Ibid.

51 Ibid.

52 Ibid.

53 *Young Woman's Journal* (December 1893), 164–65.

54 Wells, Transcript Diary, May 21, 1893, vol. 16 (1893), 22.

55 *Young Woman's Journal* (December 1893), 164–65.

56 *Young Woman's Journal* (January 1894), 212–13.

57 Cannon, 25.

58 Ibid.

Now the time has come when the women
of the International Council feel that they
should demonstrate before a wider public their
determination to remove the causes which lead
to war.

—CIRCULAR LETTER, JANUARY 19, 1924

CHAPTER 6

Internationalist Peace Activism at the 1924 British Empire Exhibition

Anne Clendinning

In a letter to the National Councils of Women, Lady Ishbel, Marchioness of Aberdeen and Temair, and the executive director of the International Council of Women (ICW),[1] made the above declaration to the membership. That "time" was early 1924, when Aberdeen feared that Europe was teetering on the verge of another war; by "wider public" the writer was referring to the visitors to the British Empire Exhibition, where the ICW erected a women's pavilion and hosted an international peace conference. Aberdeen envisioned the pavilion (open from April to October 1924, the duration of the exhibition) as an information center for women visitors and a "home" for members of National Councils of Women (NCW) from "all over the world."[2] The ICW conference, scheduled for early May 1924, addressed the prevention of a future war. Of paramount importance was the recruitment of women, both existing NCW members and "ordinary home-staying women," to this important cause by developing their interest in international matters that affected all women regardless of national boundaries.[3]

Without any apparent sense of irony, Aberdeen determined that, via its pavilion and its peace conference, the ICW would use the British Empire Exhibition to further its mandate for peace and international cooperation. An imperial fair that celebrated the economic and political strength of Britain's dominions, colonies, and protectorates, the exhibition seemed an odd place for a women's group to initiate plans for a world without war. The British Empire was the result of centuries of conquest and conflict on land and sea, while colonialism itself, manifested in the competition for territory and trade, was the frequent cause of hostilities between rival European nations, including the First World War.[4] Leading up to the exhibition, the official royal patron, Edward, Prince of Wales, touted the event as a means of strengthening imperial connections, a highly exclusive form of internationalism. Aberdeen admitted that "it might seem strange" to hold their peace conference at the British Empire Exhibition, but she justified the decision for financial and logistical reasons.[5] Upon further reflection, and in light of women's participation in previous world's fairs in the United States, the exhibition was the ideal meeting place for an international sisterhood.

Like earlier world's fairs in Europe and the United States, the British Empire Exhibition at Wembley represented a utopian world, allegedly free from political, racial, and class tensions. As outlined in the introduction to this collection, existing scholarship has shown that world exhibitions were important sites for the display of innovative technologies associated with progress, modernity, and material prosperity. World's fairs provided a venue for international feminist gatherings. Following the 1888 inaugural meeting of the ICW, held in Washington, D.C., the ICW organized conferences in conjunction with the exhibitions in Chicago (1893), Brussels (1897) and Paris (1900).[6] In addition, exhibitions were important forums for the articulation of social and political change, and as scholars have shown and the chapters in this section demonstrate, "organized womanhood" used world's fairs to celebrate the expansion of the women's sphere outside the home and to illustrate the significance of women's participation in these events as visible signs of modernity.[7] The 1893 Columbian Exhibition in Chicago encouraged women's participation: its Board of Lady Managers organized a Woman's Building that celebrated women's role in the exhibition as indicative of American modernity, progress, and the emancipation of the "new woman."[8] Aberdeen and her organizing committee drew inspiration from the successes of women's groups that had participated in previous world's fairs. However, the ICW faced several additional challenges. In contrast to the efforts of American women's sections at exhibitions in the United States, Aberdeen and Zimmern worried that the British Empire Exhibition Authorities were less supportive of women's participation than their American counterparts had been. Furthermore, the ICW's ambitious vision—to end the causes of war—extended beyond the national and imperial concerns of earlier exhibitions and represented a truly cosmopolitan challenge.

Despite these difficulties, the ICW accomplished several goals. It created politically significant gendered spaces for women at the exhibition—both physical and intellectual—wherein women were not addressed as consumers, casual workers, or objects of display—the typical roles assigned to women at the Wembley event. Instead, the ICW appealed to women as educators, potential activists, and members of a transnational sisterhood. And most important, the ICW used its conference and its women's pavilion to negotiate a new definition of nationalism, one that reconciled the goal of international peace with the idea of national and imperial patriotism so intrinsically promoted at the British Empire Exhibition. Gender figured prominently in these discussions, since many ICW speakers equated women's maternal instincts with an innate female pacifism. In both cases, the ICW worked against the grain and their successes appear limited. That said, the minimal impact of the ICW's efforts only underscores the courage of its members, their work in support of peace, and their attempts to unite women on a political level at the 1924 British Empire Exhibition.

International Women at Wembley

During the summers of 1924 and 1925, the small north London suburb of Wembley hosted the British Empire Exhibition. Encompassing 220 acres, the exhibition celebrated imperial unity and increased economic cooperation within this "family of nations." Part trade fair and part theme park, it included national pavilions representing the dominions, colonies, and protectorates, along with industrial-commercial displays housed in the palaces of industry and engineering. There were also art exhibitions, an amusement park, an artificial lake, and an electric "never-stop" railway—the first of its kind in Britain. It slowed down (but did not come to a complete stop) in order to pick up visitors and convey them around the periphery of the grounds. The exhibition attracted approximately 25 million visitors, 17 million of them in 1924. After nearly five years of planning and construction, King George V opened the exhibition on April 23, 1924, with a royal address delivered at the Imperial Stadium to over one hundred thousand spectators. That structure, later known as Wembley Stadium and soon to be a national symbol for British football fans, had been designed specifically for the British Empire Exhibition but was completed a year earlier, in April 1923, for the Football Association's Cup final. A resulting association between Wembley Stadium and sport, spectacle, and national pride heightened and served to shape its value as a destination and locale for the exhibition.

Aware that organizers of the exhibition would not naturally turn their attention to the needs, perspectives, or talents of women, Aberdeen contacted Sir Travers Clarke, the exhibition's managing director. In a letter dated March 1923,

Fig. 6.1. Palace of Industy from North Entrance Gardens, British Empire Exhibition, 1924. Fleetway Press, London. Collection of the author.

Aberdeen and the ICW recording secretary Elsie Zimmern requested facilities to hold an ICW conference at the exhibition. Their letter raised the question of whether fair organizers included in their design special facilities to address the needs of women exhibition patrons, particularly with regard to childcare, for example. Following up on their written communications, in a meeting at the offices of the British Empire Exhibition (1924) Incorporated, the private consortium that coordinated the event, Zimmern proposed the creation of a nursery, staffed by trained nurses, "where women could leave their young children while visiting the exhibition."[9] The Central Council for Infant and Child Welfare managed the resulting crèche; however, Aberdeen and Zimmern's intervention successfully persuaded the exhibition organizers to meet the gender-specific requirements of women.

To further address the needs of female visitors, Aberdeen pushed for the establishment of a Women's Section. She was inspired by the success of a similar committee, the Woman's Board, created for the 1915 Panama-Pacific International Exposition, held in San Francisco and whose efforts Aberdeen had witnessed for herself as an attendee.[10] With this precedent in mind, Aberdeen invited Mrs. Gaillard Stoney, the honorary secretary of the San Francisco exposition's Woman's Board, to consult with the ICW in London. Mindful of potential resistance from the all-male exhibition executive, Zimmern cautioned that, in contrast to the ICW's modest financial circumstances, the American women appeared to have had "money and the interests of the directors and the whole state behind them,"[11] thereby suggesting that the ICW should not count on the same level of official support from Clarke and his staff as their American counterparts allegedly received.[12] Nevertheless, the British Empire Exhibition's management committee formed a Women's Section that was responsible for arranging hospitality and accommodations for female visitors from the dominions and the colonies. It was also the body to which the exhibition's all-male board of directors referred matters that affected what they considered "women's interests," including the arrangements for Women's Week at the exhibition and the organization of various social events for visiting dignitaries.[13] The Women's Section also represented the interests of female workers employed at the Wembley exhibition.[14] The duties of the British Empire Exhibition Women's Section resembled those of the Panama-Pacific International Exposition's Woman's Board: both saw themselves as active, working committees—and therefore different from the female dignitaries and lady managers of previous world's fairs.[15] The British Empire Exhibition Women's Section included imperial boosters, like the Victoria League, alongside representatives from social and political women's groups such as the Young Women's Christian Association and the International Woman Suffrage Alliance.

Although the ICW initiated plans for both the children's nursery and the Women's Section, and assisted on committees for both, the ICW concentrated on its own Wembley projects, the organization of an international conference, and the arrangements for the women's pavilion. According to Aberdeen, both projects were intended to "bring the special women's point of view prominently before the public."[16] Despite the avowed desire to have a prominent place at the exhibition, the ICW's financial constraints imposed restrictions. To reduce construction costs, the ICW building was small; at 560 square feet (35 ft. x 16 ft.), the ICW Wembley headquarters resembled a gazebo more than a pavilion. The architects included skylights in an effort to make the space more capacious and to maximize display area.[17] Although the ICW planned to include a small tearoom and a free lavatory for their women visitors, the exhibition organizers prohibited those arrangements since all catering and restroom facilities were contracted to private companies.[18] But even if the ICW could not offer the kind of hospitality they had envisioned, the pavilion was intended as a social center where women learned about the work of the ICW and other women's organizations.

By providing a feminine space where women were seen as political activists and citizens with responsibilities to promote change, the ICW envisaged an alternative to the usual roles assigned to female exhibition participants and visitors at the British Empire Exhibition. The exhibition's displays of manufactured goods, processed foods, and abundant produce from around the empire addressed women as consumers whose purchase of British-made products and empire foods was a loyal testament of their imperial citizenship.[19] Magazine articles addressing the "housewife at Wembley" urged middle-class women to give expression to their imperial sentiments by purchasing empire products. The shopping pages aimed at the fashionable feminine elite with disposable income targeted Wembley's upper-class female visitors, whose desire for luxury items, such as fine textiles, designer gowns, and quality home furnishings could be satisfied in a patriotic manner by purchasing items manufactured in Britain and the empire as seen on display at the exhibition.[20] In addition to the assigned role of patriotic consumers, women were presented as objects of consumption. As stand attendants, demonstrators, and models employed in the commercial displays, young female workers were closely identified with the products they represented, from baked goods and confectionaries, to domestic appliances for the home.[21] In contrast to this consumerist image, the ICW saw women as political actors with a more important role to play in imperial and international affairs than the mere reliance on their purchasing power or their ability to shill domestic products and empire goods.

With the pavilion under construction, plans for the ICW's conference proceeded simultaneously, with invitations to all NCW branches. To those members who might have seen the goal to end war as beyond their mandate, Aberdeen contended that "the cause of permanent peace and arbitration was the first question which the ICW undertook to work for and it has always been kept in the forefront of our programme." Aberdeen defended the decision to hold the conference at Wembley. The exhibition's conference halls were free of charge, and by having the conference at the British Empire Exhibition, Aberdeen hoped to attract an audience "composed of visitors from all quarters of the globe," knowing that the exhibition brought the wives and daughters of businessmen, diplomats, and politicians to London. Wembley also drew visitors from all over England, and the ICW encouraged the "ordinary rank and file of women" to attend their conference.[22] It was a broad sweep for an organization known for its aristocratic connections and its conservatism.[23]

Expecting a large attendance, Aberdeen booked enough space for 550 people, but by March 1924, only 140 delegates had confirmed.[24] The executive issued one-day conference passes as well as tickets for single lectures, hoping to attract the exhibition public and casual passersby. Early in May, when the conference was held, nearly two weeks after the British Empire Exhibition's official opening, the grounds were awash in mud, and many of the pavilions remained unfinished. General attendance failed to meet the expectations of the exhibition organizers, and attracting even same day crowds to the ICW conference would have been a challenge. In the end, about one hundred international delegates attended, in addition to the unreported number of women from local branches of the British National Council of Women.[25] Despite the low turnout, Aberdeen was optimistic that, via the published conference proceedings, the spirit of international cooperation—"exceptional in character and tone"[26]—that had prevailed at the Wembley conference would be communicated to a wider audience, thereby inspiring women across Europe and the British Empire to work for peace.

In addition to the conference, Aberdeen and the ICW used their pavilion to increase the public profile of female activism by bringing women together at the British Empire Exhibition. A lounge area and a permanent display of ICW information occupied half of the pavilion, with the remaining half rented for two-week periods to other societies, including the Six Point Group, Women's International League, and the British Women's Temperance Association. Sharing the pavilion offset the financial costs of running the building, since Aberdeen confessed that the ICW had "no funds" but they were "proceeding in faith."[27] Nevertheless, Zimmern maintained that the ICW was "the important society and in charge."[28] The ICW moved its London offices to their pavilion where Zimmern worked six days a week, assisted by "splendid voluntary helpers."[29] Despite the ICW's best efforts, the pavilion incurred a deficit of 300 GBP, and although Aberdeen and Zimmern declared the pavilion a success as a political space for women, economic constraints prevented its reopening in 1925 for Wembley's final season.[30] The children's crèche and the women's section, also credited to Aberdeen and Zimmern's efforts, remained in operation during 1925, probably because neither of them were under direct ICW supervision. Even if the ICW's work at Wembley was not an unmitigated success, the ICW created physical and intellectual spaces for women at the British Empire Exhibition. And it was within these spaces that the ICW hoped it could recruit women to work for peace.

Preventing the Causes of War

In her initial letter to Sir Travers Clarke in March 1923, Aberdeen expressed her interest in a conference for the national councils of women from the dominions to address matters that affected "the women of the Empire."[31] The question of what issues should be raised and to whom the conference would address itself framed these discussions. The ICW's plans for a peace conference had been circulating since 1922, and upon the recommendations of the Provisional Committee of Women's Organizations, a joint committee of women's international groups, Aberdeen redirected the Wembley conference toward the broader question of preventing war.[32] In August 1923, when Aberdeen announced plans for the conference to the ICW membership, the outbreak of another continental war appeared imminent. In early 1923, tensions between France and Germany over defaulted reparations payments resulted in the deployment of two divisions of French troops to occupy the Ruhr Valley. In August

1923, Italian naval forces, under orders from Benito Mussolini, bombarded the Greek island of Corfu in retaliation for the assassination of an Italian general. Both incidents challenged the authority of the League of Nations and its ability to guarantee collective security and international arbitration.[33] In view of the deepening European crisis, Aberdeen called upon women to act because it was women "who can do more than anybody else to change the present atmosphere of mutual fear and suspicion among the nations to one of mutual trust and good will."[34] Estimating the ICW's membership at 35 million women worldwide, Aberdeen's organization had the potential to make a genuine impact if everyone adopted this urgent cause.[35]

The conviction that women could make a political difference by providing a model of international cooperation in place of aggression derived from the essentialist assumption that women, instinctively maternal and nurturing, were inherent pacifists, with an aversion to war that men did not possess.[36] This "maternalist" perspective, a fundamental tenet of the ICW, frequently informed women's efforts to shape social policy in the public sphere, particularly with respect to programs for maternal and child welfare.[37] The avoidance of war had always been a central concern for the ICW since 1899 when it responded to the first intergovernmental conference on peace and disarmament, held in The Hague, with the formation of its own International Standing Committee on Peace and International Arbitration. The ICW's adoption of the Golden Rule— "Do unto others, as you would have them do onto you"—applied to this pacifist stance.[38] By 1904, the ICW supported a range of causes that pertained to women, the workplace, and public morality; however, in the early 1920s, political tensions in the postwar era underscored the urgency of their pacifist policy.

By redirecting the theme away from dominion concerns and toward the prevention of war, the ICW encountered the challenge of ensuring the attendance of European delegates. The ICW defined itself as a transnational federation, composed of women of "all races, nations, creeds and classes," and as such, it attempted to maintain a decidedly neutral stance with regard to international conflicts. Aberdeen reminded participants that the ICW constitution "excludes from its program political and religious questions of a controversial nature affecting the inter-relationship of two or more countries," and, consequently, all speakers and delegates to the 1924 conference were prohibited from making references to the recent war or the continuing tensions on the continent.[39] Instead, Aberdeen asked participants to reflect on the systemic causes of war: education systems that inculcated aggressive patriotism and glorified war, and international economic competition for markets and resources.

Support for the conference was not unanimous. Henni Forchhammer, an ICW executive member from Denmark, feared that the program was "too extensive and perhaps too controversial," and that the ICW could not "influence the present situation by such necessarily academic discussions." Peace in Europe depended on the settlement of the reparations issue by the League of Nations; however, Forchhammer acknowledged the relevance of women to creating a more "enlightened public opinion and a burning desire for peace."[40] Whether this conference would provide an effective venue for women to shape public opinion toward these ends remained to be seen.

Persuading German women to participate was a difficult task. In private, Dr. Alice Salomon, a German national and the ICW vice president, expressed her enthusiasm for the conference and her hope that German National Council of Women members would attend.[41] Germany's NCW voted against participation, and even though both Salomon and Forchhammer questioned Aberdeen's determination to avoid specific political issues at its conference, their objections failed to sway the general membership of the German NCW. With regret, Aberdeen accepted the German women's decision.[42] Anna Lindemann, a German national and the vice president of the International Woman Suffrage Alliance, expressed her reservations about attending the conference. Lindemann stated that due to the continued occupation of the Rhineland, Germans were living under "special conditions of tensions," while the inability of the international community to resolve the situation forced them "to realize the unworthy place our country has been relegated to in the council of nations."[43] Lindemann acknowledged the ideal of maintaining an apolitical stance; however, she warned Aberdeen that she might feel differently at the conference itself and be compelled to address the Rhineland crisis, by saying "a word or two that might be useful."[44] Above all, Lindemann wanted the freedom to speak about the political situation between France and Germany, if she so desired. Understandably, German women found it extremely difficult to set aside their national grievances, even for a conference dedicated to peace and the eradication of war.

Presiding over the first day's meetings, ICW vice president Mrs. Ogilvie Gordon, noted that the causes of conflict were similar everywhere, and as women they "recognize[d] the essential sameness of the problems that determine peace or war in every land." Gordon called for collective action: one individual was ineffective, but if every woman, in every home, in every nation used her influence "to inculcate ideals of peace in the minds of the children, and to foster those ideals in the social life around them," then the "sum of those labors of womanhood would be enormous."[45] Gordon beseeched women to use their newly acquired political power, the outcome of suffrage campaigns and recently created democratic states, to ensure more open dealings between nations and to send a strong message to their statesmen demanding new methods of international arbitration.

Over the six-day conference, the speakers addressed the question of sustainable peace from several perspectives. Some appealed to women's maternal instincts as the basis of an international sisterhood that could prevent future wars. In her "Call to the Mothers of All Races," Aberdeen condemned the fallacious idea that warfare was a necessary expression of a social Darwinist rhetoric, arguing instead that the fittest should strive to preserve liberty, security, and the welfare of all.[46] Evolution should lead to greater cooperation and international peace. She urged all women to encourage and appreciate an understanding of each country by the study of languages, by travel and by receiving guests from other nations. But most important, women had to inspire the children to see theirs as the generation to end war. Bereft of the "old halo of glory or heroism" that characterized past conflicts, "men of science" had provided a glimpse of the devastating technologies to be expected in "the next war," technologies that caused massive destruction and targeted civilian populations.

Given the impact of modern science on warfare and the advent of more lethal technologies, Aberdeen stated that war was no longer honorable or sportsmanlike, in the way that it might have been in the past. Although it was difficult for any society to divest itself of "the associations of war, of Armies and Navies, and War Offices, and Warships," which were "part and parcel of life," it was incumbent on this generation to accept their collective responsibility to rear the next generation with new associations and ideals.[47] In the early 1920s, it would have been difficult indeed to reject the militaristic associations, given the proliferation of war memorials and commemorative statues throughout Britain.[48] Furthermore, both the commemoration of war and the recognition of the importance of the armed forces to the collective strength of the empire received tribute at the British Empire Exhibition with patriotic enthusiasm.

From its inception, references to war permeated Britain's contribution to the British Empire Exhibition. In the immediate postwar years, when the Lloyd George coalition government struggled to deliver on its reconstruction promises, Minister of Labour Thomas Macnamara justified public and private investment in the exhibition as a means of creating jobs for the unemployed. Edward, Prince of Wales, the official royal patron of the event, promoted the British Empire Exhibition as a make-work scheme for his "old comrades," unemployed ex-servicemen.[49] The Department of Overseas Trade, the government office responsible for the planning and construction of the British government's pavilion, recommended the hiring of ex-soldiers as stand attendants for the exhibition, although this patronage did not extend to the employment of ex-soldiers with disabilities.[50] To support the work of disabled ex-servicemen, the Department of Overseas Trade commissioned the Lord Roberts Memorial Workshops, a training initiative for disabled veterans, to decorate the interior of a suite of rooms prepared for the royal family for their use when visiting Wembley.[51] The government pavilion also displayed specimen work produced by the Disabled Soldiers and Sailors Handicrafts Association.[52]

At the British Empire Exhibition, the British government commemorated the events of the recent war in Europe in a variety of other ways. Britain's pavilion included dioramas of several famous battle scenes from the Great War, including the first Battle of Ypres and the first Battle of the Somme. The British pavilion's Admiralty Theatre staged a mechanical model reenactment of the British naval victory over the Germans at Zeebrugge, Belgium, with several performances daily to audiences of up to three hundred visitors. Military recruitment films, commissioned by the War Office, also featured on the theatre program.[53] In addition to the prominent displays in the British government pavilion assembled by the Royal Navy, the Army, and the Royal Air Force, the Department of Overseas Trade organized evening performances by military bands in the form of a "services tattoo" held in the stadium for several weeks during the month of July.[54] The celebration of Britain's military strength was a pervasive theme in the government pavilion and at the stadium performances. Despite the economic crunch that shelved many reconstruction schemes, during the 1920s Britain maintained a well-funded military with the highest expenditure on armaments of any nation at the time.[55]

Britain's military expertise, proudly displayed at Wembley, underscored the challenge the ICW faced in promoting peace and international cooperation at this imperial exhibition. The ICW also addressed the issue of disarmament and international arms trafficking. C. Delisle Burns, a writer and lecturer in philosophy at the University of London, lamented the high cost of arms expenditure as a drain on the postwar economy, estimating that 60 percent of Britain's annual income was spent on "war services," including armaments, servicing the Army, Navy, and Air Force, and repaying "the war debt."[56] In response to the paradoxical argument that arms production promoted international security and peace by serving as a deterrent to war, Burns argued that the state investment in armaments hampered the development of peace, while "the inevitable growth of armaments to obtain security," along with the reliance on private industry to manufacture armaments, actually increased the likelihood of war.[57]

Aino Kallas, an NCW delegate from Estonia, had the final word on disarmament. Representing one of the Baltic States that regained its independence after 1918, Kallas noted that the burden of disarmament falls most heavily on the new nations who were unable to afford the high cost of armaments and yet were forced to maintain defensive forces. For the goal of universal disarmament to succeed, Kallas believed, all humanity had to be "born anew," to revolutionize current human values by replacing "martial virtues" with the instinct for peace.[58] This was the great task for women, not just to attend peace conferences, but also to create "a new being with the peace instinct in his blood"—to pass on this peace instinct to the next generation. More than men, women knew "the value of life purchased with pain" and were better suited to inculcate the peace instinct in the next generation.

In grappling with the controversial issue of militarism and disarmament, the ICW accomplished several goals. First, they attempted to educate the conference attendees about the efforts of the League of Nations and the role of international arbitration in arms reduction in order to politicize women and help them recognize the value of supporting the efforts of this organization. The conference speakers also noted the fundamental connection between permanent peace and disarmament, pointing to the future dangers of new types of weaponry. In this respect, the ICW helped sustain the women's peace movement in Britain during the early 1920s, working alongside more activist feminist groups, including the Women's International League for Peace and Freedom.[59] Finally, the speakers invited women to imagine a world without armaments, war offices, and military spending where resources were not wasted on arms production, and reconstruction promises were not forfeited in favor of weaponry. It was a bold vision, but it was one that women might affect via their influence on the next generation as mothers and educators. It was also an appeal to a newly enfranchised group of female voters to use their new power for real political change.

Reconciling Peace with Patriotism, Women's Style

The prevention of war and the creation of peace were issues of national self-interest and patriotism, and few nations were willing to sacrifice either in the interests of collective and mutually guaranteed security. Acknowledging this dilemma, the ICW speakers challenged women to reinvent patriotism and move it beyond national boundaries. In her appeal for peace and international solidarity, Clara Guthrie d'Arcis, the president of the Union Mondiale de la Femme pour la Concorde Internationale (World Union of Women for International Understanding), asked women to learn from their past mistakes. Rather than allowing national interests and narrow prejudices to take precedent—sentiments that prevented women from collectively asserting a united resistance to prevent the previous war—she asked women as "educators of the world" to break down prejudice by teaching tolerance and understanding for all races and religions. Anticipating an enlightened future, she mused: "How strangely ignorant we shall seem perhaps to the mothers of the year 2000, very much like women who had failed to teach their children to walk upright."[60] Women needed to create a new patriotism, to educate "real internationalists without sacrificing love of one's own country." Patriotism, d'Arcis recognized, was a powerful and complex emotion that called forth the greatest sacrifice and drove men to give up their businesses, homes, wives, and children in the service of their country. She observed that "no other emotion has had so much money spent upon its cultivation." Unfortunately, patriotism was also the most manipulated and exploited emotion. But true patriotism, she posited, was not limited to loving one's own country, but in making one's nation loved by all and others, thereby enabling patriotism to extend beyond narrow self-interest to a new form of patriotism: internationalism.[61]

For some conference delegates, internationalism as a new form of patriotism was itself an indication of the scientific evolution of humanity. Charlotte de Geocze, the secretary of the NCW of Hungary, noted that at the British Empire Exhibition, they were surrounded by the spectacle of industrial and mechanical progress. Material progress, however, failed to ensure happiness but served instead to extend competition and thereby hasten the outbreak of another war. Observing that the Darwinian theory of the "survival of the fittest" had contributed to the "bankruptcy of Western civilization," de Geocze posited that Darwinian progress was not determined by material and intellectual strength, but rather by "moral power." The real claim of women, de Geocze argued, was the feminine gender's superior morality and more highly evolved sense of social justice; this was women's contribution to social evolution and the advancement of the human species.[62]

Female solidarity and the identification with women of other nations based on their common maternal instincts were expressions of what historian Leila Rupp has called "the international bonds of womanhood." Women could also articulate and inculcate a new form of patriotism—internationalism—which Rupp describes as more of a phenomenon or movement than an ideology.[63] For those who attended the Wembley conference, this internationalist ideal was based on tolerance, understanding, and friendship, and it could foster "a spiritual movement concentrating on peace, enrolling individuals everywhere regardless of nationality, religion, station or politics."[64] International exchanges for teachers, students, and organizations that promoted humanitarian assistance, such as the Red Cross, would foster international cooperation and understanding.[65]

The ICW's articulated ideal of international citizenship contrasted with the popular expression of national and imperial identities as conveyed at the BEE. In their respective studies of international and colonial exhibitions, John MacKenzie, Peter Hoffenberg and Benedict Burton note that the colonial system figured prominently at these events. Imperial exhibitions presented empires in miniature to the citizens of the dominant culture, but also reflected racial and cultural hierarchies that validated the colonial project.[66] It is unlikely that this paradox escaped the notice of the conference organizers, and by having the conference at the British Empire Exhibition, the ICW walked a fine line between the acknowledgement that the colonial system itself was a cause of war and oppression, and the alternate view, that imperialism was a form of internationalism. The latter perspective was explicitly defended by at least one speaker. Major Frank Fox, the secretary of the Fellowship of the British Empire

Exhibition, a club that promoted imperial cooperation and fraternity via the Wembley exhibition, expressed a different interpretation of international feeling than that articulated by Aberdeen, d'Arcis, and de Geocze. Fox agreed with his fellow speakers on the need for greater intellectual cooperation and supported the cause of peace, but he also believed that the "basis of true and sound internationalism must be in the first instance at home . . . [that] men and women must have a real pride in their own nation." National pride provided individuals with the basis on which to build a "sound and true international spirit." On this premise, Fox asserted, the British Empire stood as the best example in the world of the movement toward internationalism. Fox asked all peoples of the empire to realize what a great heritage they had and to develop that imperial heritage "for the benefit of our race, for the benefit of those races which are leagued with us in the work of the empire and also for the benefit of humanity at large."[67] In cultivating pride in one's own culture, but with tolerance for that of others, Fox asserted that the British Empire was a great organization for the British people, for their colonial subjects, and for humanity in general.

Although Fox used the ICW conference to promote his fraternity of empire, his definition of internationalism rested on a firm loyalty to nation and empire first, with the assumption that internationalism naturally would follow. This sentiment was shared by some of the delegates. Leaving the conference, Louisa Macdonald, a retired teacher and Australian delegate, had this to say: "Coming from such a meeting day after day, it was not difficult to see that the wonder of the Exhibition lies in this: that it stands for a symbol of what can be wrought by justice, freedom and peace."[68] And yet the absence of the NCW's German delegation, in protest over the French occupation of the Ruhr Valley, compounded by the suppression of all political discussion at the conference reinforced the divisive power of patriotism and national self-interest.

Conclusion

The International Council of Women put women on the map at the 1924 British Empire Exhibition by creating political spaces for women in the physical and the intellectual sense. Despite their limited financial resources and the apparent indifference of the exhibition authorities, the ICW built and staffed a modest pavilion where women met and shared information about various participating organizations, and where female exhibition patrons were treated as political subjects and not merely the consumers of goods and services. The ICW's Wembley conference highlights the complexities and contradictions of internationalism expressed within the colonial context, wherein empire itself was an acknowledged cause of war, and discussions about peace and disarmament might have appeared ironic when contrasted to the British government's celebration of its armed forces. Amid these reminders of conflict and conquest, the conference delegates envisioned a world without war where resources were dedicated to education, social programs and international cooperation. According to conference speakers, the prevention of war depended upon the maternalist efforts of women to foster a spirit of peace, to end the association of patriotism with militarism, and to demand new methods of international arbitration by rejecting violence as a solution. Framing the discussion as a matter of evolutionary progress, women's ability to cultivate the instinct for peace, not war, in the next generation was an indication of women's contribution to the social and moral evolution of humanity. If women failed in this, they would appear uncivilized and barbaric to their sisters in the future.

In place of nationalism and patriotism, the old ideals that lead to war, women must cultivate a new value—internationalism—founded on peaceful arbitration between nations. However, the difficulty of reconciling peace and patriotism—even the difficulty of producing a nationally neutral space to discuss this aim—within the setting of an exposition ostensibly celebrating empire was evident in 1924. Even as the conference rejected any overt political references, the German women's absence and the well-known liberal connections of many of the British conference organizers and speakers, including Aberdeen, belie that point, as do the frequent references to the League of Nations and the problem of disarmament. In addition, the strategies for peace, as presented at the conference, had distinct class underpinnings. This is particularly true since the proposed means of cultivating internationalism—language study, travel, and hosting foreign guests—were worthy activities for upper- and middle-class women but were hardly within the reach of women of the working classes. Even the ICW pavilion appears to be a class-exclusive space, despite the efforts and intentions of Zimmern to welcome all women. Its pamphlet displays, volunteer staff, and sections rented out to other liberal-minded women's organizations were unlikely attractions for the majority of female exhibition goers who might have dropped their children at the crèche but then headed for the Palace of Industry, to see the displays of food, fashions, and furniture, or ventured into the amusement park for a bit of fun. Were Aberdeen and the ICW demanding too much by asking women to take seriously the cause of peace, internationalism, and the prevention of war? Perhaps so, but in the process, they expressed their reservations about the high cost of war, even in times of peace. They urged newly enfranchised women to look beyond national interests and embrace internationalism, and in so doing, to try reconciling the quest for peace with a new form of patriotism. This was the only cause worth fighting for.

Thanks to all who facilitated this research and offered suggestions: the Social Science Humanities Research Council of Canada, Nipissing University, Richard Rempel, Katrina Srigley, Hilary Earl, TJ Boisseau, and Abigail Markwyn, and also Matthew Hendley for his comments on a version of this paper presented at the 2005 North American Conference on British Studies.

1   Founded in 1888 by American suffragists, the ICW affiliated women's groups in individual countries, organized as National Councils. Lady Aberdeen, a Scottish aristocrat, was president of the ICW from 1893 until 1936. See Leila R. Rupp, *Worlds of Women: The Making of an International Women's Movement* (Princeton: Princeton University Press, 1997), 15–21, 42.

2   Circular letter, January 19, 1924, National Archives, Ottawa, MG 28, I 245, 27, 398.

3   Ibid.

4   Eric Dorn Brose, *A History of Europe in the Twentieth Century* (Oxford: Oxford University Press, 2005), 74–75.

5   Circular letter, January 19, 1924, National Archives, Ottawa, MG 28, I 245, 27, 398.

6   Maria Grever, "Reconstructing the Fatherland: Comparative Perspectives on Women and 19th Century Exhibitions," available at www.vrouwengeschiedenis.dds.nl/nl/dossiers/grever.html (accessed January 16, 2010).

7   Introduction, note 3.

8   Tracey Jean Boisseau, "Where Every Woman May Be a Queen: Gender, Politics, and Visual Space at the Chicago World's Fair, 1893," in *Space in America: Theory, History, Culture*, ed. Klaus Benesch and Kerstin Schmidt, 288–93 (Amsterdam: Rodopi, 2005).

9   Letter, July 30, 1923, National Archives, Ottawa, MG 28, I 245, 27, 404.

10   Letter, September 4, 1923, National Archives, Ottawa, MG 28, I 245, 10, 156. Thanks to Abigail Markwyn for her comments on Aberdeen at the Panama-Pacific International Exposition.

11   Letter, September 10, 1923, National Archives, Ottawa, MG 28, I 245, 10, 156; Anna Pratt Simpson, *Problems Women Solved* (San Francisco: Woman's Board, 1915), 12–14, 30–34, 62–84.

12   Abigail Markwyn, "Constructing 'An Epitome of Civilization': Local Politics and Visions of Progressive Era America at San Francisco's Panama-Pacific International Exposition" (PhD diss., University of Wisconsin–Madison, 2006), 125–28.

13   Directors' Report, British Empire Exhibition (1924) Incorporated, October 1–31, 1923, 2, National Archives Ottawa, RG 25, 455, 11; Women's Section, *Women & Wembley: The British Empire at Home: April to October 1924* (British Empire Exhibition: Fleetway, 1924), 3–4.

14   Marie Carola Galway, *The Past Revisited: People and Happenings Recalled* (London: Harvill, 1953), 232.

15   Markwyn, 121–23.

16   Circular letter, July 1923, National Archives, Ottawa, MG 28, I 245, 27, 404.

17   Letters, May 22, 1923; June 26, 1923; July 20, 1923, National Archives, Ottawa, MG 28, I 245, 10, 155.

18   Letters, August 16, 1923; September 25, 1923, National Archives, Ottawa, MG 28 I 245, 10, 15.

19   Anne Clendinning, "Consuming the Commonwealth: Women and the British Empire Exhibition," unpublished paper, Pacific and West Coast Meeting, North American Conference on British Studies, Santa Barbara, Calif., March 2000; Keith McClelland

and Sonya Rose, "Citizenship and Empire, 1867–1928," in *At Home with the Empire: Metropolitan Culture and the Imperial World*, ed. Catherine Hall and Sonya O. Rose, 294–95 (Cambridge: Cambridge University Press, 2006).

20 "The Housewife at Wembley," *Home and Politics* 36 (June 1924): 11; "I Saw: ——," *Gentlewoman* 68, no. 1769 (May 24, 1924): 545; "A Lace Romance, as Told at Wembley," *Gentlewoman* 68, no. 1771 (June 7, 1924): 606.

21 "The Seven Ages of Woman," *Gas Journal*, June 4, 1924; "A Housewife's Paradise—the Electric House," *Illustrated London News*, July 19, 1924; "Peek Freen, Huntley & Palmer and W. R. Jacobs," *Illustrated London News*, July 19, 1924.

22 Letter, January 19, 1924, National Archives, Ottawa, MG 28, I245, 27, 398.

23 Rupp, 19.

24 Minutes of the Directors, ICW, March 12, 1924, National Archives, Ottawa, MG 28, I 245, 2, 23.

25 International Council of Women, *The Prevention of the Causes of War: Addresses Delivered at the Conference Held at the British Empire Exhibition, Wembley, May 2–8, 1924* (International Council of Women, 1924), 321.

26 Ibid., ii.

27 Letter, December 5, 1923, National Archives, Ottawa, MG 28, I 245, 10, 156.

28 Letter, December 28, 1923, National Archives, Ottawa, MG 28, I 245, 10, 157.

29 Letter, November 7, 1924, National Archives, Ottawa, MG 28, I 245, 151.

30 National Council of Women, Great Britain, Executive Minutes, November 21, 1924, 1026, London Metropolitan Archives/ACC 3613/01-006.

31 Letter, March 31, 1923, National Archives, Ottawa, MG 28, I 245, 10, 154.

32 Circular letter, October 21, 1922, National Archives, Ottawa, MG 28, I 245, 27, 402.

33 Brose, 124–26.

34 Circular letter, August 20, 1923, National Archives, Ottawa, MG 28 I 245, 37, 555.

35 ICW, *Prevention of the Causes of War*, 312–13.

36 Rupp, *Worlds of Women*, 84–86; Susan Zeiger, "Finding a Cure for War: Women's Politics and the Peace Movement in the 1920s," *Journal of Social History* 24, no. 1 (Autumn 1990): 75–80.

37 Seth Koven and Sonya Michel, eds. *Mothers of a New World: Maternalist Politics and the Origins of Welfare States* (New York: Routledge, 1993), intro.

38 Leila Rupp, "Constructing Internationalism: The Case of Transnational Women's Organization, 1888–1945," *American Historical Review* 99, no. 5 (December 1994): 1595–96.

39 Letter, April 17, 1923, National Archives, Ottawa, MG 28, I 245, 27, 400.

40 Ibid.

41 Letter, September 17, 1923, National Archives, Ottawa MG 28, I 245, 27, 403.

42 Letters, January 21, 1924; February 9, 1924, National Archives, Ottawa, MG 28, I 245, 27, 404.

43 Letter, April 23, 1924, National Archives, Ottawa, MG 28, I 245, 27, 402.

44 Ibid.

45 ICW, 3–5.

46 Ibid., 6–10.

47 Ibid., 7–9.

48 Jay Winter, *Sites of Memory, Sites of Mourning: The Great War in European Cultural History* (Cambridge: Cambridge University Press, 1995), chap. 4.

49 "British Empire Exhibition: Appeal to MPs," *Times*, October 11, 1921; "The Prince and the Unemployed: Work on the Empire Exhibition," *Times*, October 4, 1921.

50 Interdepartmental Meetings, May 10, 1923; May 24, 1923; June 12, 1923; July 26, 1923; February 7, 1924; February 21, 1924, National Archives, Kew, BT/5 part 2.

51 Interdepartmental Meetings, October 18, 1923, NA, Kew, BT/5 part 2; see also Deborah Cohen, *The War Come Home: Disabled Veterans in Britain and Germany, 1914–1939* (Berkeley: University of California Press, 2001), 29, 34–37.

52 Interdepartmental Meetings, November 29, 1923, NA, Kew, BT/5 part 2.

53 Interdepartmental Meetings, May 24, 1923; July 26, 1923; September 6, 1923; March 29, 1924; October 27, 1924, National Archives, Kew, BT 60/5/ part 2; the Pavilion of H.M. Government, *The Raid on Zeebrugge: An Illustrated Souvenir of the Model Display in the Admiralty Theatre of H.M. Government Pavilion* (British Empire Exhibition: H.M. Government, 1925).

54 Interdepartmental Meetings, May 24, 1923; July 5, 1923; July 19, 1923, National Archives, Kew BT 60/5 part 2.

55 David Edgerton, *Warfare State, Britain, 1920–1970* (Cambridge: Cambridge University Press, 2006), 21–24.

56 ICW, 289.

57 Ibid., 290–91.

58 Ibid., 297–99.

59 Jill Liddington, *The Road to Greenham Common: Feminism and Anti-Militarism since 1820* (Syracuse: Syracuse University Press, 1991), 134–40.

60 ICW, 11–16.

61 Ibid., 18.

62 Ibid., 115–16.

63 Rupp, *Worlds of Women*, 108.

64 ICW, 12.

65 Ibid., 83–95; 98–116.

66 John M. MacKenzie, *Propaganda and Empire: The Manipulation of British Public Opinion, 1880–1960* (Dover, N.H.: Manchester University Press, 1985); Peter Hoffenberg, *An Empire on Display: English, Indian and Australian Exhibitions from the Crystal Palace to the Great War* (Berkeley: University of California Press, 2001); Burton Benedict, *The Anthropology of World's Fairs: San Francisco's Panama-Pacific International Exposition of 1915* (Berkeley: University of California Press, 1983).

67 ICW, 96–97.

68 Louisa Macdonald, "The International Council of Women at Wembley," National Archives, Ottawa, MG 28, I 245, 27, 402.

CHAPTER 7

The Woman's World's Fairs (or The Dream of Women Who Work), Chicago 1925–1928

TJ Boisseau

The souvenir program for the 1927 Woman's World's Fair greeted visitors with a buoyant and woman-centered highmindedness: "Woven from the shimmering web of a dream—a woman's dream—into the enduring fabric of an exposition, planned by women, made and installed by women, for the benefit of all women everywhere, the Third Annual Woman's World's Fair opens its doors and bids you welcome."[1]

More than a generation after the 1893 Woman's Building closed its doors to the public, an emphatic insistence on showcasing women's accomplishments persisted among that city's most energetic female organizers. They endeavored to produce a venue in which women's ideas about themselves could be expressed and a context in which they could come to appreciate and celebrate each other's contributions to the world. To do so, they turned toward the form that had best represented one of Chicago women's greatest triumphs: the world's fair. The results of their efforts were the week-long Woman's World's Fairs held in Chicago each spring in 1925, 1926, 1927, and 1928.

Fig. 7.1. 1927 Woman's World's Fair *Souvenir Program*. Cover. Used by permission of the Chicago History Museum.

This time in Chicago, sentiments regarding Woman's advancement and achievements would be expressed entirely apart from the distinctively classist, racialist, and colonialist rhetoric that had saturated the meaning of its predecessor—the Columbian Exhibition held in Chicago in 1893. Promotional materials announcing the Woman's World's Fairs were free of elitist metaphors, such as the "white queenliness" that had characterized so much of that earlier Chicago fair.[2] Instead a determinedly, even if somewhat naïve and certainly idealistic, celebration of Woman as productive contributor to society expressed a sex-consciousness unrent by class division, racial prejudice, or national hierarchy. Absent such ideological crutches, and at a time that both contemporaries and historians since have often derided as manifesting a decline in self-consciously politicized, woman-centered organizing, a fair "planned by women, made and installed by women, for the benefit of all women everywhere" drew hundreds of thousands of visitors each June and managed to pay for itself as well as turn a profit for four years running.[3]

The principal setting for the Woman's World's Fairs was the acclaimed American Exposition Palace located along Lake Shore Drive. The exposition space was located on the first floor of what was said to be, at the time, the largest building ever built, at 466 feet deep, 218 feet wide, and sixteen floors high—and that was before the tower added in 1927 increased its height to 474 feet.[4] This structure was apparently designed with the idea in mind that it would frequently house expositions such as the Woman's World's Fairs on its first floor and, more permanently, a furniture mart, club, restaurants, and a gallery on its upper floors. The anticipation that expositions and fairs would be an ongoing function of the building is demonstrated by the enlarged entrances to the American Exposition Palace that were placed on the grandest facades of the building off Lake Shore Drive and Huron Street, with extra-wide doors provided at the north end of the Erie Street furniture mart entrance "so that, should occasion demand, this entrance can be opened up into the Exposition Palace."[5] Thus the American Exposition Palace, unlike the vast majority of world's fair buildings, was made to endure. Its foundation rested on piles driven 50 and 60 feet below the level of Lake Michigan; its walls were reinforced concrete, its floors marble, its paneling and woodwork solid oak. The main entrance to the Exposition Palace, on Lake Shore Drive, opened onto a room of "truly majestic proportions," according to *Architecture* magazine—120 feet by 55 feet, with a height of 35 feet.[6] In 1925,

H-3307.   THE AMERICAN EXPOSITION PALACE, LAKE SHORE DRIVE, CHICAGO, ILLINOIS. © 1925 FRED HARVEY

Fig. 7.2. American Exposition Palace. Postcard. Image supplied by chicagopc.info.

the building drew over one hundred thousand visitors to a week-long exhibit which included several hundred booths. By 1927, the Woman's World's Fair had outgrown even the first floor of even this building and had to be housed in the nearby Coliseum.[7]

However majestic the spaces that harbored the Woman's World's Fairs, these expositions must be viewed as tiny compared to more well-known, male-dominated, and often federally or commercially supported international expositions. Lasting for only a week instead of the usual five months of summer, and with attendance representing a mere fraction of the tens of millions who attended more widely known world's fairs, there are many aspects of these fairs that are not comparable with their mammoth cousins. Still, though the overall scope of the Woman's World's Fairs was small, the crowds they drew cannot be considered paltry. Total attendance figures—from 160,000 to 200,000 visitors each year, according to local news accounts—were figures most international exhibition organizers would have found enviable for a week's attendance to one building. Likewise, the organizers and backers of more prominent early-twentieth-century fairs would have envied the $50,000 that the first of these fairs, staged without loans or government funding, reputedly netted in just eight days.[8] And, though these world's fairs were less widely publicized than most, their organizers purported to address women the whole world over. Foreign participation of exhibitors from Europe, including Greece, Ukraine, Germany, and Great Britain to the 1928 fair, places these fairs firmly within the family of "international expositions," even when the definition is parsed on technicalities.[9] Most significant is that in their rhetoric and promotional materials, the Woman's World's Fairs communicated an idealistic and global ethos that all world's fairs shared.

Moreover, lest we imagine that a world's fair limited to purely women's accomplishments and interests went forward bereft of the aura that recognition by the national government lent to larger and more studied fairs, bookending the opening and closing of the first of these annual fairs were tributes from United States President Calvin Coolidge and Vice President Charles G. Dawes. Borrowing an opening format from the 1904 St. Louis World's Fair, the disembodied voice of Calvin Coolidge opened the Woman's World's Fair of 1925 on the morning of Saturday, April 18. Unlike the 1904 fair, however, and in keeping with the woman-centered purposes of this fair, the wireless mechanism carrying the president's voice was triggered by the touch of a button wielded by First Lady Grace Coolidge.[10] Indeed, the first day of what would become an annual event for four years was marked by several layers of nationalist iconography twisted to locate women at the center of expressions of nationalist spirit. Just as the president's voice was broadcast to the assembled crowd, a woman named

Betty Turner Matthews—but declaring herself a latter-day "Paulette Revere"—took off at a galloping pace, tracing the shoreline of Lake Michigan between two heralding trumpeters to deliver the message to throngs of mostly female attendees that "the Woman's World's Fair is coming!" The orchestration of this reenactment of a founding moment in the origin of the nation may have been lighthearted enough, but it and the rest of the hoopla of the day were meant as no spoof. Lending gravitas, masculine acknowledgement, and nationalist import to the fair were the several companies of soldiers emptying out the nearby garrison at Fort Sheridan to pass in review and stand dramatically in attendance while an artillery unit in front of the fair building fired a presidential salute of twenty-one guns. The Woman's World's Fair of 1925 was a small, compact affair, but it declared itself firmly within the family circle of world's fairs with such officiousness and demonstrations of nationalist pomp.

Vice President Dawes's concluding speech on the last day of the fair articulated—albeit in a most condescending manner—the principle theme that would animate all of the Woman's World's Fairs held in the late 1920s. In his speech he congratulated the assembled all-female board of directors for being "serious-minded women" and went on to remark approvingly on how "happy is the enterprise like this for which earnest women are willing to give their time, means and unselfish hard work."[11] Dawes's patronizing attitude notwithstanding, his final words likely struck members of the board of directors as on point at least in one respect. *Work*, more specifically the work of women, was indeed the watchword at this fair and to an extent that was never explored at a world's fair previously or since. The Board of Lady Managers at the Columbian Exposition thirty years before, for instance, had not encouraged an appreciation for women's work as such. Although the unusual exploits of particularly accomplished women became focal points in the celebration of the modern woman in 1893, the most important criteria of modernity enshrined at that fair was a certain dignified bearing as well as an effective display of imperial sovereignty over racialized or colonized "others." It was this quality combined with the exhibition of middle-class "true womanly" traits that drew the highest praise from the organizers of the 1893 Woman's Building.[12] As for remunerative work or ordinary industrial labor—the socialite status of the leisured women who dominated the 1893 Board of Lady Managers had produced only an awkward silence.

In contrast, the women who oversaw the administration of the 1920s Woman's World's Fairs chose work as the primary theme of the event each year, purposefully erasing distinctions between the work of urban working-class and rural women and between the experience of both those groups and that of educated, professional women. At these fairs work itself figures as the centerpiece of women's lives and identities as women. Neither were women's domestic lives dismissed as insignificant; instead, the rhetoric of the 1920s Woman's World's Fairs re-imagined the domestic sphere as a productive one and domestic labor as something that served to connect women rather than as alienating drudgery that separated them from one another and from the world at large. Such a vision represents a departure from the romanticized notion of middle-class domesticity shorn of labor (a labor typically made invisible by female servants) as was often presented by the Board of Lady Managers in 1893. It also countered a presentation of modern domesticity typical of corporate depictions.

In the 1920s, as many historians have shown, popular culture texts often presented for public consumption the fantasy of the leisured modern domestic woman as liberated by technology, her home transformed into a site of ease and consumption as a consequence of this liberation. Commercial advertisements in the 1920s implicitly and explicitly proffered technology as a replacement for women's work in the home while imputing a certain valuelessness to the actual reproductive work of rearing children and homemaking. This effect was frequently achieved through a set of contrasts between successfully modernized women and primitivized or "backward" women in desperate want of liberation from preindustrial toil that dovetailed with their submission to patriarchal men. No such diminution of physical labor, devaluing of reproductive labor, or dismissal of traditional crafts is in evidence in the literature of the Woman's World's Fairs. These expositions did not promise to liberate women from productive or reproductive labor, nor was there a splintering of women into consumers and producers or into those who had achieved modernity and those who had not.[13] Modernity was presented by fair organizers as a state of mind that acknowledged no limits on work—whether domestic, agricultural, industrial or professional— for women. Work, as defined by these fair organizers, was all-inclusive of what women did and how women best expressed themselves as women. Modernity was redefined in their visions as the state of being within which women would be encouraged and enabled to choose and succeed at work.

The Beauty of Work

Press surrounding the first Woman's World's Fair in 1925 made clear that *work* was to be its central message. Work was what Woman's World's Fair organizers believed women had in common with each other, regardless of their status as wives, "home girls," or single "spinsters," and regardless of whether they were working-class, middle-class, or affluent women. According to the *Woman's Viewpoint,* even "society women who have changed hobbies into vocations" are included in the list of women for whom life's meaning is found in work. One aspect of life that was not highly touted by fair organizers was marriage, not only because of its tendency to obscure a married woman's identity behind that of her husband, but more particularly, and explicitly, because a society that only valued women as wives pitted women against one another by tending to stigmatize unmarried adult women and devalue domesticity when it was performed as paid labor: "Somebody else's babies and somebody else's fireside," the magazine insisted, "was all there was left to the spinster and home girl of yesterday." The sentence was finished in a way that refused to assign to married and unwaged mothers a higher status than that of "working girls." "Now the young girl and the middle aged woman," the passage went on to say, "go forth to their work in the morning and have their own children—brain children."[14] Whether maternalizing women's nondomestic work (professional accomplishment = "brain children") or lending social value to their domestic labor, the women behind the fairs held in Chicago in the late 1920s declared all women united as valuable producer-laborers. The centrality of work as a mainstay of woman's identity produced a leveling and a unity among women as workers regardless of social rank, marital status, class, or type of work.

The main impetus of the fair was to bring the tidal wave of work that women were and had been performing for ages "by the light of a candle and under a bushel" into the national spotlight and in concentrated form such that it provided a mirror for women to know themselves as a constituency of pro-ducers.[15] Clearly, organizers of the Woman's World's Fair saw themselves as working women, though they came at least in part from the same social strata of industrially prominent families that the Board of Lady Managers had in 1893. However, the fair's self-advertising makes it apparent that gendered notions regarding work held by women within this class had undergone much change in the intervening years. An enlarged middle class of professional women had emerged whose class status stemmed less from the position of their fathers and husbands than it did from their own professional training and roles. As the first sentence of Managing Director Helen M. Bennet's dedication in the souvenir program for the 1927 fair proudly asserted, "The Woman's World's Fair comes into its third year a firm foundation under the dreams of women who work."[16]

Bennet and the contrast she makes with the 1893 Board of Lady Managers' President Bertha Honore Potter Palmer make most obvious the changes in gender ideology and the new centrality of work to women's identity in the 1920s. While Palmer was the fashionable wife of a powerful Chicago-based businessman and civic leader—and was an influential woman as a result of the social circle this tie made available to her—Bennet was a simply dressed, unmarried, "self-made" career woman devoted to the mission of putting education and vocational training within reach of both the working- and middle-class girls of Chicago. She was co-founder and first manager of the Chicago Collegiate Bureau of Occupations, an organization whose purpose was to place women college graduates in jobs. In 1917, Bennet had authored *Women and Work: The Economic Value of College Training*, a study of the presence of women in occupations and opportunities for career advancement including an assessment of obstacles women experienced in education and training and the social value of providing women with college-level education. Even decades later, the *Chicago Tribune* would credit Bennet for leading the charge in Chicago to "get women hired in jobs which had been denied them, at wages equal to that of men."[17] Although at the Collegiate Bureau Bennet's work was primarily with middle-class girls and young women from the city, her vision emphatically embraced an international, interregional and cross-class continuum of woman's work, as the language she uses in the introduction to the Woman's World's Fair 1925 souvenir program illustrates:

> From the far West came the nation's first woman Governor of a state. . . . From Canada came a girl prospector bringing pottery made after old Indian designs from Saskatchewan clays she herself had discovered. From France, Czecho-Slovakia, Italy, Greece, and Germany came the beautiful embroidery and other needle work of the peasants, and exhibits showing what the women of those countries have accomplished. Large department stores, railroad companies and other great corporations made exhibits showing the almost incredible share women have had in their success.[18]

Noteworthy in this passage is the leveling between those labors and productive pursuits associated with industry and those associated with nonindustrial societies. The program does not, as it certainly would have in 1893, measure "modern" woman's achievements against "primitive" women's labor, with the latter figured as either drudgery or quaint craftwork befitting societies of lesser social advancement. At this fair imperial attitudes are nowhere in evidence; elitist metaphors had no bearing on the celebration of woman as modern sovereign subject. Instead, industrial workers and peasants, governors, craftswomen, and prospectors all were to be equally celebrated as evidence of woman's ability to free herself through work.

The fair that Bennet envisioned celebrated women's work as a priori proof of women's individual capacities and of Woman's collective contribution to human achievement. The purpose of the fair was to advertise this fact to other, particularly younger, women and to articulate in concentrated ways the contribution to society that women were already making through a "visualization of the vocations of women." Bennet was very clear that the fair was simply another tool with which to educate the public to see women as workers first and foremost. A woman's world fair, for Bennet, should also serve as a "picturization of facts," a "visible demonstration," a "symbol," and a "parable" by which women could come to know themselves as workers.[19] The fair, Bennet boasted, paints "a series of pictures of the efforts and accomplishments of women. Showing the beauty of work. Lifting these [facts] into the white light of publicity that all may see what women, both within and without the home, are giving to the world."[20]

In explicit contrast to recent world's fairs, Bennet and the dozens of women who sat on the Woman's World's Fairs' boards of directors and committees imagined that other women wanted to visit fairs that hearkened back to "the original idea of a medieval fair—an exchange of wares and of thought." The rampant consumerist and sensational pleasures of the midway and the pike—the entertainment zones of world's fairs that had become so prominent on fairgrounds since 1893—were given no quarter at these fairs. Although there were some musical and dance performances offered each day of the fair and some consumption took place (such as the buying and selling of the items that women exhibitors offered as examples of the product of their labor), consumerism was not the point of these fairs. Nor were consumerist activities situated as the central draw as they had come to be in the far grander world's fairs men organized and administered. Bennet's vision of a world's fair "planned by . . ., made and installed by . . ., for the benefit of all women everywhere" concentrated its visitors' attentions virtually exclusively on production rather than consumption.[21] This emphasis asserted that all women were equally deserving of having what they did be celebrated as work, that no kinds of work should be denied to women, and perhaps most radical of all that the work of women should be both valuable and valued, rewarding and rewarded. The souvenir program from 1925, in explaining the fair's origins and intents, raises women's work and women as workers to a plane not only commensurate with men but—entirely apart from that measuring stick—to a sublime level of self-generating fulfillment. The fair, the program asserted,

> flashed a white spotlight into the dim corners where women have been doing their work [to] reveal not only an undreamed of multiplicity of occupations in which women have scored successes, but unlimited opportunities and a new attitude toward women's work. . . . The idea of a Woman's World's Fair has blossomed into a revelation of a new order of things. Work no longer is the scorned necessity of the few. The lovely idler no longer is popular or happy. The typical charming woman shown in the white light that beats around the booths of the first annual Woman's World's Fair, is the woman who does things.[22]

The standard that the organizers of the Woman's World's Fairs proclaimed put leisured and middle-class women on notice that the value of their lives was to be measured not in terms of the attainment of heretofore unequaled ability to avoid work, or in professional accomplishments imagined as antithetical to labor and typically outside the range of women's lives, but in the innate value fair organizers ascribed to work itself.

The contrast with the sorts of messages that President Palmer and the Board of Lady Managers had communicated to fairgoers in 1893 is a profound one—one that fair organizers in the 1920s were highly conscious of and proud of despite the relatively smaller scale of their own endeavor. The 1925 souvenir program provides a compact history from 1893 to 1925 of women's advancement and of women's fair organizing. It presents the 1893 Woman's Building as a notable but comparatively *less* impressive monument to women's work than the Woman's World's Fairs of the 1920s. "Thirty-two years ago," the text begins, "a single building in the shimmering white city that was the great World's Fair of Chicago, housed all that was important in women's achievements. . . . [As] occupations open to women in those days were limited both in number and in the opportunities they afforded the few women who braved public opinion or were driven by the wolf to go to work . . . the one generally recognized vocation for women was marriage."

In the eyes of Bennet and her cohort three decades later, the widening of employment for women meant that the Woman's World's Fairs had more to offer female fairgoers than the Woman's Building in 1893 could have, irrespective of the size and the grandeur of that earlier fair's sumptuous spaces. Without suffering from the contextualization within a larger, male-dominated fair that largely ignored or excluded women, what the 1925–28 fairs offered visitors was a glimpse onto a virtual "woman's world" that had emerged since 1893, as the literature of the 1925 fair made plain: "Even the women themselves scarcely realized the revolution they were creating. Then Mrs. Coolidge touched a button in the White House in Washington and the wide doors of the American Exposition Palace opened on a woman's world."[23]

At the 1893 Columbian Exhibition, though women's accomplishments in new fields of endeavor had been celebrated, such accomplishments were rarely described as "work" and when women's work was touted it was usually carefully distinguished from "labor." Neither rural women's lives nor working-class women's lives in the factory, the tradesmen's shop, dry goods store, restaurant, department store, or office were celebrated in any significant way—despite the fact that a major theme of that fair had been industrial progress and productivity. A discomfort with rusticity (with farmwomen as agricultural workers, for example) and with remunerative work meant that the high-society members of the Board of Lady Managers were unable to wed Woman's progress with industrial progress explicitly or to any effective degree. In 1893 the Lady Managers chose instead to emphasize a vaguely defined "progress" that lent itself to the linked rhetorics of civilization and colonialist discovery, and they crowned exceptionally accomplished white women as exemplars of civilized society.

By contrast, in 1925 no neocolonialist theme or rural/urban contrast emerged through which elite and white women would declare themselves "modern." Instead, women's contributions to the modern world were measured by their labors, and an effort was made to equate all labor as equally fulfilling to the human spirit residing within women. Not only national differences and colonialist preconceptions about women but also class chauvinism were deliberately, and from all available evidence, effectively laid aside in favor of a kaleidoscopic celebration of women's labor. Fair organizers consistently emphasized the diversity of women's experiences as workers. Their radical intermingling of rural and urban, working class and professional, domestic and waged work appeared in the form of promiscuous lists of employment sprinkled throughout the souvenir programs as well as journalistic reports of the Woman's World's Fairs. The impression these ubiquitous lists make deviates strikingly from the rank-consciousness and homogeneity comprising the notion of "womanhood" the fair "queens" wielded in 1893. The *Woman's Viewpoint* reflected the more ecumenical attitude evident in the 1920s fairs, quoting Bennet's explanation of how fair organizers had "hoped to make this not only an exposition of women's wares—*produced by hand or brain*—and of the multitude of products turned out for their exclusive use and pleasure" (emphasis added). "Happy," Bennet claimed, "are those women who do congenial work and do it well, whether it be taking care of a baby, singing in [a] grand opera, measuring timber in a forest, making candy, writing books, or bossing a gang of workmen."[24] The article let the echo of Bennet's indiscriminate listings of employments reverberate in an elaboration of women's employments whose diversity took on a dramatic, even sensual, dimension: "Women [came] from the country, . . . from the cities, from all walks of life and degrees of prominence. Hard, rough hands joined soft white ones across the common board of effort. Women lawyers, doctors, inventors, candy-makers, a girl prospector, women in all sorts of welfare and vocational work, beauty experts, authors, writers, composers, poets, doll makers, settlement houses and so on ad infinitum, brought their tangible wares and placed on display their sureness of vision."[25]

Certainly it would be considered naïve to take Bennet's classless idealism and that of the other organizers of the 1920s Woman's World's Fairs as evidenced by the souvenir program simply at their word. For example, the phrase *soft white hands* in the quote above, betrays distinctly racial connotations and weds race to class inasmuch as it assumes white skin signals professional work. Despite such problematic imagery, the aim of the article is to deny race or class any power to divide women or assign hierarchal value to the types of work women performed. Indeed, there is notable evidence of black women's participation as exhibitors and celebration of them as inventors at the 1920s Chicago Woman's World's Fairs. For example, Lillian Tolbert, an African American, was interviewed and celebrated at the 1925 fair for her invention of the Tolbert ice pitcher; as well, African American clubwomen presented a pageant at the 1927 fair. Black women's participation is notable particularly in light of the poor state of race relations in Chicago—highly segregated as this city was in the 1920s.[26] However, it is impossible to surmise much about the racial climate on the fairgrounds from such scattered evidence or language used in the promotional literature alone. One should note that, though the souvenir programs lay out a prescription for ecumenical classlessness, they do not provide a blueprint for achieving class egalitarianism in society beyond asserting it as a high-minded ideal.

My purpose here is not to assert that no racial, ethnic, or class divisions existed or expressed themselves at the 1920s Woman's World's Fairs; rather, my intention in stressing the emphatically egalitarian nature of the promotional literature designed by Chicago female fair organizers in the 1920s is to point out how much the ideal of modern womanhood they held out to their audiences differed from that wielded by female organizers in Chicago in 1893 and from that deployed by male fair organizers in Chicago in the 1930s. World's fairs, in general, present idealizations—of modernity, of national identity, of racial, class, and gender relations. The character of these idealizations hold power for fair visitors even if, or perhaps particularly for the ways in which, they clash with general prejudices and perceptions. The ideal of class egalitarianism embedded within presentations of women as workers at the 1920s Woman's World's Fairs rang so loudly probably because it represented such a contrast to representations of women at other world's fairs and to the larger urban context in which it took place.

The Woman's World's Fair organizers' dismissal and disregard for class, race, and national divisions among women in favor of a unified and female-centered revaluation of women as workers contrast sharply not only with the ways in which female fair organizers at the 1893 fair chose to represent women, such attitudes also depart noticeably from the ways in which gender was to figure at fairs held in the 1930s—fairs organized primarily by men and dominated by corporate interests. Despite the invocation of "white hands" as seen in quoted remarks above, no discussion of a racially pure world order creeps into Bennet's idealism, for instance, as it does suffuse the all-too-Nietzschean and often eugenic visions of the organizers of the "Century of Progress" Expositions. As Robert Rydell has documented, fairs held in Chicago, San Diego, Dallas, San Francisco, and New York within a few years of the Woman's World's

Fairs in Chicago held out dismayingly circumscribed roles for women as sexual objects productive of male desire or as maternal consumers freed up from productive labor in order to enjoy their own leisure. Not only do such images of women presented by male fair organizers and designers strongly contrast with the woman-as-producer image that Chicago female fair organizers asserted in the 1920s, no tendency to dichotomize women into sexualized objects versus asexual mothers characterize their portrayal of themselves. The little eroticism on display emanates directly from the seductive vision of a modern womanhood unified across class and race divisions: "Hard, rough hands joined soft white ones across the common board of effort."[27] In light of this, one can only wonder how someone like Helen Bennet, who would later become extremely important to the administration of Lenox Lohr at the Chicago Century-of-Progress Exposition, must have felt about contributing her efforts to a world's fair whose most high-profile woman was a female dancer named Sally Rand—nearly nude except for her notorious feathered white fan—and one where the greatest collective female accomplishment on display consisted of the synchronized underwater movements of a sizeable group of rubber-suited young white women known as the Modern Mermaids.

The evidence supporting this conclusion is not only positive—in the sense that we now know, in light of the Woman's World's fairs, what women would have done in this period if provided with an opportunity to design their own fairs—but is also negative, in the sense that we also find traces in the historical record of defensiveness on the part of male organizers on this very point. What should we make, for instance, of the testy insistence in 1937 of Rufus Dawes (president of the exposition board and brother to Charles Dawes, vice president in the Coolidge administration) that the few female organizers associated with the Chicago World's Fair in 1933–34 had themselves eschewed the notion of sex-segregated exhibits, presentations, and buildings? According to John E. Findling, author of *Chicago's Great World's Fairs* (1994), Dawes, responding to criticism about the Century of Progress Exposition's lack of women-centered exhibits, recalled that "it was . . . the decision of the women of Chicago that so much progress had been made in cooperation between men and women that emphasis ought to be placed on this cooperation rather than on their distinctive fields of activity."[28] To take Dawes's testimony at face-value—to conclude, as Findling seems to, that an era of woman-centered organizing was past as a result of women losing interest in such strategies—appears to ignore the significance of the criticism to which Dawes was forced to respond publicly.[29] Since many of the women in executive positions within the administration of the Chicago Woman's World's Fairs are the very same women involved in the 1933–34 Chicago Exposition (the organizing for which pulled key women away from planning of woman's world's fairs in that city starting in 1928), should we assume that such women had sudden changes of heart in their vision of world's fairs and in their ideology regarding the relationship of women to work? Helen Bennet, for example, went from her role as managing director of the Woman's World's Fair of 1928 overseeing all aspects of that fair's management to an assistant to the director of social science exhibits at the Century of Progress Exposition in 1933. Is it plausible that, within months of a successful fourth annual fair "of an exposition, planned by women, made and installed by women, for the benefit of all women everywhere," a woman like Helen Bennet might no longer have considered it necessary to display women's work in segregated exhibits because of the progress Woman had made?

Cheryl Ganz has unearthed evidence of early efforts made by former Woman's World's Fair organizers such as Louise de Koven Bowen, who had chaired the board of directors overseeing the Women's World's Fairs, and Ruth Hanna McCormick, their general director, to promote a woman-centered agenda and gender-segregated spaces at the Chicago's 1933–34 Exposition.[30] The efforts these women exerted to shape the Century of Progress Expositions collapsed when class-conscious infighting between individuals arose— triggered when Rufus Dawes passed over such organizers and activists in favor of the wives of prominent businessmen, including his own wife Helen, for key leadership roles.[31] Elite and elitist women entirely lacking a "defining feminist agenda," according to Ganz, shunted aside the experienced organizers of the Woman's World's Fairs and chose instead to unite "with the male fair organizers to promote a vision that denied women a distinctive space."[32] Women who resembled in both ideology and class stature the earlier Board of Lady Managers far more than they did the activist organizers behind the Woman's World's Fairs were not likely to challenge Dawes's personal beliefs in circumscribed roles for women as he expressed them in a speech he made at the opening ceremonies of the 1927 Woman's World's Fair: women's "greatest contributions to society," he claimed were to be found exclusively in the home.[33] Such bold disrespect for the evident theme and central message of the Woman's World's Fairs presaged his strangling of women's feminist fair organizing five years later.

Dawes's influence over women's participation at the 1933–34 Century of Progress, specifically his decision to exclude professional and experienced female organizers from positions of authority, suggest that it would be prudent of world's fair scholars to abandon their emphasis on a declining women's movement following the achievement of suffrage as a way of explaining their declining participation in world's fair organizing. Neither seems to reflect the evidence that the Woman's Worlds' Fairs presents. As Maureen Flanagan has argued, the Woman's World's Fair demonstrated "activist women's continuing

Fig. 7.3. 1925
Woman's World's
Fair Souvenir Pro-
gram. Cover. Used
by permission of
the Chicago History
Museum.

concern with supporting women's causes and organizations." The fairs' exhibitors, which included representatives from "Hull House, the Illinois Federation
of Women's Clubs, the Illinois Club for Catholic Women, the IFCWC, Business
and Professional Women, the CWTUL, the YWCA, the Auxiliary House of the
Good Shepherd . . ., the Visiting Nurses Association, and the Women's Bar
Association," reflected a broad, cross-party and "continuing women's alliance
in the city."[34] Neither female organizing in general nor specifically in the service of a world's fair appears to be in decline in the late 1920s, if the Woman's
World's Fairs are taken into account. What some see as the paltry performance
of women as organizers at major world's fairs held at most twentieth-century
fairs more likely was a direct result of the marginalization and tenuous status
of women at world's fairs dominated by men uncomfortable with the notion
of women as activists or professionals, dovetailing as these predilections did
with the influence of corporations whose interests lay in promoting women's
primary sense of themselves as consumers rather than producers.

> Every girl as she left the Woman's World's Fair . . . must have been saying
> something of this sort to herself, "Now shall I be a ceramic engineer? . . .
> Or shall I start a travel bureau? Or shall I go into insurance? . . . Or shall I
> start out in the newest of new businesses—radio?" And every middle-aged
> woman must have been saying, "think of the changes that have taken place
> in my lifetime."
>
> In those two reactions we find expressed the twofold purpose of the first
> Woman's World's Fair as conceived by Helen M. Bennet, originator of the
> Fair, and its managing director—"to make the Fair not only an exposition of
> women's wares, produced by hand and brain, but also a vocational clearing
> house for women and girls who have not found themselves."
> —HELEN BURLING, "THE WOMAN'S WORLD'S FAIR" (1925)

The 1920s Woman's World's Fairs remain the only outstanding example of independent, sovereign, female world's fair organizing—not only in
Chicago but throughout the United States. The intense organizing that went
into staging Woman's World's Fairs in Chicago for four years speaks to the
vibrancy of women's self-segregated reform activism in the 1920s, undercut-
ting our view of the 1920s as a period when sex-segregated activism was on the
decline. They deserve our attention and appreciation for the way they revise our
assumptions about women's world's fair organizing as never having achieved
much success apart from the 1893 Columbian Exposition or faltering as early
as the outbreak of World War I. However limited in scope, these fairs and their
principle message of celebrating women as workers represent a real break with
the elitist discursive tradition of what it meant to be modern and American and
a woman, best publicized and memorialized by the Woman's Building in 1893.
The centrality of work and cross-class embrace of Woman-as-producer in the
idealistic vision of Woman's World's Fair organizers presents a stark contrast
to the nearly exclusively male or corporate-dominated fairs that replaced them
in Chicago in the 1930s. The success of these carefully staged events illustrate
the ongoing utility of the world's fair as a format for women's organizing in
this period and its enduring value as a venue for the shaping of public attitudes
toward women.

NOTES

1 Woman's World's Fair *Souvenir Program* (1927), Woman's World's Fair Records, Chicago Historical Association (n.p.). Some of the material in this chapter is included in
an article ("Once Again in Chicago: Revisioning Women as Workers at the Chicago
Woman's World's Fairs of 1925–1928," *Women's History Review* 18, no. 2 [June 2009]:
265–91) triangulating the 1893 Chicago World's Fair, the 1920s Chicago Woman's
World's Fairs, and preparations made by feminist organizers involved with the (can-
celled) 1992 Chicago World's Fair.

2 For more on "queenliness" or the "white queen" as a foundational metaphor in the

rhetoric surrounding the 1893 Columbian Exhibition, see T. J. Boisseau, "White Queens at the Chicago World's Fair: New Womanhood in the Service of Race, Class, and Nation," *Gender & History* 12, no. 1 (2000): 33–81. See also Mary W. Blanchard, "Queen of A Europeanized World" in *Een Vaderland voor Vrouwen [A Fatherland for Women]*, ed. Maria Grever and Fia Dieteren, 30–46 (Amsterdam: Stiftung beheer IISG, 2000).

3   *Souvenir Program* (1927), n.p.

4   I am grateful for Eric Hartlep's research skills and his generosity for much of the information I have on the American Exposition Palace and for providing me with an article published soon after the building was finished: J. B. Loggia, "The Furniture Mart Building, Chicago," *Architecture* (March 1925), 87–96. Claim appears on pp. 87–88. According to Eric Hartlep, the building—originally addressed at 666 Lake Shore Drive—currently houses some Northwestern University offices as well as the international headquarters of Playboy, Inc. It is considered an uncommonly large building, even by today's standards.

5   Ibid., 87.

6   Ibid., 91.

7   Maureen A. Flanagan, *Seeing with Their Hearts: Chicago Women and the Vision of the Good City, 1871–1933* (Princeton: Princeton University Press, 2002), 201. See also Helen Burling, "The Woman's World's Fair" *Woman Citizen* (May 2, 1925): 14, 28–29.

8   Kristie Miller reports that part of the financial success of the fairs was due to the strategy of allowing women's clubs to sell, and profit from, tickets (of which fifty thousand were sold in advance of the first fair). According to her, board members pulled in an additional $60,000 by selling space to exhibitors, with the profits from the first fair going primarily to the Illinois Republican Women's Clubs and Roosevelt Republican Club of Chicago. See Miller, "Yesterday's City: Of the Women, For the Women, and By the Women," *Chicago History* 24, no. 2: 58–72. Relevant material appears on pages 62 and 68.

9   Miller, 71.

10 "President's Wife to Open First Woman's World's Fair," *New York Times*, April 12, 1925.

11 "Chicago's First Woman's World's Fair Closes Its Exposition" (n.a.), *Illinois State Historical Society* 18, no. 2: 452–54. Quoted material appears on pp. 453–54.

12 Boisseau, "White Queens," 40–44; and Boisseau, "They Called Me Bebe Bwana," *Signs: A Journal of Women and Culture in Society* 21, no. 1 (1995): 116–46.

13 Nancy Cott, *The Grounding of Modern Feminism* (New Haven: Yale University Press, 1987), 145–78.

14 Helene Throckmorton, "Woman's World's Fair Marks Epoch," *The Woman's Viewpoint* (May 1925): 161, 51.

15 Ibid., 51.

16 *Souvenir Program* (1927), 11.

17 *Chicago Tribune*, April 23, 1962.

18 *Souvenir Program* (1925), n.p.

19 *Souvenir Program* (1927), 7.

20 Ibid., 11.

21 Ibid., 5.

22 *Souvenir Program* (1925), n.p.

23 Ibid.

24 Throckmorton, 51.

25 Ibid.

26 Flanagan, 201. On African American women's participation at world's fairs, also see

Patricia Schechter, *Ida B. Wells-Barnett and American Reform, 1880–1930* (Chapel Hill, N.C.: Duke University Press, 2001), 226, 313n55. My point is restricted to the idealistic vision expressed in promotional literature; it would be foolish to imagine racial equality was achieved at these fairs or to overlook the highly segregated and racially intolerant character of Chicago in these years. For works that specifically address the ways that black women in Chicago were most likely to have been affected by a hostile racial climate in structural and material ways, see Anne Meis Knupfer, "'Toward a Tendered Humanity and a Nobler Womanhood': African American Women's Clubs in Chicago, 1890–1920," *Journal of Women's History* 7, no. 3 (1995): 58–76; and Andrew Wiese, "Black Housing, White Finance: African American Housing and Home Ownership in Evanston, Illinois, Before 1940," *Journal of Social History* 33, no. 2 (1999): 429–60.

27 *Souvenir Program* (1925), n.p.

28 Dawes to Anna Dunlap, April 23, 1937, COP 15–1. Quote appears in Findling, *Chicago's Great World's Fairs* (Manchester: Manchester University Press, 1994), 112; see also Findling's discussion of the same topic on p. 116.

29 Although John Findling appears to presume Dawes to be a reliable source on this point, almost all the evidence Findling brings to bear on the issue directly contradicts the claim that women themselves eschewed separate exhibit spaces, as he states: "Helen Bennet, assistant to the director of the social science exhibits, reported that many with whom she had spoken had said that a woman architect should design a women's pavilion, as had been the case at the World's Columbian Exposition, and that women's achievements as a group should 'have quarters of their own.' She also suggested an exhibit on the changing status of women over the past century." Quote appears in Findling, 112.

30 Ganz agrees with my central thesis that the significance of world's fairs for women as political actors should not be measured purely by their sanctioned participation in male-dominated fairs, which had seen a precipitous decline since 1893: "Women's autonomy, representation and presence in leadership roles steadily diminished at male-organized world's fairs following the Columbian Exposition. . . . [B]y 1933 male organizers relegated women primarily to the role of social hostess . . . [suggesting] the relentlessly constrictive role men imposed upon them." Cheryl Ganz, *The 1933 Chicago World's Fair: A Century of Progress* (Urbana: University of Illinois Press, 2008), 85–107, esp. 88–89.

31 Ibid., 90–94.

32 Ibid., 94.

33 "Woman's Progress," *Stamford (Conn.) Advocate* (June 4, 1927). Folder 1–15865 of *A Century of Progress Records*, Archives of the University of Illinois–Chicago. Quote also appears in Ganz, 90.

34 Flanagan points to the uses to which proceeds from the Woman's World's Fair were put—earmarked as they were in 1927 for the Immigrants' Protective League and the Chicago Public School Art Society—as evidence of "the connections that activist women still made between politics and female voluntary organizations." Flanagan, 201.

CHAPTER 8

Memorializing the 1897 Tennessee Centennial Woman's Building

Elisabeth Israels Perry

On June 4, 1904, a group of prominent Tennessee women installed a monument in Nashville's Centennial Park. Placed on the park's front lawn, slightly to the southwest of the park's famous replica of the Parthenon of ancient Greece, the monument marked the location of the "Woman's Building" of the 1897 Tennessee Centennial and International Exposition. Although the monument still stands, it is so dwarfed by the Parthenon that most visitors to the park overlook it. Even long-time Nashville residents do not know it is there.[1]

I first noticed the monument while walking in the park on a beautiful fall day in 1997, more than ten years after I had moved to Nashville. The monument's unusual design—a rectangular stone shaft about twelve feet tall set onto a double pedestal and crowned by a large granite sphere—caught my eye. As I walked over to take a closer look, I told myself it was probably just another Civil War memorial, a common feature of southern parks. Imagine my surprise when the inscription on the monument's bronze tablet revealed that it not only dated from the historical era in which I specialized, the Gilded Age and Progressive Era, but it honored and justified the public activism of middle- to upper-class

Fig. 8.1. Memorial to the Woman's Building of the 1897 Tennessee Centennial and International Exposition. Used with permission. Carole Bucy, photographer.

Gilded Age women. Convinced that both monument and inscription held historical significance for me, a few days later I returned to take its photograph and copy down the tablet's text.

Here is what the text says: "THIS MONUMENT APTLY MARKS THE SITE OF THE WOMAN'S BUILDING AT THE TENNESSEE CENTENNIAL EXPOSITION HELD IN THIS PARK IN THE YEAR 1897." An enigmatic aphorism follows: "THAT THAT IS ROUND CAN BE NO ROUNDER." Next comes a list of the members of the "Woman's Department": Mrs. Van Leer Kirkman, President; Mrs. John W. Thomas, Miss Mary B. Temple, Mrs. Florence K. Drouillard, Mrs. Charles N. Grosvenor, who were all Vice-presidents; Mrs. Robert Weakley, Treasurer; and Miss Ada Scott Rice, Secretary. And finally, two words: "WOMAN'S WORK," below which is Kate (Mrs. Van Leer) Kirkman's definition of this term as "WHATEVER MAY BE NECESSARY TO PRESERVE THE SANCTITY OF THE HOME AND ENSURE THE FREEDOM OF THE STATE."

When I first read these words, standing in Centennial Park a century almost to the day of the closing of the 1897 fair, I wondered what had prompted these women to memorialize their building in this way. A historic marker near the park's entrance acknowledging the work of Anne Dallas Dudley, the Tennessee suffrage leader, made sense to me; marking the site of a building, one of many temporary exhibit halls torn down after the fair, did not. I had other questions: what did the monument's aphorism mean? Why had the directors picked "Woman's Work" as the dominant theme of their monument, and why had Kate Kirkman defined this term in such a political way? I did not know anything about the specific women named on the tablet, but I knew enough about Gilded Age women to suspect that this monument sent a message to posterity about their vision of women's public and political roles.

In this chapter I reconstruct the story behind this unusual and, as far as I have been able to tell, unique monument. I identify the members of the Woman's Department, describe the building they constructed, and speculate on why they erected a monument to memorialize their work. Finally, using clues provided by contemporary reports of both the Woman's Building at the time of the 1897 fair and of the monument's installation ceremony in 1904, I analyze the monument's meaning, touching on its design, enigmatic aphorism, and cryptic definition of "woman's work." My claim is that the monument evokes a particular vision of white, upper-class women's social roles in the American "New South" of the 1890s. I conclude that, while this vision had the potential for a radical expansion of those roles, in many ways it remained heavily circumscribed by tradition.

The Woman's Building at the 1897 Tennessee Centennial

The 1897 Tennessee Centennial and International Exposition celebrated the state's centennial as well as showcased the state's industrial, agricultural, commercial, and cultural achievements. Built on the grounds of a former racetrack on West End Avenue, about three miles west of downtown, the exposition opened a year late but to great acclaim. Attracting over 1.8 million visitors, it was the largest of any southern fair. Modeled on the 1893 Chicago World's Columbian Exposition, the fairgrounds featured a man-made lake, neoclassical buildings to hold exhibits, a winding system of roads, and a midway offering popular entertainments. The fair's crowning achievement was its full-scale replica of the Parthenon. The Exposition's president, John W. Thomas, manager and chairman of the board of the Nashville, Chattanooga & St. Louis Railway, had come up with the idea to build the replica in order to evoke Nashville's reputation as the "Athens of the South." When the fair ended, no one wanted to tear the Parthenon down, but as it was made of temporary materials, over time it began to disintegrate. The city rebuilt it in concrete in the 1920s.[2]

Previous world's fairs had relied heavily on women's organizational and fundraising skills. The 1876 Centennial International Exhibition held in Philadelphia had a "Woman's Pavilion," but only after a committee of women had themselves raised the money for it. Poet, clubwoman, and suffragist Julia Ward Howe spearheaded a movement to erect a woman's building at the 1884 New Orleans World's Industrial and Cotton Centennial. Of all nineteenth-century fairs held in the United States, the World's Columbian Exposition, held in Chicago in 1893, boasted the highest-profile woman's building. Designed entirely by women architects and artists, it became a central topic of discussion in public commentary on that fair. Two years later, women led efforts to erect another woman's building at the Cotton States and International Exposition in Atlanta.[3] Thus the Woman's Building of the Tennessee Centennial had many precedents. What distinguished it from its predecessors was the directors' decision to erect a permanent memorial to their efforts.

The members of the Woman's Department of the Tennessee Centennial were typical of the era's white, middle- to upper-class activists in women's voluntary organizations. Born in Oxford, Mississippi, Katherine (Kate) Thompson Kirkman (1863–1926) was the granddaughter of Jacob Thompson, secretary of the interior under President Buchanan and avid supporter of the Confederacy. She was the second wife of Cumberland Furnace ironworks heir Van Leer Kirkman, with whom she had three children. Florence Drouillard was her sister-in-law, the wife of a former Union Army captain, James Drouillard, and co-heir with her brother to the family ironworks. Evalina (Mrs. John W.) DeBow Thomas was the second wife of the exposition's president, John W. Thomas. Vassar graduate Mary Boyce Temple (1856–1929) was the first president of Knoxville's Ossoli Circle, the South's first literary woman's club, which she had helped to found in 1885; she later served as corresponding secretary of the General Federation of Women's Clubs. Olivia (Mrs. Charles) Grosvenor, who represented West Tennessee, was a member of Memphis's Nineteenth Century Club (founded 1890), and Margaret (Mrs. Robert) Weakley helped found the Centennial Club of Nashville in 1905. According to an article in the *Nashville Banner,* Ada Scott Rice graduated from Nashville's Ward Seminary for Young Ladies, the city's prestigious girls' school, and wrote "numerous sprightly articles for the daily and weekly papers"; by 1904 she was society editor for the *Nashville American.*[4]

All of these women were well known among the social elites of Tennessee's three largest cities, Nashville, Memphis, and Knoxville. They all boasted ancestors from the time of the American Revolution or earlier. Generally well educated, they all pursued a variety of cultural and philanthropic interests. Mary Boyce Temple, described by the *Banner* as a "woman of great intellect and culture," and Ada Scott Rice had attended the most demanding women's schools, but the others had also been educated well and traveled extensively abroad.

As the organizers of women's literary clubs and charitable projects in their home cities, all of the women had strong connections to people who could help them raise the funds for a Woman's Building. They used a variety of techniques. They put out special "woman's editions" of local newspapers; their edition of the *Nashville American* netted $3,000. After pledging to raise not less than $25 each, Woman's Board members hosted entertainments in their own homes and organized ward and district "Centennial" clubs that held other special events. After these methods had brought in more than $30,000, they met the rest of their expenses through exclusive control over all of the privileges and concessions of their building. As one newspaper put it, "They simply worked. And worked indefatigably."[5]

Except for its actual construction, the members of the Woman's Department managed everything concerning their building. Local artist Sara Ward Conley, daughter of William E. and Eliza Hudson Ward, the founders of Ward Seminary, designed it. Instead of imitating the open, "barn-like" design of other exhibition buildings, Conley created "a somewhat idealized" reproduction of the two-story, classic-styled Hermitage, the home of Andrew Jackson, located just outside Nashville. Tall columns holding up the roof of the building's portico dominated the façade. Above the front entrance sat two groups of heroic statuary, one representing "Maternity," the other "Woman in Art." An observatory over the portico served as a café. Inside, a grand stairway connected the building's two floors. Women's groups from Tennessee and beyond took charge of the exhibit room decorations, which illustrated "woman's work" in the household as well as women's contributions to the fine arts, literature, inventions, and scientific discovery. A library displayed four thousand volumes of works written primarily by American women but also from other parts of the world.

Fig. 8.2. The Woman's Building. W. G. and A. J. Thuss, *Art Album of the Tennessee Centennial and International Exposition: held at Nashville, May 1 to October 31, 1897* (Nashville: Marshall and Bruce, 1898).

Women from Cheatham County equipped a model kitchen and held cooking demonstrations. And finally, throughout the months of May and October, the Woman's Department organized a series of convocations and congresses to address issues of importance to women, such as women's higher education and political rights.[6]

The members of the Woman's Department were immensely proud of their building. The many compliments they received during the fair led them to believe that much of the fair's success had been due to their own hard work. Two weeks after the Woman's Building opened, for example, the Nashville American extolled the women's contribution, writing, "A great day it was for Tennessee when the women said, let's lend our hand. Their share towards the phenomenal success of the Centennial cannot be too largely estimated. Even the men prefer this building." The following month, the New York Times heaped praise on the "Woman's Board," saying that without the women's "enthusiastic and never-failing encouragement," the fair would have fallen far short of the success it has enjoyed. In his farewell speech at the fair's closing, its president, railroad executive John W. Thomas, echoed this sentiment. The fair's buildings, he said, "would have been a wilderness and a desert without a spring, were it not for the Woman's Board. There would have been no attendance, the men would have all gone where the women were, and these grounds would have been without an inhabitant."[7] And yet in 1904, when Nashville's newly formed park commission, in cooperation with the Tennessee Historical Society, unveiled a large memorial in Centennial Park to the directors of the 1897 centennial, the women's contribution was acknowledged, but from their viewpoint inadequately.

The general public learned of this memorial when, on May 2, 1904, the Nashville American announced that a "mammoth slab" of granite honoring the directors of the 1897 fair would be placed in Centennial Park at one end of its artificial lake. The dedication of this memorial took place on May 21. During the ceremony, only men, such as former Governor James D. Porter (who was then president of the Tennessee Historical Society), Governor James B. Frazier, Senator E. W. Carmack, and Nashville Mayor Albert S. Williams, delivered addresses. With their names prominently listed in the center of a bronze tablet affixed to the slab, the male leaders of the fair also received the highest honors for having run a successful Centennial. As for the women, their names were listed too, but only on a small corner on the lower right-hand side.[8]

It is not known when the women directors learned of the paltry recognition they would receive on the centennial memorial or when they made the decision to put up a memorial of their own. Since they installed their memorial only two weeks later (on June 4), they must have had considerable advance warning, perhaps through a Woman's Board member, Evalina Thomas, who was married to the fair's former president. Indeed, Nashville park historian Leland R.

Fig. 8.3. Monument to the directors of the Tennessee Exposition. Used with permission. Carole Bucy, photographer.

Johnson writes that it was in 1903 that the city's park board "turned the former site of the Woman's Building at the 1897 Exposition over to the ladies who had directed the exhibits in that building for development as they saw fit."[9] Hence it seems likely that they had heard of the men's plans in 1903 and at that point appealed to the park board for a piece of the land on which their building had stood. It also seems likely that the news of the insufficient honor their efforts would receive on the main centennial memorial is what had motivated the women directors to take compensatory action.

The Meaning of the Woman's Building Memorial

Everything about the Woman's Building memorial—from its design to its enigmatic aphorism and Kate Kirkman's cryptic definition of "woman's work"—had a special meaning for the women who put it up. They left no record of their discussions on this score, but contemporary newspaper accounts of both the 1897 Woman's Building and the memorial's installation in 1904 provide helpful clues.

First, its design: the square pillar contrasted with the "mammoth slab," which expressed solidity and groundedness but did not soar upward to catch the eye. The shaft of the women's memorial did this, but not in an overbearing way, and therefore seems to convey both the women's aspirations as well as the "modesty" with which the era's "true women" were supposed to be endowed. The monument's crowning sphere came from the Southern Marble Company of Marblehill, Georgia, and had been part of the Georgia Railroad exhibit at the 1897 fair.[10] The aphorism about "roundness" was probably inspired by a rule of grammar. As John Bechtel wrote in a popular 1895 book called *Slips of Speech*, "When a thing is round or square it cannot be rounder or squarer. These adjectives do not admit of comparative and superlative forms."[11] Had the Woman's Building been beyond compare? So "perfect" that it could not have been "perfecter"?

Speaking at the installation ceremony, Maj. E. C. Lewis, who had been director general of the exposition, confirms this meaning for the sphere. Referring to the sphere's "purity and perfection," its "completeness and whiteness," Lewis called it "a sermon in stone." He continued, "The words are aptly spoken—the capital of this monument is perfection itself: 'That that is round can be no rounder.'" A newspaper reporter shed further light: "Emblematic as [the marble ball] is of perfection and beauty," the reporter wrote, "it eminently commemorates the work of the Woman's Department and the corps of fair Tennesseans composing its directorate."[12] In short, the women thought of their work as "perfect," a phenomenon nonpareil, and they had chosen the sphere and its accompanying aphorism to symbolize this assessment.

Of greater import is the other phrase the women chose to memorialize their contribution of 1897, Kate Kirkman's definition of "woman's work," which was drawn from Kirkman's address to the throng attending the formal opening of the Woman's Building on May 3, 1897. After reviewing Tennessee's hundred-year history and praising men for all they did to lead the state from rude forest into blooming civilization, Kirkman urged her audience not to suppose "that in all this century of struggle and triumph woman has been an idle spectator. She has been a potent if not an equal factor in the march of human progress." She continued: "If ever we are to attain the highest ideals of civilization, it must be by the persistent and united effort of man and woman, all of them toiling in their own God-appointed sphere. But it may be asked: What is woman's work? I unhesitatingly answer, anything and everything that may be necessary to preserve the sanctity of the home and freedom of the State."[13]

By using the phrase "God-appointed sphere," Kirkman was bowing to the separate-sphere convention of late Victorian America by which men led in the public sphere, women in the private. Yet in her speech she emphasized the "united effort" of both sexes and, in selecting the text for their bronze tablet, her co-directors of the Woman's Department did not include her reference to separate spheres. Perhaps they simply lacked the space for a longer quote; perhaps they omitted the reference because they did not fully accept it.

Kirkman's linkage of "home" and "state" also challenged the idea of separate spheres. Through this simple wording Kirkman seemed to be stressing a point that the social feminists of the Progressive Era would make repeatedly in succeeding years: that while domestic life remained women's prime area of concern, they were living in a time when the "sanctity" of the home, that is, its "protection" from the evils of the world, depended on the "freedom of the state." In the industrial age, if women were to perform their "God-appointed" task of preserving the home's "sanctity," then they also had to ensure the state's freedom.[14]

We may never know exactly what Kirkman meant by "the freedom of the state." Several possibilities come to mind. She may have been thinking of the need to empower the state to protect the home from the "social evils" that harm families, such as liquor, impure food and drugs, and venereal disease. Another possibility is the idea of preserving the state from control by the "monied interests," such as the liquor industry, whose efforts to prevent the passage of both woman suffrage and prohibition were notorious, and whom reformers accused of corrupting the nation's political process. Yet a third, less "progressive," interpretation is that "the freedom of the state" meant "states' rights," that is, a state's right to oppose the power of the federal government to interfere, for example, in a state's race relations.

Whatever Kirkman's precise meaning may have been, it remains significant that she linked the home's "sanctity" and the state's "freedom" and insisted that "woman's work" involved preserving the one and ensuring the other. Her words certainly challenge separate sphere ideologues, who argued against women "meddling" in public affairs. That Kirkman's colleagues chose her phrase for reproduction on their memorial suggests that, if nothing else, they agreed with whatever meanings and associations she hoped to evoke with this phrase and saw themselves as active participants in public affairs.

The term "woman's work" itself invites analysis. Although we think of these wealthy Gilded Age women as "leisured," they did not see themselves that way. For them, what they had done to bring about the Woman's Building at the Tennessee Centennial *was* "work," and serious work at that. By giving this idea prominence on the face of their monument, they were asking the general public to view their work as meaningful too. They were also asking the public to accept such work as constituting an important, if not vital, contribution to the advancement of civilization. In composing her definition of woman's work, however, Kirkman first mentioned "the sanctity of the home," perhaps thereby indicating that, for her, domestic agendas still took priority. Hence her and her colleagues' challenge to contemporary gender boundaries did not go too far. They were not so much overturning the tradition of separate spheres as *using* it to justify their involvement in tasks they believed important.

The convocations held in the 1897 Woman's Building underscore the cautious message of the monument.[15] Throughout the months of May and October, the Woman's Department hosted a series of meetings on intellectual, cultural, economic, and political topics that revolved around the general theme of "woman's mission and woman's work." Widely reported on in the press, many of these "Special Days," as the meetings were called, attracted large audiences, predominantly of women, although not exclusively so. Female musicians—vocalists, pianists, and string players—gave performances, and women's contributions to the fine arts received considerable attention. Speeches, however, almost all given by women, with many reproduced verbatim or summarized in the press, dominated the events.

Many of the speeches began by looking at women in the past and then forward to the widening realm of women's opportunities. Angie (Mrs. Charles H.) Perkins, a graduate of Wesleyan University and the first of four women to receive the A.B. degree in New England, talked of the thirteen women who had founded Knoxville's Ossoli Circle in 1885 and of how the membership had since grown to a hundred. Women's clubs, she said, moved a woman's intellectual outlook beyond her own "gateposts" to consider more than "the compounding of a cake and . . . the fit of a gown." Ossoli's founder, Mary Boyce Temple, one of the Woman's Board's vice presidents, sounded a note of caution, however. Suggesting that women "keep back something of her old home life and home duties," she advised women against demanding "equal privileges in business, financial, social and professional life." Instead, they should develop "well-defined fields" as "woman's work."[16]

The meetings on suffrage were somewhat less equivocal, but even they avoided taking positions that some might consider too "extreme." In introducing one speaker, Virginia Clay Clopton, Tennessee suffrage leader Lide Meriwether called her "the Moses who is to lead the children of Alabama out of bondage," thereby suggesting that women without the vote were slaves. Clopton hailed the "legions" who, after only two years since a visit by Susan B. Anthony to her state, have joined in the work to end prejudice and ignorance. "Southern men enjoy a reputation for chivalry," she said, "but the age has advanced and all must change with it." Kentucky suffragist Laura Clay gave a long speech arguing that the Bible laid a foundation for women's equality.

As in the convocation on women's clubs, however, the speakers at the suffrage meetings set clear limits on their ambitions. Alabama's Frances E. Griffin, introduced by Meriwether as an "Aaron to her people," denied that women were interested in holding office, a view echoed by Flora C. Huntington of Memphis, who said, "Woman prefers, as a general thing, a home, not public office." Meriwether read a paper by a Colorado suffragist, who emphasized that women "did not want to be office seekers" but wanted only to establish "good government" and win appointments to school and hospital boards. And, when attorney Belva Lockwood, whose two runs for the presidency had made her a nationally known but controversial figure, was rumored to be a future speaker, Clara Conway, chair of the May convocations, informed the press that "the proposition has not been considered favorably."[17]

Other Special Days celebrated women's advances into the professions but also reaffirmed women's traditional pursuits. Sophonisba Breckenridge, Kentucky's first woman lawyer, who was "daily winning laurels" for her successful cases, was honored. Representatives of the nation's women's colleges gave papers on the value of a college education. In representing the Mississippi Industrial Institute and College, the first such college for women in the world, a speaker claimed that its establishment showed that the "sentiment which revolted at the idea of women working" had at last disappeared. On the other hand, several of the speakers on women's higher education assured audiences that the pursuit of a college education would not unfit women for the "practical duties of life."[18]

Finally, nationally prominent settlement workers Florence Kelley and Jane Addams spoke, Kelley on the importance of industrial education for children and Addams, during a "Social Science Convocation," on the need to apply the "spirit of social science" to women's philanthropic pursuits. Although reporters hearing Addams's speech were deeply impressed with her "strong character" and "true woman's heart," they noted that only a small audience turned out to hear her.[19] One can speculate why so few were interested in Addams. The women who organized the Special Days were committed to doing "good works," but more in the traditional spirit of women's charitable giving than in the application of scientific principles to achieve far-reaching social reforms. Nor were they fully ready to incorporate into their mindset the needs of wage-earning women or of racial and ethnic minorities, a population of explicit concern to settlement workers like Kelley and Addams.

In fact, none of the Special Days focused on issues of race. The organizers extended invitations to the Daughters of the American Revolution, Ladies' Hermitage Association, General Federation of Women's Clubs, National Council of Women, National Council of Jewish Women, and other organizations of white membership to make presentations of their work, but not to the National Association of Colored Women, which met in Nashville the same year as the centennial. As far as can be surmised from the newspaper reports of the Special Days, not one African American woman appeared on the Woman's Building programs.[20] During the suffrage convocations, several speakers gave emotional recognition to the validity of the South's "lost cause." Frances Griffin, for example, had opened her speech on suffrage by insisting that the South's heroes "were right in defending their rights, regardless of whether slavery was right or wrong." Virginia Clopton claimed that a prominent "negro professor" had attributed "to slavery" "the good results now being reached" in the education of black people, a view of the "benefits" of slavery that would have made any African American attending—or someone like Jane Addams, for that matter—cringe.[21]

There is no doubt that the Woman's Building's Special Days sent a message that a new era of possibility and progress for women was dawning. Echoing a prominent theme of the fair, Memphis writer Louisa Preston Looney exclaimed, "This century upon whose summit we are standing has been called the woman's century. In this century she has recognized intellect and has been recognized in exchange." Foreseeing a future filled with women in prominent roles, she quoted George William Curtis, the editor of *Harper's Weekly,* as saying of "woman" that she "troops into the twentieth century at the head of every organization for good."[22] And yet, as excited as some speakers were about the future, the organizers of the 1897 Woman's Building could gesture toward uncharted territory but dared not venture too far beyond the comforts of what they knew. They still saw themselves, in their private lives at least, as "angels" in homes of elegance, comfort, and good taste. Such a vision necessarily excluded vast numbers of their contemporaries who lacked the privileges of wealth and social status that they enjoyed. Indeed, the very metaphors used to describe the perfectly round sphere atop their monument, and by analogy, their work—"whiteness" and "purity"—made quite clear that the underprivileged would never be included in their endeavors.

Conclusion: Honoring Women's Past

The full story behind the Tennessee Centennial Woman's Building monument may never be known. One point is clear: the women who put it up did so because they thought it would preserve a memory of their deeds. It has not. Few visitors to the park take the time to look at it closely, and even those who do are puzzled by it.[23]

In short, memory of the work of the Woman's Department of the Tennessee Centennial has faded. This is not what Kate Kirkman and her hard-working Woman's Department thought would happen. The closing words of her report speak to their hopes: "Nothing perishes that is worth preserving. So woman's part in the Centennial will live on, shining through another century, stimulating women to a higher endeavor; but worth more than woman's work was the example set of the character of the women of Tennessee. And what is owing to the Woman's Department for this? A debt which the unceasing praise of a cycle of years can not repay."[24]

How optimistic she was! Like so many other middle- and upper-class organized women in the decades surrounding the turn of the twentieth century, Kirkman was utterly convinced of her and her colleagues' potential for "doing good" and of the lasting importance of their work. Yet they never received the "unceasing praise of a cycle of years" they wished for. It's likely, in fact, that the last time they received much praise at all was on June 4, 1904, when they dedicated their monument in Centennial Park.

That event, attended by some 450 people, was impressive. Costumed in white dresses adorned with light blue ribbons (the official color of the Woman's

Department), the women who had worked so hard to make the Centennial Exposition a success entered the park in twenty-five carriages. They then mounted a speakers' platform festooned with a vast network of flowers and asparagus vine. In contrast to the unveiling of the centennial directors' monument, no major politicians attended, and although both women and men spoke, pride of place still went to the men. Park commission chairman Maj. F. P. McWhirter noted how often history did justice to man, but to woman, "never": "The pages of history lie open to the one, but the meek and unobtrusive excellencies of the other sleep with her unnoticed in the grave," he said. In continuing, he evoked the standard gender conventions of the day, saying, "In her have shone the genius of the poet, with the virtue of the saints; the energy of the man, with the tender softness of the woman." He promised that his commission would "vigilantly guard and protect" the Woman's Building monument "in order that it may be handed down to generations yet unborn that they may catch the inspiration of the spirit that actuated these good women." Finally, in noting that there were other memorials on park land, including one soon to be dedicated to the "dead soldiers of the lost cause," he called the ground on which they were now standing "well nigh holy." Still, he concluded, "[W]hatever is good, and whatever is noble, none will be more illustrious, than that which was directed by the gentle touch of woman."[25]

All eloquent words, no doubt pleasing to the assembled crowd, despite their patronizing tone. One of the women attending, Woman's Building architect Sara Ward Conley, remained dissatisfied. To her, the marble monument was not enough. Twice, in 1906 and again in 1907, she tried to persuade the newly founded Centennial Club to put up a "Woman's Gate" as a grand entrance to Centennial Park. Only such a gate, she argued, would be a fitting memorial to women's work for the Exposition. But she failed to arouse the club's interest in her idea, and it was dropped.[26] Had she succeeded, the Woman's Board of the Tennessee Centennial might have boasted a memorial much more visible to future generations than the one now so easily overlooked.

At least the marble shaft still stands, for now. But suppose that someday the powers-that-be decide to redesign Centennial Park, and no one remembers why that marble shaft with its strange ball on top stands on the park's front lawn so near to the much more important Parthenon. Who would protest its relocation to some even more obscure corner, or maybe its removal altogether?

Perhaps this chapter might inspire someone, maybe the current members of Nashville's Centennial Club, to place a historical marker at the monument to explain how it got there and what it means. Should that happen, then the monument will continue to speak even more eloquently, as it did to me the first day I saw it, of the women of the "New South" who worked so hard to bring about the Tennessee Centennial and International Exposition of 1897. While they did not think of themselves as "progressives," they spearheaded later movements for civic improvements, gave critical support to the South's woman suffrage campaign, and through their building provided opportunities for networks of women to form which, in succeeding decades, reconnected in the reform networks of the Progressive Era.[27] Modern women might not identify with their definition of "woman's work"—that is, as "preserving the sanctity of the home" and "ensuring the freedom of the state." But progressives like Jane Addams would have found the definition compatible with her sense of why women had to have the vote and be involved in politics and public life.[28] Thus, even though their challenge to the powerful gender conventions of their era was not radical, their contribution to the Tennessee fair had promoted a re-envisioning of "woman's work" in ways that would bear fruit in later decades. For that alone, they deserve to be remembered better than they have been.

NOTES

1 The monument is no longer in its original spot. According to Leland R. Johnson, "The monument was moved from its original site in 1928 when the roads in the park were relocated." See his book *The Parks of Nashville: A History of the Board of Parks and Recreation* (Nashville: Metropolitan Nashville & Davidson Co. Board of Parks & Recreation, 1986), 288. I extend thanks to Carole Bucy for sharing with me her knowledge of Nashville women's history, to Robyn Muncy and Rebecca Edwards, who gave critical readings to an earlier draft of this essay, and to Jamie Schmidt Wagman, who combed Nashville's 1904 newspapers to find coverage of monument dedications.

2 The nickname "Athens of the South" (originally "Athens of the Southwest") was the brainchild of Philip Lindsley, president of the University of Nashville. See *The Tennessee Encyclopedia of History and Culture* (http://tennesseeencyclopedia.net), at entries "Philip Lindsley 1786–1855," "The Parthenon," and "Tennessee Centennial Exposition." According to *Appleton's Annual Cyclopaedia and Register of Important Events of the Year 1897*, 1,886,714 visitors passed through the fair's turnstiles (New York: D. Appleton, 1899), 764. See also John E. Findling and Kimberly D. Pelle, eds., *Historical Dictionary of World's Fairs and Expositions, 1851–1988* (New York: Greenwood, 1990), 146–48; and Bruce Harvey, "World's Fairs in a Southern Accent: Atlanta, Nashville, Charleston, 1895–1902" (PhD diss., Vanderbilt University, 1998), 265–74.

3 On women's participation in the 1893 World's Columbian Exposition, see Jeanne Madeline Weimann, *The Fair Women* (Chicago: Academy Press, 1981). By using the singular "woman" to designate their buildings and organizations, nineteenth-century women evoked a generic bond among all women.

4 Van Leer Kirkman's family was very wealthy. His grandfather, Anthony Van Leer (b. 1783), had turned Cumberland Furnace into a successful ironworks, which his grandchildren, Mary Florence and Van Leer, inherited in 1863. Van Leer Kirkman served on the executive committee of the Tennessee Centennial. Mary Florence's 1864 marriage to a Union captain "shocked" Nashville society, but the couple were eventually accepted, especially after Florence bought out her brother's interest in the ironworks in 1870, reopened them, and made the business prosper. She helped improve life for Cumberland Furnace villagers, building St. James Episcopal Church and a parish school for white and black children. See *The Tennessee Encyclopedia of History and Culture*, at entry "Mary Florence Drouillard 1843–1905"; http://www.vanleerplus.org/9anthony

.htm#vanleertn; and Rick Hollis, *A Brief History of Dickson County, Tennessee "200 Years of Pride, Promise and Progress,"* available at http://www.dicksoncountychamber.com/community/dickson_county_history.pdf (both accessed February 12, 2007). The Ossoli Circle was named in honor of the transcendentalist intellectual Margaret Fuller Ossoli; see http://www.discoveret.org/ossoli/ (accessed February 26, 2007). Mary Temple was the daughter of Judge Oliver P. Temple, a prominent Knoxville politician and literary figure; she herself later served as a regent of the state of Tennessee and of the "Bonny Kate" chapter of the Daughters of the American Revolution (named after the wife of Tennessee's first governor, John Sevier). On the Nineteenth Century Club, see Marsha Wedell, *Elite Women and the Reform Impulse in Memphis, 1875–1915* (Knoxville: University of Tennessee Press, 1991), ch. 4. On the Centennial Club, see Robert W. Ikard, "The Cultivation of Higher Ideals: The Centennial Club of Nashville," *Tennessee Historical Quarterly* 65, no. 4 (2006–7): 342–69. Articles about the fair published almost daily in the *Nashville Banner* and *Nashville American* between May and October 1897 provide much information about the women, describing many of the other women involved in the planning and execution of the Woman's Building.

5   Much of this information comes from "Work of the Woman's Department," *Nashville Banner*, May 1, 1897.

6   For more on these convocations, see below. In her speech at the monument's installation, Evalina Thomas described the building as "classic in its architecture, beautiful in its surroundings, elegant in its furnishings, and contain[ing] innumerable evidences of the proficiency of the women of the nineteenth century in handiwork, music, art and literature." (*Nashville American*, June 5, 1904). See also *Catalogue, Woman's Department, Tennessee Centennial and International Exposition, May 1 to October 31, 1897* (Nashville: Burch, Hinton, 1897); "The Woman's Department," in Herman Justi, ed., *Official History of the Tennessee Centennial Exposition, Opened May 1, and Closed October 30, 1897* 143–58 (Nashville: Committee on Publication, Tennessee Centennial and International Exposition, 1898); and *The Tennessee Encyclopedia of History and Culture*, at entry "Sara Ward Conley 1859–1944." See also "In the Woman's Building," *Nashville American*, May 4, 1897.

7   See "About the Woman's Building," *Nashville American*, May 21, 1897; "Nashville's Exposition," *New York Times*, June 20, 1897. Thomas's statement appears in *John W. Thomas: A Memorial by the Nashville, Chattanooga, and St. Louis Railway* (Ambrose and Boselman, 1906): 22. The women ran their building with great economy, spending the smallest amount of any fair department, $749.48; as they explained: "After the preliminary work the women paid their own running expenses and raised the money themselves."

8   See "To Dedicate Shaft," *Nashville American*, May 2, 1904. An article headlined "Centennial Park" (March 21, 1904) mentions the "mammoth slab which was erected on a line with the center line of the Parthenon" and which would be dedicated to the "directors of the exposition early in May." See *Nashville American*, May 20, 1904, and May 22, 1904, 21.

9   See Johnson, 288. In early May the *Nashville American* treated the park board's grant of land to the women as "news" ("To Dedicate Shaft," May 2, 1904) and claimed that the women had not yet decided how to use the land. As the women could not have installed their monument only a month later, I conclude that the newspaper was misinformed and that the women had been planning their use for the land for many months.

10 See Johnson, 288.

11 John Bechtel, *Slips of Speech* (Philadelphia: Penn, 1895), 63, available at http://www.gutenberg.org/etext/4983. I thank Jamie L. Schmid for finding this reference.

12 "Unveiling Memorial," *Nashville American*, June 5, 1904.

13 Kirkman's speech appears in full in Justi, 146, and in local newspapers (*Nashville Banner*, May 3, 1897, and *Nashville American*, May 4, 1897). The *American* reproduced Mary Boyce Temple's address that day as well. Entitled "The Woman of Yesterday," it swept through the history of "woman," referring pointedly to her struggles against obstacles "thrown in her path" and announcing her "final recognition by the world as a leader in every respect."

14 In "Women Progressives and the Politics of Americanization in California, 1915–1920," (*Pacific Historical Review* 64, no. 1 (1995): 71–94), Gayle Gullett provides an excellent explanation of the long tradition of American women's political activism on behalf of "home defense" (75). Kate Kirkman was speaking in that tradition.

15 Women at previous fairs had organized similar meetings, bringing together women from across the nation and abroad, thereby stimulating interests in reform. Topics included suffrage, emancipation, professionalization, legal reform, and education. The National Council of Jewish Women was one national network that grew out of the 1893 Chicago fair; see Faith Rogow, *Gone to Another Meeting: The National Council of Jewish Women, 1893–1993* (Tuscaloosa: University of Alabama Press, 1993). At the 1895 Atlanta fair, attorney Belva Lockwood, a presidential candidate for the National Equal Rights Party twice in the 1880s, urged women to pursue a higher mission than "pickles and preserves" (see Harvey, 261). On Lockwood, see Jill Norgren, *Belva Lockwood: The Woman Who Would Be President* (New York: New York University Press, 2007).

16 "Club Life Discussed," *Nashville American*, May 8, 1897.

17 "More Talk of Suffrage," *Nashville Banner*, May 12, 1897; "Great Day for the Women," *Nashville American*, May 12, 1897; "About the Woman's Building," *Nashville American*, May 21, 1897. A prominent Tennessee educator, Clara Conway had founded the Clara Conway Institute in Memphis.

18 "Pleasant Mention of Prominent Women," *Nashville Banner*, May 7, 1897; "College Day Convocation," *Nashville American*, May 19, 1897; "Federation of Women's Clubs," *Nashville Banner*, May 25, 1897. Founded in 1884, the Mississippi Industrial Institute and College became Mississippi State College for Women, and then Mississippi University for Women.

19 "Social Science Convocation," *Nashville Banner*, October 8, 1897. For more on Kelley, see Kathryn Kish Sklar, *Florence Kelley and the Nation's Work* (New Haven: Yale University Press, 1995); on Jane Addams, see Victoria Bissell Brown, *The Education of Jane Addams* (Philadelphia: University of Pennsylvania Press, 2004), and Louise Knight, *Citizen: Jane Addams and the Struggle for Democracy* (Chicago: University of Chicago Press, 2005).

20 Anita Shafer Goodstein, "A Rare Alliance: African American and White Women in the Tennessee Elections of 1919 and 1920," *Journal of Southern History* 64, no. 2 (May 1998): 223. Goodstein discusses interracial cooperation in Nashville some twenty years after the centennial. The fair had a "Negro Department," but the Woman's Building does not seem to have interacted with it.

21 "More Talk of Suffrage," *Nashville Banner*, May 12, 1897.

22 "Second Day of Convocation," *Nashville Banner*, May 5, 1897. Josephine St. Pierre Ruffin's "Woman's Era Club" and her club's newspaper, *Woman's Era*, is another manifestation of turn-of-the-twentieth-century American women feeling that women had truly "arrived" in the 1890s. Looney later published *Tennessee Sketches* (Chicago: McClurg, 1901), a collection of short stories.

23 Robert W. Ikard's "The Cultivation of Higher Ideals: The Centennial Club of Nashville"

mentions the monument but makes no effort to figure out its meaning, calling Kate Kirkman's definition "broad and cryptic" and leaving it at that (350).

24 Justi, 154.

25 *Nashville American,* June 5, 1904. See also *Nashville Banner,* June 6, 1904, which reported that McWhirter "paid an eloquent tribute to the good women to whom so largely the success of the Centennial Exposition was due," but did not report his actual words.

26 *The Centennial Club of Nashville: A History from 1905–77* (Nashville: The Centennial Club, 1978), compiled by Charlotte A. Williams, contains two references to Conley's attempt to memorialize the women's work at the centennial. At the 1906–07 First Central board meeting: "Mrs. Sara Ward Conley, fine arts chairman at the Exposition, suggested making a beautiful gate to Centennial Park to be called the Woman's Gate as a memorial to the work done there. Obviously that was a time a reach exceeded its grasp, for no action was taken" (27). Later that year, "Mrs. Conley again suggested a grand gate for the main entrance to Centennial Park, as a seal on the work done at the Exposition and as a crown for the work of the Centennial Club. Again she got nowhere" (46). Since members of the Woman's Department were all later founders of the Centennial Club, I asked the club's current leaders for access to its early archives to see if I could find out more about Conley's suggestion, but I was turned down on the basis that the organization is a "private ladies' club" and does not want any publicity (letters and telephone call, April 23, 2007).

27 In 1916, six thousand women in 150 clubs belonged to the Tennessee Federation of Women's Clubs. See Carole S. Bucy, "Quiet Revolutionaries: The Grundy Women and the Beginnings of Women Volunteer Associations in Tennessee," mss. draft, p. 18, in my possession. Anita Goodstein's article, cited above, discusses Tennessee women's pursuit of Progressive Era feminist goals, such as controls on political machines, the passage of social welfare legislation (especially for mothers and children), public funding for recreational resources, and moral campaigns for prohibition, an end to red-light districts, and stricter supervision of movie theaters and dance halls.

28 See Jane Addams, "Why Women Should Vote," *Ladies' Home Journal* 27 (January 1910): 21–22: "As society grows more complicated it is necessary that woman shall extend her sense of responsibility to many things outside of her own home if she would continue to preserve the home in its entirety." For historian Victoria Bissell Brown's contextualization of Addams's argument, as well as for a reproduction of the article, see http://www.pbs.org/wgbh/amex/wilson/filmmore/fr_addams.html (accessed May 30, 2007).

PART III
Gendered Spaces

CHAPTER 9

Encountering "Woman" on the Fairgrounds of the 1915 Panama-Pacific Exposition

Abigail M. Markwyn

On the evening of September 16, 1915, a visitor to San Francisco's Panama-Pacific International Exposition might have stumbled upon an impressive and unusual spectacle. Ten thousand men, women, and children packed the Court of the Universe to view a pageant marking the conclusion of the first-ever Woman Voter's Convention, sponsored by the Congressional Union for Woman Suffrage. Hundreds of women in colorful costumes from nations where women were enfranchised filled the stage. The young female students of the city's Oriental School occupied one end of the stage, while the members of the Congressional Union, dressed in the group's official purple, white, and gold colors, took center stage. The event culminated in a grand send-off of the two women chosen to escort a now three-mile-long right-to-vote petition on its cross-country automobile trip to Congress. The next morning, city residents opened up their newspapers to accounts of the event, and two days later subscribers to the *San Francisco Bulletin* read an entire edition dedicated to women's issues. Thanks to the efforts of women at the exposition, suffrage and women's rights had spilled out of the fairgrounds and into the public consciousness of San Franciscans.

Images of women and womanhood greeted fairgoers to the Panama-Pacific International Exposition from the opening day through the closing ceremonies nine months later. Women performed in events held across the grounds—in county-day celebrations, in parades, and in Zone (midway) attractions. In addition, thousands of women came to San Francisco to participate in the hundreds of congresses and conventions held in conjunction with the fair.[1] While the groups promoted sometimes radically differing opinions, each event offered a platform for women to discuss and share their opinions with other fairgoers. Both male and female visitors could visit the booth maintained by the Congressional Union in the Palace of Education, one of a number of similar displays created by women's reform groups. Or fairgoers could rest their feet in the Young Woman's Christian Association building, a structure erected to both assist women and to forward the group's ideas about women's place in society. Even without purposefully aiming for it, visitors to the fair could hardly have missed encountering the centrally located *Pioneer Mother* statue, one of the most prominent and popular pieces of public art at the fair, its erection the result of a campaign run by the exposition's Woman's Board. Fair visitors encountered female generated ideas about gender in a variety of forms and format; indeed, at this fair, although there was no official "Woman's Building"—or even perhaps, in part, as a consequence of having no building so designated—fairgoers encountered the idea of "Woman" and a promotion of women's interests as a sex at every turn.

As we note in our introduction and as the evidence explored in many chapters in this volume attests, too many scholars have concluded that Chicago's 1893 Columbian Exposition, with its active Board of Lady Managers, impressive Woman's Building, and Congress of Representative Women, exhausted the possibilities for white women's participation in international expositions.[2] Most observe not only that women's exhibits, after Chicago, became integrated into the larger fair, they assume that such integration resulted in a depoliticization of women's fair organizing and participation.[3] Exposition scholar Paul Greenhalgh, for instance, contends that in the pre–World War I period, "non-political women's organizations ... transformed Women's Buildings from arenas for discussions of rights to comfortable bazaars, where the unequal status quo was accepted and even lauded." He further asserts that, after 1893, "It was far less usual however to find the socio-political debate that had accompanied the Columbian, women's sections being rapidly appropriated by anti-suffrage forces to construct a vision of womanhood exclusive of the vote. This was the case in the Cotton States Exposition in Atlanta in 1895, in Buffalo in 1901, St. Louis in 1904 and San Francisco in 1915."[4] Robert Rydell, on the other hand, has argued that women continued to use fairs to "consciously . . . enlarge their involvement in the public sphere," but he has not yet fully explained just how that worked.[5] What Greenhalgh misses in his analysis, and what Rydell does not fully explain, are the many ways that the visual and performative aspects of fairs—which, as the chapters in this volume make clear, are absolutely integral to understanding the way visitors *experienced* expositions—offered extensive opportunities for conveying ideas about womanhood and gender to fair visitors. Although the one published study of women at the Panama-Pacific International Exposition argues that women were relegated to a "decorative" role, the ubiquity of expressions of politicized gender activism and Woman's presence at this fair, in fact, demonstrates that ideas about Woman and womanhood thoroughly saturated fairgoers' experiences of the Panama-Pacific International Exposition.[6]

Only by training our attention on the powerful examples of women's participation and Woman's representation enshrined in the public art, performance, and organization of politicized space at the 1915 San Francisco exposition can we fully appreciate the ideas about women that early twentieth-century fairs generated and promoted. In this chapter, I give equal weight to the spatial, experiential, and rhetorical encounters with "Woman" the Panama-Pacific International Exposition offered fairgoers, analyzing a few of the many ways in which women turned the purposes of the fair to their own sex-conscious intentions. My aim in doing so is not only to challenge our assumptions about the manifestations of women's activism at fairs that lacked veritable "Woman's Buildings" but also to illustrate the degree to which fairgoers' experience of the gendered spaces of this fair were far more bound up with racial and nationalist ideologies than previous scholars (overly focused on the lack of a Woman's Building per se) have discerned.[7]

Organizers of the Panama-Pacific International Exposition staged the fair ostensibly to celebrate the completion of the Panama Canal and the four hundredth anniversary of Vasco Nuñez de Balboa's "discovery" of the Pacific, but, like all such events, the fair was more about boosting the economic fortunes of the host city. Boosters hoped to draw business, tourists, and potential settlers to San Francisco, and close to 19 million visitors passed through the gates of the 635-acre fairgrounds during the nine months of the exposition. What these fairgoers would find, in addition to proof that San Francisco was firmly on its feet following the devastating 1906 earthquake and fire, was a world where women's rights—to vote, to participate in the imagined life of the nation, and to see themselves as central to the history of their nation—was everywhere evident. That this was also a world where some women—particularly nonwhite women and colonized women—were imagined outside that nation and readily available for consumption was also a foundational element of the gendered experience that the Panama-Pacific International Exposition offered.

As Sarah Moore notes in this volume, the Panama-Pacific International
Exposition featured a strong focus on the nation's imperialist fortunes in the
Pacific and Caribbean, with what she argues was a masculinist overtone. The
official designation of the exposition's Woman's Board as simply "hostesses,"
however, did not mean that women's voices were absent on the grounds. The
overtly political activities of woman suffragists, who took advantage of the fair to
stage a campaign for a national amendment, the reform and outreach activities of
the YWCA, and the campaign by the Woman's Board to memorialize their vision
of "pioneer" motherhood on the grounds all suggest that visions of "Woman"
were present—and openly debated—at the fair. At the same time, other women
performed for visitors—as hostesses, in ceremonies, and as entertainers—in
roles that at times reinforced the imperialist and racist messages of the fair.

The exposition's Woman's Board constituted the official voice of women
on the grounds, privileging these white, elite women with the ability to speak
for and represent all women at the fair. One pre-fair guidebook assured potential visitors that the Woman's Board would "assist in the care and guidance of
visitors and will be especially helpful to women," and the images of these staid,
respectable women in the pre-fair publicity assured concerned visitors that the
fair would be morally "clean."[8] Woman's Board authority was officially limited
to two major areas: hostess duty and moral protection. The board occupied and
ran the California Building, a structure that reflected the style of the California
missions, thus symbolically linking the Women's Board to the conquest of California and the state's current racial hierarchy. There, they staged receptions and
dinners for visiting dignitaries and fulfilled their roles as hostesses of the fair.

Visions of white womanhood greeted those who encountered many of the
ceremonies and events held on the grounds. During the days set aside to celebrate California counties, young, attractive, white women showcased local produce. After Orange County's day at the fair, a local newspaper reported that the
"orange girls [were] wearing orange ribbons in their hair and tossing oranges by
the armful to the crowd." Alongside the story appeared the picture of "Miss Freda
Sander, one of the pretty orange girls distributing oranges from Orange County
yesterday at the exposition." Her face and upper body appeared superimposed
on a gigantic orange, as if to emphasize the link between oranges, California
agriculture, and youthful beauty.[9] These women represented California's fe-
cundity, and their beauty was used to advertise the state's natural bounty. That
they were white was not incidental; displaying young, white women reassured
potential settlers that despite the state's indigenous and Mexican past and its

multiracial present (one in which many orange-pickers were in fact of Mexican origin or descent), the future of the state lay with its white inhabitants.

In contrast to these visions of white women designed to reassure potential visitors of the fair's racial and moral purity, images of a racialized and sexualized "other" existed to titillate visitors. On the "Zone," the amusement section of the fair, women of all races became the bearers of culture and of "otherness." Exposition-produced newspaper publicity and guidebooks emphasized the costumes and appearance of women, often linking them to the exotic, quaint, or nostalgic. These tactics fixed the women—and their cultures—in place as objects to be consumed or fetishized. Without the belly dancers of the Mysterious Orient, the concession would lose much of its cachet, and without the "Spanish senoritas" of the Gold Rush, nostalgic white Californians would not be able to experience fully their idealized vision of their history. Although women did not make up the majority of workers on the Zone, publicists continually remarked on and heralded their presence as key attractions of the fair. *The Blue Book,* the most comprehensive official souvenir view book of the fair, included many references to women in its photographs of the Zone and its attractions.[10]

Local newspaper reports carried this discussion of womanhood off the fairgrounds and into San Francisco society. Helen Dare, a feature columnist for the *Chronicle* dedicated an entire column to the question "Feminine Fashions Seen On (and Off) the Zone: Are the Beauties Beautiful Because of, or in Spite of What They Wear?" She emphasized their exotic costumes, detailing for the reader exactly what women in the Hawaiian Village, the Samoan Village, and so on, wore everyday as well as what they wore to perform. The undercurrent of the article was not only what the women wore, but also what they did not wear. Many of these women dressed in considerably less than was considered acceptable for white woman (of any class) at the time. Dare's emphasis on their clothing drew attention to this, reemphasizing the inherent difference between these "dusky beauties" and an audience she presumed to be white.[11] Stories like Dare's marked the women of the Zone as racialized others in relation to white society, providing another example of the way that discussions of "Woman" extended beyond the bounds of the fair into the public dialogue of San Francisco society.

Making Way for Women's Rights: Suffrage at the Fair

California's status as a suffrage state meant that the Panama-Pacific International Exposition offered politically motivated women the opportunity to take advantage of the space of the fair and allowed its visual and performative aspects to assert a politically active vision of "Woman" for fair visitors. Members of the Congressional Union for Woman Suffrage, the radical arm of the suffrage movement, erected a booth, held meetings and conventions, and staged pageants and parades, all with the intent of convincing fair visitors to embrace the vision of a world in which women were political actors. Suffrage activity at the fair revolved around the Congressional Union booth in the Palace of Education. A part of the fair's extensive exhibit on "social economy," the booth highlighted the accomplishments of the white woman suffragists of the nineteenth century. Banners reading "The world has progressed in most ways, but not yet in its recognition of women" and "We demand an amendment to the United States Constitution enfranchising women" greeted passersby who glanced into the comfortably furnished booth.[12] A petition demanding the passage of the "Susan B. Anthony Amendment" to the United States Constitution, which would enfranchise women, held center stage, and suffragists urged visitors to sign it. Other features included portraits of Anthony and other leading suffragists, along with a reading area with extensive literature on voting rights.

Suffragists also staged numerous meetings, speeches, parades, and pageants during the nine months of the fair. According to Congressional Union organizer Sara Bard Field, "the booth had of course to be publicized and to that effect we had many prominent people (both that were living out there and those that came to the convention and cared about woman suffrage) speak for us at the booth. The result was that it became one of the well-known and publicized portions of the . . . Exposition."[13] In April, for instance, Crystal Eastman Benedict, Mary Beard, Kate Waller Barrett, and May Wright Sewall spoke at the YWCA, with a reception following at the suffrage booth.[14] These events continued throughout the fair, ensuring that suffrage remained in the news both on and off the grounds.

Suffragists did not confine their actions, however, to the suffrage booth—they took possession of the streets and avenues of the fair, deploying strategies they had developed in the fight for California suffrage to draw attention to their campaign and to advertise meetings held on the grounds. Their tactics paid off.[15] In August 1915, the *Chronicle* featured a photograph of a woman dressed in "fantastic garb"—not a Samoan or Hawaiian woman in native dress but a suffragist adorned as a set of purple and yellow dominoes and sporting a sandwich board advertising a mass meeting of the Congressional Union at the YWCA auditorium. Three women, Jessie D. Hampton of New York, Mrs. M. B. Stone of Boston, and Miss Ruth Miller of Berkeley, wore the costumes and paraded the grounds, waving flags and exhorting onlookers to listen to their message. According to the report, this was but one of a series of such attempts to publicize the upcoming September convention of the Congressional Union.[16] When suffragists exploited the attention that the fair paid to women to forward their

Fig. 9.1. Woman's Party Booth at San Francisco Exposition Spring 1915. *Left to right (front, seated):* May Wright Sewall, Kate Waller Barrett; *(rear, standing)* Anita Whitney, Mary Bear, Vivian Pierce, Margaret Whittemore. Library of Congress.

own political message, they turned the objectification and commodification of women to their own advantage.

Yet this vision of womanhood was not completely at odds with the larger vision of society fostered by the fair, for it relied on assumptions about white racial dominance that were integral to the vision of an imperial United States created by fair directors.[17] Alongside celebrations of white women's political activism was at least one display that referenced contemporary concerns about the nation's relationship to its colonial subjects. One exhibit case in the suffrage booth contained a collection of cartoons reflecting the history of suffrage, including one that depicted President Wilson as "a two-headed orator raised upon a monument of his own historic literature which is crowned by his work on the New Freedom. One of Mr. Wilson's heads, wreathed in smiles, is turned toward a little Filipino man; the other head, directed toward a disfranchised American woman, wears an extremely nipped and frosty expression."[18] The racial subtext of this cartoon is clear and must not have escaped visitors to the booth. The Filipino man was depicted child-sized, bowing toward President Wilson and wearing a vacant smile on his face, while the respectable white woman was drawn as an adult, with the caption "womanhood" on her dress.[19] This image played on popular perceptions of Filipinos as "little brown men" who were not equal to whites.[20] Yet President Wilson continued to grant Filipino men more political autonomy in the U.S.-held protectorate. How, wondered white suffragists, could Wilson justify extending the vote to Filipino men but not to white women?[21]

The international nature of the fair offered the group the opportunity to juxtapose the enfranchised women of foreign nations against the disenfranchised white women of the United States. The California branch of the Congressional Union's June convention featured a session on the status of woman suffrage around the world in an attempt to draw attention to the inadequacies of the United States in this area. This "International Suffrage" meeting held at the Inside Inn featured Dorothy Morrell, the popular cowgirl of the 101 Ranch on the Zone, who represented her home state of Wyoming, as well as speeches from representatives from all of the nations and states in which women had been granted the vote. Mrs. Ch'en Chi, wife of the Commissioner General to the Exposition from China, described her experience with suffrage, as did Rouva Mayi Maya from Finland; Coodalook Eide, an Alaskan Inuit; and Neah Tagook, an Alaskan Indian. These five women were featured in a photo in the *Chronicle*, in which they wore their "native" costumes—including a full fur hood for Eide, a blanket for Tagook, and Morrell's cowgirl outfit, hat and all—on a June day in California.[22]

Why were these particular women singled out for attention? The appearance of these women in native costume both at the meeting and in newspaper reports suggests that organizers hoped to play on the tropes of an exposition by displaying women dressed in "exotic" costume in order to make a political statement. What, however, was that statement? As Louise Newman has argued, white women's claim to social power in the late nineteenth century rested in part on their role as participants in what she calls "civilization-work," which included all activities designed at "uplifting" a race. Bringing Christianity and the ideals of white, middle-class society to native peoples and African Americans at home and to "primitive" nations abroad was all a part of that work.[23] Of the women described above, both Coodalook Eide, and Neah Tagook qualified as representatives of cultures that many white Americans would identify as "primitive." Similarly, the dominant anti-Asian rhetoric of Progressive Era California characterized Chinese women as either prostitutes or as unnaturally submissive.[24] To honor these women as female voters created a curious paradox. Displaying them in their customary costumes drew attention to their racial otherness and their fundamental difference from white American society.[25] But suffragists invited these women to speak as voters, to discuss their experiences with voting and participating in the political process, and the resulting publicity portrayed them as voters, reprinting parts of their speeches for readers. Whatever the motives of organizers, the presence of these women served a subversive purpose, because to have nonwhite women speak as voters in front of a white audience upended the fair's imperial hierarchy.

The rights of women were not only proclaimed, they were performed on the fairgrounds of the Panama-Pacific International Exposition that summer. The elaborate September pageant described in the opening vignette marked not only the beginning of the trek to deliver the three-mile long petition to Congress but also the end of the first ever national convention of woman voters. The pageant drew on the spectacle of the fair to celebrate the culmination of a politically revolutionary event designed to showcase women's political power. Opening speaker Alva Belmont urged attendees to "forego alliances with any existing man's political party, and to work for a new, woman-made civilization."[26] Organizers designed the convention to show western women voters their political possibilities and to inspire eastern women tired of fighting what often appeared to be a losing battle that success was indeed possible. The fair offered space for a combination of politics and performance that sparked the political imagination of suffragists across the country.[27]

The mere presence of the suffrage booth in the Palace of Education validated the organization's existence and provided a headquarters for these activities. And of course, millions of visitors passed by the booth over the nine months of the fair. Even if only a few stopped each day, that number was far more than organizers could hope to reach in more commonplace venues. The fair and its location in San Francisco provided these female activists with the space and opportunity to convey their vision of politically active public womanhood to large numbers of people in a short time. In their campaign to expand women's political role in American society, these suffragists appropriated the fair's tropes of display and spectacle, offering at times contradictory visions of the relationship between white and nonwhite women and complicating the fair's racial and social hierarchy.

Spaces that Served the Needs of Women: The YWCA

Suffragists often cooperated with members of the Young Women's Christian Association (YWCA), another group of active, organized women that appropriated space at the fair to exhibit themselves, their work, and their worldview to fairgoers in ways that reveal the extent to which women's work extended across the grounds of the fair. The YWCA building, located just inside the main entrance to the exposition, combined utility with display and performance in an extraordinarily effective way. The building offered an attractive combination of services—good, cheap food, friendly advice about the city to women (and men), and plentiful sitting areas, along with movies depicting the work of the YWCA across the nation and a series of speakers on "home economics, hygiene, physical training, recreation, questions of thrift and efficiency, and kindred subjects."[28] Although geared toward female visitors, the building was open to all who entered. The YWCA also developed a working relationship with women's clubs in San Francisco and with organizations holding conventions during the fair in an effort to coordinate activities and to advertise its facilities for visiting women. The decision to combine service with exhibits showed a canny understanding of how best to use the space the fair offered.

YWCA leaders hoped that by displaying their work for all to see, they might inspire others to follow suit and work to ensure the safety of young working women. Films featuring the work of YWCA branches across the country ran daily in the assembly room on the second floor, also the site of "lectures, and debates on different subjects of interest to women."[29] Glass cases exhibiting the results of a series of national contests that reflected the YWCA's values and goals lined the halls of the building. One such series of competitions determined the most skilled in a variety of fields—dressmaking, wardrobe design, writing, and art.[30] Another display featured the winning model wardrobes designed for the "college girl" and the "business girl."[31] These nationwide contests and the resulting displays served both as a widely distributed advertisement for the fair and as a convenient way for the YWCA to showcase its values and benefits to society for fair visitors.

Although YWCA officials staged this elaborate exhibit for visitors, they understood that the real value of their presence depended on the interactions they had with visitors and workers at the fair. An article on the exposition published in the YWCA's monthly journal described their work as "not a moving picture film, nor a stand of statistical charts, but a throng of living people—this is the exhibit of the National Board of the Young Women's Christian Association at the Panama-Pacific International Exposition in 1915."[32] By providing friendly and helpful services to visitors—meals, a place to rest, referrals to safe lodgings, a children's day nursery, and Sunday church services—YWCA workers hoped to serve the needs of visitors and in so doing to convince visitors of the value of the world they created in the YWCA building.

But the YWCA also staged a less public presence on the grounds that directly affected the working lives of exposition employees. YWCA workers dedicated much of their time to reaching out to the female workers of the fair, to promote "the economic, physical, social, intellectual and spiritual interests of young Women employed" on the grounds.[33] They provided classes, dinners, parties, and individual counseling to the thousands of women employed at the fair, in the hopes of protecting them from the dangers of the city and the fair, and of helping them "lead . . . straightforward, normal, Christian, li[ves]."[34] Through the clubhouse they erected on the Zone, they provided the women of the Zone—from the cashiers to the dancing girls and the women of the native villages—with cheap, hot meals, hot water, a sewing machine, foot baths, books, and comfortable chairs. There, YWCA workers hoped women might gain courage "for another day of this life which she believes she is forced to lead; or the greater courage necessary to make a fresh start in a more normal and less perilous career."[35]

Through this "personal work" YWCA workers hoped not only to provide necessary services to young women, but also to convey to them the value of their vision of womanhood.[36] This vision relied on assumptions about race, class, and female sexuality that privileged the ideals of white, middle-class womanhood.[37] YWCA organizers believed that the city teemed with dangers for the unaccompanied young woman, and they made it their mission to "protect" young women from sexual exploitation.[38] They assumed, as the above quote indicates, that the female performers of the Zone, along with other women who seemed to have "fallen," were misguided and lost. Despite these biases, YWCA workers provided physical benefits for young women at the fair, offering them hot baths, a restroom, and home-cooked meals.

In short, the YMCA served many nonwhite women who society—and the fair—willfully disregarded. A report by a YWCA worker about her forays onto the Zone also illuminates the relationships of race, class, and gender at work. She reported that "one thing that seems quite evident is that we do not regard the show girl and the foreigner as womankind, but rather as belonging to some strange species entirely outside of any need for friendly interest."[39] If we assume her turn of phrase to be a critique of society—"we" being society rather than the YWCA—we see that she challenged society's—and the fair's—disregard for the welfare of these young women. When she described the presence of Hawaiians, "colored young women," cowgirls, and Japanese women all attending the dinner intended to help young women get to know each other on the grounds, that assumption is supported.[40] It seems that women of the YWCA provided for the physical, and presumably the moral, needs of all women on the grounds, without regard to their racial or ethnic background. Bringing them together and serving their needs simultaneously at a time when many such facilities were segregated held the potential to undermine assumptions about racial hierarchy, both for both the young women involved and for interested visitors who might encounter the YWCA's work on the Zone.[41]

These displays of the YWCA's welfare work—and the efforts themselves—served a variety of purposes and contributed to the dialogue about American women created at the fair. They publicized the work of the YWCA, raising awareness of the dangers facing young women in the city, as well as the necessity for reformers to outfit those same women with the skills to survive in the sometimes risky urban environment. In so doing, these activities bolstered the organization's basic philosophy that women must be able to live in a world in which female sexuality was not commodified and in which young working women could live and support themselves in the city without risking the fall to prostitution. YWCA workers also emphasized the commonalties between these young working-class women, opening the space for them to form relationships and friendships that provided a counter to other exhibits emphasizing the inherent differences between whites and people of color.

Centering White Motherhood: *Pioneer Mother*

Visitors to the Panama-Pacific International Exposition viewed not only the thousands of exhibits contained in the fair buildings but also the murals and statuary that adorned the grounds. Two prominent statues came to define the exposition's California roots: *The Pioneer* and *The End of the Trail*. These statues helped solidify the fair's visual and rhetorical celebration of the white conquest of native California.[42] Another statue also captured the hearts of fairgoers, for it celebrated the female pioneer and her role in westward expansion. This third statue, *Pioneer Mother,* was erected through a fundraising campaign sponsored by the exposition's Woman's Board. The statue, the campaign for its funding, and the accompanying rhetoric all asserted the dominance of the white middle class in California culture, erasing the presence of nonwhites in the state and the culpability of white women for the results of conquest. Although this example of women's activism proves much less ambiguous than either of the above accounts, it demonstrates that white women actively created a vision of American womanhood that probably most, if not all, fair visitors would have encountered.

Like the male pioneer envisioned on the grounds, this female pioneer was depicted as a white participant in the mid-nineteenth-century overland migration that contributed to the devastation of native cultures in California. By calling on a monument to the white pioneer mother to stand in for a monument to the "Motherhood, the Womanhood of the nation," the Woman's Board was asserting in strong terms the link between white women, civilization, and nation building. The pioneer mother *was* the mother of the nation, according to this formulation, a position that vested in white, middle-class women the power to turn a rough camp of men into a home—and a state, ready for inclusion in the national polity. White, middle-class mothers became absolutely essential to the creation of "civilization."

Fig. 9.2. The *Pioneer Mother* at the Panama-Pacific International Exposition. San Francisco History Center, San Francisco Public Library.

The finished statue depicts a mother with two small children in front of her. The mother wears a small sunbonnet, a homespun dress, and a short cape around her shoulders. Arms outstretched, she holds the arm of her small daughter. The son echoes his mother's gesture, wrapping his other arm around his sister. Both children are nude and appear to be walking forward with their mother, whose rough boot peeks out from beneath her skirt.[43] She was no Californio, born and raised under Mexican rule—nor was she a native Californian, or a Chinese immigrant. Many kinds of women lived in California, but the woman memorialized in this statue was clearly marked as white. By defining her as the *Pioneer Mother* the Woman's Board erased the experiences of the many other women who lived in California at the same time.

The rhetoric surrounding the statue reified its message about the dominance of the white woman in California and the erasure of nonwhite women from the state's history. The inscription on the base of the sculpture read: "Over rude paths beset with hunger and risk she pressed on toward the vision of a better country. To an assemblage of men busied with the perishable rewards of the day she brought the three-fold leaven of enduring society, faith, gentleness, and home with the nurture of children."[44]

The inscription reinforced the "Pioneer Mother's" race and class by drawing on traditional Victorian middle-class associations of women with domesticity, religion, and home. Ironically, from the perspective of the state's native inhabitants, this argument lays the blame for the devastation that followed the intrusion of Anglos into the state on white women, since it was white women who created the settlements that drove out native peoples and replaced their culture with a highly stratified, racialized society. White Californians generally failed to see this perspective on westward expansion, however, and for white viewers *Pioneer Mother* perpetuated the idea that conquest was a benign process through which white "civilization" took its rightful place as the dominant society in California.

Once erected in a prominent location near the Palace of Fine Arts, *Pioneer Mother* stimulated a great deal of local interest and debate, suggesting the power of the image for many Californians. Many supporters of the projects objected to the final design for class-based reasons. Ella Sterling Mighels, the originator of the movement for the statue, disliked the statue because it failed to sentimentalize the journey west. She remembered, "There was nothing holy about that mother, and the poor little boys and girls who went to view the statue . . . were filled with shame at the sight of the naked children."[45] Those who objected wanted a romanticized, sentimentalized portrait of a refined, middle-class matron rather than the more realistic image of a woman in homespun and half-soled shoes. It is not surprising that white, middle-class visitors who felt personally invested in the statue would object to an image that displayed a woman unable to clothe—or properly take care of—her own children. Such an image suggested the "primitive" rather than the "civilized," and boosters of the statue did not want to imagine their mothers or grandmothers as "primitive."[46]

Many fairgoers commented on *Pioneer Mother*, suggesting their investment in the gendered and racial issues it raised and confirming that the Woman's Board efforts to centralize motherhood within their vision of Womanhood as well as California history had succeeded in striking a nerve. Many would take home with them the ideas this statue engendered and then amplify its power as they shared their impressions of the fair and of this statue in particular with their friends and families. Laura Ingalls Wilder, famed children's author of the *Little House on the Prairie* books, who spent the summer with her daughter in San Francisco, wrote home to her husband about *Pioneer Mother*: "A woman in a sunbonnet, of course pushed back to show her face, with her sleeves pushed up, guiding a boy and girl before her and sheltering and protecting them with her arms and pointing the way westward. It is wonderful and so true in detail. The shoe exposed is large and heavy and I'd swear it had been half-soled."[47]

This was the only piece of art Wilder described in detail in any of her many letters home. Her response demonstrates the statue's power for those, like her, who had experienced the move west. It reinforced her sense of the "pioneer" and of westward expansion, affirming her experience as "the" definitive one and erasing all others, while also denying the destructive repercussions of the conquest of the west. The emphasis Wilder placed on this statue evinces the centrality of the idea it conveyed to ideologies of Womanhood promoted at the exposition.

Through the campaign for *Pioneer Mother*, the members of the Woman's Board inscribed the role of white women as civilizers onto the grounds of the fair. They staked out a space—one that was visual, three-dimensional, and rhetorical—for a vision of white womanhood in which women were absolutely essential to westward expansion. In a fair that celebrated the conquest of California and America's position as an imperial power, this claim was a powerful one. They denied the very existence of California's native peoples and other nonwhites in the state as well as the culpability of white women in perpetuating a society based on racism and discrimination. The presence of the *Pioneer Mother* in a place of honor on the fairgrounds reinforced the racial overtones of a fair that celebrated the conquest of the Pacific and of the Panama Canal and the dominance of white Europeans on the Pacific Rim while inscribing an enthusiasm for Woman's place in that history.

Conclusion

Visitors found no designated "Woman's Building" at the Panama-Pacific International Exposition, but that did not mean that they did not encounter visions of society crafted by politically minded women. On the contrary, women's voices and images were found throughout the fair, in a sometimes clashing multiplicity of visions. The activities of the Congressional Union, Young Women's Christian Association, and exposition's Women's Board reveal that women at the fair went far beyond simply a "decorative role." Rather, they actively appropriated the space of the fair in order to further their own visions of American society and of women's place therein. As white, middle-class women, they perpetuated racial and class assumptions that privileged their status and assumed the inferiority of nonwhite and lower-class women. They also, however, insisted on the significance of women as actors in history and in public life, a fact that fair directors ignored in their deployment of female gender at the fair, and which made the activities of all women into oppositional spectacles that in some ways reinforced and in other ways challenged the official narratives of the fair. These female-created spaces and the activities they housed challenged the Panama-Pacific International Exposition's larger story about American race and empire, and they remind us to pay close attention to the ways women exploited the opportunities made available by fair organizers. Women carved out spaces for themselves under the guise of serving visitors' needs, captured attention by centering themselves through exhibits and statuary, and transformed spaces through their performance of their gender. Activists' ability to exploit space allocated by fair authorities and to politicize traditionally feminine roles at the Panama-Pacific International Exposition demonstrates that feminist theorizing of space and performance can offer new insights into the role of world's fairs as both reflections and transformers of societal norms.

NOTES

1 For a complete list of congresses and conventions held at the fair, see Frank Morton Todd, *The Story of the Exposition, Being the Official History of the International Celebration Held at San Francisco in 1915 to Commemorate the Discovery of the Pacific Ocean and the Construction of the Panama Canal* (New York: Putnam, 1921): 100–121.

2 Mary Francis Cordato, "Representing the Expansion of Women's Sphere: Women's Work and Culture at the World's Fairs of 1876, 1893 and 1904" (PhD diss., New York University, 1989); Virginia Grant Downey, "Women and World's Fairs: American International Expositions, 1876–1904" (PhD diss., Emory University, 1982); Gayle Gullett, "'Our Great Opportunity': Organized Women Advance Women's Work at the World's Columbian Exposition of 1893," *Illinois Historical Journal* 87 (1994): 259–76; Ann Firor Scott, *Natural Allies: Women's Associations in American History* (Urbana: University of Illinois Press, 1991), 128–34.

3 Cordato.

4 Paul Greenhalgh, *Ephemeral Vistas: The Expositions Universelles, Great Exhibitions and World's Fairs, 1851–1939* (Manchester: Manchester University Press, 1988), 183.

5 Robert W. Rydell and Ron Kroes, *Buffalo Bill in Bologna: The Americanization of the World, 1869–1922* (Chicago: University of Chicago Press, 2005), 65.

6 Susan Wels, "Spheres of Influence: The Role of Women at the Chicago World's Columbian Exposition of 1893 and the San Francisco Panama Pacific International Exposition of 1915," *Ex Post Facto* 8 (1999) (published by the History Students Association of San Francisco State University), available online at http://userwww.sfsu.edu/~epf/1999/wels.html (accessed May 30, 2006). For a more critical look, see Jamaica Hutchins, "Constructing Womanhood: Women's Work and Participation at the Panama-Pacific International Exposition, San Francisco, 1915," (master's thesis, University of California Santa Cruz, 2005).

7 The dominant interpretation of world's fairs in the early twentieth century is that they conveyed racial and gender messages that reified the dominance of white, Anglo-Saxon Americans. See Robert Rydell, *All the World's a Fair: Visions of Empire at American International Expositions, 1876–1916* (Chicago: University of Chicago Press, 1984). Newer

interpretations of fairs argue that fairs conveyed more complex messages. See Paul Kramer, "Making Concessions: Race and Empire Revisited at the Philippine Exposition, St. Louis, 1901–1905," *Radical History Review* 73 (1999): 74–114.

8 *The Panama Pacific International Exposition* (San Francisco: PPIE Co., 1914).

9 "Orange County Holds Notable Celebration," *San Francisco Chronicle*, April 20, 1915.

10 *The Blue Book: A Comprehensive Official Souvenir View Book of the Panama-Pacific International Exposition at San Francisco 1915*, 2nd ed. (San Francisco: Robert A. Reid, 1915), 321.

11 "Feminine Fashions Seen on (and off) the Zone: Are the Beauties Beautiful because of or in spite of What They Wear?" *San Francisco Chronicle*, April 24, 1915.

12 Sara Bard Field, *Sara Bard Field, Poet and Suffragist* (Berkeley: Regional Oral History Office, the Bancroft Library, University of California, Berkeley, 1979), 294; Donna Ewald and Peter Clute, *San Francisco Invites the World: The Panama-Pacific International Exposition of 1915* (San Francisco: Chronicle Books, 1991), 72.

13 Field, 294.

14 "Four Notable Women at Suffrage Meeting," *San Francisco Chronicle*, April 4, 1915.

15 Jessica Sewell, "Gendering the Spaces of Modernity: Women and Public Space in San Francisco, 1890–1915," (PhD diss., University of California–Berkeley, 2000), 300; Gayle Gullett, *Becoming Citizens: The Emergence and Development of the California Women's Movement, 1880–1911* (Urbana: University of Illinois Press, 2000); Margaret Finnegan, *Selling Suffrage: Consumer Culture and Votes for Women* (New York: Columbia University Press, 1999); Rebecca Mead, *How the Vote Was Won: Woman Suffrage in the Western United States, 1868–1914* (New York: New York University Press, 2004).

16 "Fair Boosters in Fantastic Garb," *San Francisco Chronicle*, August 20, 1915.

17 On the race-based arguments of women suffragists, see Louise Newman, *White Women's Rights: The Racial Origins of Feminism in the United States* (New York: Oxford University Press, 1999).

18 "Suffrage at the Panama-Pacific Exposition," *Suffragist*, April 10, 1915. The cartoon appeared on the cover of the *Suffragist* on September 5, 1914, in an issue that contained a number of articles deriding the U.S. government's decision to enfranchise Filipino men (in the Philippines) but not white women at home, a situation to which white suffragists vehemently objected.

19 The cover of the *Suffragist*, September 15, 1914.

20 For a discussion of the national anxieties attached to the U.S. relationship to the Philippines, see Matthew Frye Jacobson, *Barbarian Virtues: The United States Encounters Foreign Peoples at Home and Abroad* (New York: Hill and Wang, 2000).

21 "The Federal Amendment and the Race Problem," *Suffragist*, February 6, 1915.

22 "Women Gaining from Iceland to China," *San Francisco Chronicle*, June 3, 1915.

23 Newman, 8.

24 Abigail Markwyn, "Economic Partner and Exotic Other: China and Japan at San Francisco's Panama-Pacific International Exposition," *Western Historical Quarterly* 39, no. 4 (2008): 439–66.

25 Hazel Carby argues that the presence of six black women at the World's Congress of Representative Women during the 1893 Chicago Fair was "part of a discourse of exoticism that pervaded the fair." See Carby, 5.

26 Belmont's comment echoed the Congressional Union's controversial political strategy of campaigning against the party in power for refusing to support woman suffrage. "First Ever Political Campaign of Women Opened at Exposition," (San Francisco) *Bulletin*, September 14, 1915.

27 See Michael McGerr, "Political Style and Woman's Power, 1830–1930," *Journal of American History* 77 (1990): 864–85, for a discussion of the evolution of women's political style in the early twentieth century.

28 "Women's Club Interests Center on the Exposition Activities: Young Women's Christian Association Commands Attention," *San Francisco Chronicle*, February 14, 1915.

29 "Welfare Work at the Panama-Pacific International Exposition," Social Service, Panama-Pacific International Exposition Vertical Files, San Francisco Public Library (PPIE-SFPL).

30 "Y.W.C.A. Will Exhibit Results at Exposition," *San Francisco Chronicle*, January 15, 1915.

31 "Social Service at the Panama-Pacific International Exposition," Social Service (PPIE-SFPL).

32 Wilson, "By the Fountain of Energy," 424.

33 Ibid., 425.

34 Ibid., 429.

35 Ibid., 428.

36 Ibid.

37 Adrienne Lash Jones notes that although the YWCA served black women, its practices perpetuated segregation. Adrienne Lash Jones, "Struggle among Saints: African American Women and the YWCA: 1870–1920," in *Men and Women Adrift: The YMCA and the YWCA in the City*, ed. Nina Mgakij and Margaret Spratt, 160–87 (New York: New York University Press, 1997). In San Francisco, separate branches served both the Chinese and Japanese populations of the city.

38 For an expression of this attitude, see "Little Stories from the Exposition," *Association Monthly* 9 (1915): 465.

39 "Report of Work: YWCA Building, Exposition Grounds, March 8, 1915," YWCA (#2), Carton 10, Phoebe A. Hearst Papers, Bancroft Library, University of California–Berkeley (BL).

40 Ibid.

41 On the YWCA's racial policies, see Jones, "Struggle among Saints."

42 See chap. 4 of this volume for additional discussion of the statuary of the Panama-Pacific International Exposition.

43 According to art historian Anna Andrzejewksi, picturing children (and others) nude was a common artistic convention that Grafly might have used to try to evoke the primitive nature of the group. Alternatively, displaying nudes was also a nod to classical artistic conventions. Personal communication with Dr. Anna Andrzejewski, Madison, Wis., June 21, 2006.

44 *Blue Book*, 9.

45 Aurora Esmeralda [Ella Sterling Mighels], *Life and Letters of a Forty-Niner's Daughter* (San Francisco: Harr Wagner, c. 1929), 152.

46 In 1914 a debate between the artist and the Women's Board emerged over a design by the artist that was too "primitive," clearly revealing the class and racial bias of its supporters. See "The Pioneer Mother's Monument—What It Should Be," *San Francisco Call*, June 26, 1914.

47 Laura Ingalls Wilder, in *West from Home: Letters of Laura Ingalls Wilder to Almanzo Wilder, San Francisco, 1915*, ed. Roger McBride, 37 (New York: Harper and Row, 1974).

CHAPTER 10

Woman's Buildings at European and American World's Fairs, 1893–1939

Mary Pepchinski

Situated on the outskirts of the White City at the Chicago World's Columbian Exposition, the 1893 Woman's Building was the first major world's fair structure whose organization was directed by female administrators. It was also the first world's fair structure planned to house women's exhibits exclusively, and the first to be designed by a female architect. Women from all over the United States and from more than forty nations sent examples of their work and that of their countrywomen—all to be displayed in this pavilion. While some traveled to Chicago, either to participate in the administration of the fair or to examine the building and its contents as curious spectators—many of whom also recorded their impressions through letter-writing, as professional journalists, or as official representatives of their home nation—others who stayed at home were also caught up in the excitement. These women collected funds and prepared exhibits destined for display in the Woman's Building. Still others received messages from friends who had attended the fair, read accounts about the building in popular journals, or attended lectures by those who had undertaken the sometimes long, expensive, and arduous journey to Chicago.

Although "woman's buildings" and "women's divisions" had appeared at several international fairs prior to 1893,[1] the Woman's Building erected in Chicago that summer captured attention around the world in ways unimaginable prior to its fabrication. For the next half century, officials would consider the inclusion of a gendered building—that is, a pavilion devoted to exhibiting women's work and, most important, to exploring feminine ideals—at subsequent world and national fairs.

Between 1893 and the outbreak of the Second World War, inspired by the Chicago Board of Lady Managers' accomplishment, Woman's Buildings were erected at as many as seven world and national fairs held in U.S. cities as well as fourteen that were organized in European nations.[2] As significant as these achievements may seem, these buildings have been overlooked in most histories of modern architecture. While this may be due to their lack of technical or aesthetic innovation, qualities that we have come to expect from the memorable architecture of the world's fairs, the roughly two dozen or so Woman's Buildings that millions of fairgoers visited between 1893 and 1939 were noteworthy for their use of more ephemeral aspects of architectural production—authorship and reception, sequence and symbolism, space and memory—in ways that challenged emerging conventions of modern architecture and introduced gender as a legitimate theme animating exhibition architecture during the first half of the twentieth century.

The great popularity of the 1893 Woman's Building notwithstanding, subsequent Woman's Buildings were neither overtly imitative of the Chicago precedent nor closely similar to one another. While their content was somewhat consistent (most included galleries and rooms for refreshment), the architecture—that is, the style, means of construction, material, interior organization and exterior articulation—was extremely diverse. Some buildings included references to well-known monuments meant to evoke particular associations. Some displayed novel architectural forms created expressly for a specific fair and executed in styles ranging from the international style to the art nouveau and the neoclassical. Others utilized an existing structure that was temporarily converted to use as a Woman's Building.

While this heterogeneity may seem a fitting response to the New Woman, when considered as architecture it seems illogical, conflicting deeply with the fundamental conventions of this discipline. Architectural classification, or typology, assumes that buildings serving the same purpose closely resemble one another. Because each typology is understood as having been derived from a particular archetype (an innovative building, the first of its kind to accommodate a new function), all members of this group are expected to be similar in their appearance and layout.[3] Regarded in this manner, the Woman's Buildings constructed after 1893 comprise a paradoxical typology, or one which is not One, because the archetype (the 1893 Woman's Building) did not give rise, as expected, to subsequent types that shared the same purpose and closely resembled one another.

In addition to typology, it is difficult to regard Woman's Buildings as outstanding examples of modern architecture. Canonical histories of this discipline uniformly emphasize how modern architecture resulted from ongoing technical innovation or artistic experimentation and focus on the visual and tangible qualities of buildings to advance their arguments. These texts also portray the exemplary buildings constructed at national and world's fairs along these lines, a product of bold engineering concepts, new urban planning ideals, and, especially after 1900, novel aesthetic propositions.[4] When measured by this standard, the 1893 Woman's Building was not a meaningful work of modern architecture due to its unremarkable organization (a symmetrical structure with a central atrium, recalling a generic public building[5]) and its lack of technical innovation[6]—both of which failed to break new ground. Although created in reaction to a pressing issue confronting modern society—identifying a role for women—Woman's Buildings do not readily conform to the framework put forth by historians to define and quantify the significant architecture of the past century.

Whether considered as a typology or regarded as modern architecture, Woman's Buildings challenge architectural conventions and inspire several questions: How is it possible to regard these pavilions collectively, as a group of related buildings created to explore gender ideals? In light of the diverse pavilions it inspired, if the 1893 Woman's Building was not an archetype in the traditional sense, can it be viewed in another manner, as a paradigm containing not one but multiple strategies to "gender" architecture? And if they were not technically or aesthetically innovative, how is it possible to view these buildings as legitimate architectural responses to modernity?

One must be cautious when identifying a work of architecture as inherently gendered in terms of its design, material, or decoration. As Thomas Markus and Deborah Cameron have observed, "Buildings themselves are not representations." These scholars, among others, argue that as language alone has the power to represent reality, buildings only acquire meaning when language is used to describe them. The language we select to represent architecture also governs how a building is "experienced and used."[7] Following their argument, the name *Woman's Building* often assigned to these structures immediately and unequivocally conferred a gendered context to the structure, while descriptions of the pavilion offered a gendered lens through which its architecture, sponsored exhibits, and even the behavior of its visitors would be viewed.

Guided by the premise that language lends and reveals architectural meaning, one might consider how the written descriptions authored by the organizers of the 1893 Woman's Building influenced the way the structure would be expe-

Fig. 10.1. Women's Rose Court, German Art Exhibition, Cologne, 1906. Author's collection.

Fig. 10.2. The Woman, the Child, and the Family, International Exposition, Paris, 1937. Author's collection.

Fig. 10.3.
Palace of
Feminine Work,
International
Exposition,
Brussels,
1910. Author's
collection.

rienced. Which architectural, spatial, or linguistic strategies did they articulate
to identify it as a gendered building? Following the fair, how were these strategies adapted to "gender" subsequent buildings? Two noteworthy commentaries
published in *Art and Handicraft in the Woman's Building* (1894) shed light on
how the meaning of the 1893 Woman's Building was purposefully shaped by fair
organizers and also hint at subsequent interpretations. An essay by Maud Howe
Elliot, the catalogue's editor, describes the pavilion's design and exhibits, while
another, authored by Bertha Honoré Palmer, president of the Board of Lady
Managers, recounts the project's origin and analyzes the contributions from
foreign women. Drawing upon concepts borrowed from architectural theory
along with linguistics, history, and philosophy, I suggest that their arguments
illuminated four distinct strategies, which I have chosen to identify as inventions, metaphors, narratives, and spaces. These essential conceptual strategies
lent particular gendered meaning to the 1893 Woman's Building, creating a
context for future such pavilions at subsequent fairs. Productive of a particular
set of meanings about buildings, artifacts, and spatial practices, they gave rise
to Woman's Buildings that challenged established concepts of architectural
classification and confronted emerging notions of modern architecture. As they
reflected on these buildings, architects, organizers, and observers considered
how architecture not only propagated specific ideologies—particularly regard-

ing women's "advancement" in society and women's "natural" role—but also complicated the content and scope of the world and national fairs during the late nineteenth and early twentieth centuries.

Inventions

Throughout the nineteenth century, buildings were erected for such unprecedented purposes that they might most usefully be considered inventions in themselves. Railroad stations, department stores, and skyscrapers all required ingenious new materials (fire-proofed steel, plate glass, reinforced concrete) and exploited novel methods of construction (wide-span structural systems, prefabrication) to serve burgeoning urban populations.[8] Although the 1893 Woman's Building did not enlist new materials, require pioneering feats of engineering, or provide previously unknown municipal services, organizers were well aware that the building's unique purpose itself represented a kind of invention: it was a new type of exhibition pavilion, and inasmuch as it was devoted to wholly feminine concerns and ideals, it represented "a hitherto untrodden path" for exposition organizers.[9]

At the heart of the 1893 Woman's Building's novelty was its authorship by a female architect, Sophia Hayden. Her well-publicized presence—in concert with her calculated design—encouraged organizers and fairgoers to consider the pavilion as a gendered exhibition building. Whereas typical exhibition buildings enclosed vast, unadorned halls most often punctuated by slender columns and housing rows of merchandise,[10] Hayden decorated and concealed the 1893 Woman's Building's supporting construction, placed the elaborate Hall of Honor at the pavilion's center, and divided the capacious interior into finely furnished rooms, including a library, an assembly room, a model kitchen, offices, parlors, and galleries. In another departure, she located gardens and an observation deck on the building's roof. Like the other major pavilions in the White City, she articulated the facades with an array of architectural details, derived from . Italian Renaissance models, yet she arranged them to lend a sense of human scale and delicacy to her monumental structure. Augmenting Sophia Hayden's vision, scores of female artists contributed decorations, sculptures, and murals to adorn the building.[11]

The Board of Lady Managers consisted of moderate reformers who believed that women should have some economic and social rights, particularly in the areas of education, property, and health. But they were also mostly privileged women who enjoyed great leisure and social status and had little interest in directly challenging the notion of separate spheres or surrendering their class-specific "elevated womanhood" in favor of political equality with men. They were proud of their building in part because it set them apart from men and because it provided a haven from the masculine spaces of the exposition in ways that drew attention to certain womanly pursuits—support of the arts, social and charitable engagement, domestic design and decoration—within which they felt they reigned supreme. Believing that women were to act demurely, offering support and sympathy, while men were to be chivalrous, bold, and strong, they projected these qualities onto the architecture they had commissioned. Convinced that a building designed by and devoted to women should appear different from the other pavilions in the White City, all created by male architects and dedicated to the masculine pursuits of trade and commerce, the Board of Lady Managers identified with Sophia Hayden's Woman's Building, finding its scale (it was one of the smallest pavilions in the White City), elaborate decoration, and welcoming ambience to be an appropriate expression of their feminine ideal.[12] These women considered the 1893 Woman's Building to be successful precisely because its unique design and distinct atmosphere revealed the gender of its architect.

Maud Howe Elliott expanded on this conviction, arguing that as women were rising to prominence in the arts and design professions, they should now celebrate their gender in their creative works. Women, she asserted, were no longer required to "cloak their womanhood under noms de plume" or imitate male artists because, as she said, "Today we recognize that the more womanly a woman's work is, the stronger it is."[13] She praised the 1893 Woman's Building in precisely these terms: "Our building is essentially feminine in character." Maud Howe Elliott asserted the building possessed the qualities of an ideal woman, embodying her temperament ("reserve, delicacy, and refinement"), appearance ("every line expresses elegance, grace, harmony"), and disposition (the building's innate ability to "soothe, to rest, to refresh the great army of sightseers who march daily through the fair").[14]

Following Chicago's example, as a strategy to "gender" subsequent pavilions, female architects were engaged to design representative Woman's Buildings at two national fairs held in the United States soon after the Chicago exposition. Elise Mercur created a Woman's Building for the 1895 Cotton States and International Exposition in Atlanta, while Sarah Ward Conley authored the one at the 1897 Tennessee Centennial in Nashville. Both women developed two-story, multifunctional buildings modeled on a regional paradigm, the Southern antebellum plantation house.[15] At the 1915 Panama-Pacific Exposition in San Francisco, a less prominent pavilion, sponsored by the Young Women's Christian Association (YWCA) and designed by Julia Morgan, was inserted behind a facade previously fashioned by an official fair architect. Julia Morgan's functional, wood-paneled interior provided practical amenities, including a cafeteria and clubrooms, while in lieu of arranging a display of women's work, the organizers sponsored an array of services ranging from childcare to Sunday vespers.[16]

Around 1900, representative Woman's Buildings also appeared at European fairs. As design academies and technical universities on this continent were slow to admit women,[17] the first female-designed pavilions were constructed in 1914, roughly two decades after the Chicago Woman's Building. In this year, two separate Woman's Buildings were erected at competing fairs in Germany. For the Werkbund Exhibition in Cologne, where consumer products from German-speaking nations were showcased, Margarethe Knüppelholz-Roeser created the Woman's House, a one-story building, with stark, unornamented facades, colored in deep ochre tones. At the International Book and Graphic Exhibition in Leipzig, Emilie Winkelmann arranged twenty-five finely furnished exhibition rooms, each differing in size and decoration, into a long building, also called the Woman's House, clad in light gray, neobaroque facades.[18]

By the late 1920s, the international style—stark, undecorated buildings with flat roofs, functional plans, constructed using industrial materials, and articulated with bold colors—emerged in major European cities and was adopted by progressive female architects for the design of Woman's Buildings at national and world's fairs in Poland, Scotland, and Germany. At the 1929 National Exhibition in Poznań, for example, Anatolia Hryniewiecka-Piotrowska created for the Pavilion of Women's Work a design that included the use of striking gray and yellow facades with bold signage, an oversized display window, and a pronounced circular staircase leading to a rooftop café.[19] For the 1938 Empire Exhibition in Glasgow, Margaret Brodie enclosed the Women of Empire pavilion in "dove grey, blue and silver" facades and arranged a café, exhibition and reception rooms, as well as a large theater to accommodate daily fashions shows in the sprawling building.[20] The House Women's Ring, initially erected for the 1931 Berlin Building Exhibition, should also be mentioned in this context. Not solely authored by a woman (both Peter Behrens and Else Oppler-Legband collaborated on the design), the pavilion, a one-story, cylindrical volume surrounded by gardens and reflecting pools, occupied the center of the city's fairgrounds until 1935. It served as a social center for women.[21]

Contemporary critics evaluating these pavilions tended to echo Maud Howe Elliott's descriptions of the Chicago Woman's Building, drawing attention to the thoroughly feminine character of architecture created by women. One local newspaper felt the efforts of Elise Mercur, the Atlanta Woman's Building's architect, assured spectators, "This is really a woman's department."[22] The Woman's House in Leipzig was seen to "blend demurely and contentedly into the exhibition's overall impression,"[23] and the YWCA pavilion's interior was judged a "remarkable airy, cheery, welcoming arrangement."[24] While these comments portray femininity as being pleasing, accommodating, and hospitable, they also demonstrate how the implied presence of the female architect, in concert with an appropriate design, was perceived as an acceptable strategy to "gender" a building. Pavilions designed by women architects that seemed to diverge from this premise, however, were thoroughly condemned. Architects and progressive women, for example, scorned the Woman's House in Cologne, finding its unadorned facades displayed "an exaggerated masculine character,"[25] devoid of "all charm"[26] and "womanly gentleness."[27]

In the 1920s and 1930s, despite some legal and economic gains, progressive European women now turned a critical eye on the notion of political and social emancipation for women, questioning many of the more strident goals set forth by feminists prior to the First World War or choosing to view motherhood in a more positive light. Meanwhile, rising unemployment and fiscal uncertainty turned popular sentiment against the New Woman and her perceived individualism, seemingly unnatural competition with men, and rejection of the traditional family.[28] In evaluating Woman's Buildings, critics now articulated this unease and viewed these pavilions as less of an ideal state—an embodiment of the perfect woman—and more of a conflicted site, a place that revealed the tensions accompanying the growing antifeminist backlash on the European continent. In Great Britain, a leading architectural publication equally praised and belittled the Women of Empire pavilion, finding "its ingenious and wholly charming little fashion theatre . . . more than makes up for the rather indeterminate elevations."[29] In Poland, as progressive women had come to abhor the word "feminist," feeling it implied undue individuality and an abnegation of women's essential maternal role,[30] it is not surprising that one prominent female journalist appropriated these sentiments to assess the bold design of the Pavilion of Women's Work. While she felt its bright yellow facades positively evoked the "youthfulness of feminine labor," she asserted the striking architecture, with its "excessive originality," lent expression to the "totalitarianism of the feminist movement."[31]

Although the invention, the selection of a woman architect who went on to design a suitably feminine building, was understood as an effective means to "gender" a pavilion, not all organizers of subsequent Woman's Buildings embraced this strategy. The failure to commission women architects to design other pavilions can be ascribed to their paucity in this discipline as well as to the deep-rooted and enduring prejudice toward female professionals. When women architects were not forthcoming, strategies that relied on the more symbolic and conceptual aspects of architecture were adopted to make these Woman's Buildings gendered feminine as well.

Metaphors

If *invention* encouraged viewers to speculate on the gendered nature of buildings created by women architects, then another strategy, which I have chosen to identify as *metaphor,* relied on the symbolic power of architecture to confer and reinforce the gendered meaning these buildings conveyed. Metaphor is a culturally determined concept that defines an experience, justifies inferences or draws attention to certain features while concealing others. It is produced through a process of displacement, where symbols that are rooted in one context are removed and inserted into a new one.[32] Applied to architecture, the metaphor can be seen as the practice of reconstructing a specific building on a new, often unexpected, site and at a much later time. Woman's Buildings retained the meanings inherent to the historic types of structures they cited by way of explicit physical references, but these meanings were complicated by the change in their programming (their functions as Woman's Buildings) and by their settings—the themes, site planning, and architectural design of the particular fairs of which they were a contextual part.

In designing the 1893 Woman's Building, Sophia Hayden manipulated architectural metaphors to comment upon the status of women at the Chicago fair. Maud Howe Elliott observed that the building's decoration recalled "the style of the villas of the Italian Renaissance," while the design of the second-story arcades surrounding the Hall of Honor had been "treated in the way of a cloister, with graceful arches springing from well-proportioned columns."[33] Both the Renaissance villa, accommodating an extended family and a large household, and the cloister, a secluded place for a community of women, called to mind the idea of a public (or a less intimate) residence. Interpreted as a villa or a cloister, these sentiments conveyed a sense of the pavilion's ambiguous status at the Columbian Exposition. Similar to a villa, it was a private place among the White City's public structures; not unlike a cloister, it was a secretive and an enriching place, secluding women while enabling them to establish a community of like-minded sisters. Sophia Hayden's architectural metaphors, however, were generic references. She did not reproduce a particular "villa" or "cloister" but freely interpreted historical forms, "the expression of what I felt and liked," as she noted,[34] to inscribe meaning upon her building.

Subsequently, the design of other Woman's Buildings found inspiration in generic domestic architecture, as if to negotiate the contradiction proposed by femininity and publicity. Although the Woman's Palace at the 1900 World Exposition in Paris resembled a villa articulated with various French rococo and art nouveau details, it functioned more like a service center for the female fairgoer, providing space for a hairdresser, a seamstress, and even a patisserie.[35] In contrast, a religious reference was chosen for the design of the Women's Rose Court, erected for the 1906 German Art Exhibition in Cologne. Constructed from red sandstone blocks and surrounded by gardens, the pavilion called to mind the intimacy and serenity of a small cloister. At the entrance to the Rose Court, an arcade led visitors to a lofty, chapel-like hall, an exalted space to accommodate feminine activity (women lectured here during the fair) and display finely crafted, feminine attire (jewelry, toiletries, and decorative arts), arranged in elegant vitrines.[36] The Woman's Building at the 1907 Jamestown Centennial in Hampton Roads occupied a more familiar reference, a simple, clapboard house where the Woman's Christian Temperance Union dispensed refreshments and provided temporary lodgings.[37] By the 1920s, however, pointedly domestic references declined, although one notable example was found at the 1929 National Exhibition in Poznań. There, as conservative, rural women rejected the progressive message of the Pavilion of Women's Work, they constructed a competing building, the Pavilion of the Female Farmers and Estate Owners, modeled on an eighteenth-century, neo-baroque country residence. It contained meeting rooms and areas to display traditional crafts.[38]

Another metaphor, the reconstruction of a well-known monument, brought associations to the fore that were specific to particular historic buildings that would have been well-known to fair visitors. The 1897 Tennessee Centennial Exhibition in Nashville, for example, sported numerous monuments citing the Greek Acropolis, Renaissance Venice, and ancient Egypt,[39] yet it was a regional landmark that female fair organizers selected to orient their civic work and lend expression to their modern identity. In choosing the Hermitage (the antebellum plantation home of Andrew Jackson and his wife Rachel Donelson Jackson) to orient their design of the Woman's Building, white southern women paid tribute to pre–Civil War culture and identified a feminine contribution to contemporary civic life. The Hermitage's mistress, Rachel Donelson Jackson, whose reputed displays of hospitality in the face of adversity were legendary, embodied the womanly ideals they intended to champion with this building.[40] Such efforts to preserve and maintain this particular residence pointed to an emerging feminine public role as the protectors of historic memory in the New South.[41]

At European fairs diverse feminine ideals were promoted. At the 1905 World Exhibition in Liège, the Palace of the Woman and Lacework referred to a specific historical model, the Grand Trianon. This baroque summer palace had been erected at Versailles for Louis XIV in the late seventeenth century. The 1905 palace's distinct design (actually two pavilions that were joined by a central, columned porch) housed examples of lace and textiles. Organized by bourgeois and aristocratic women alike, the Palace of the Woman and Lacework's august source underscored male organizers' need for the reassurance offered by tradition and by conservative social ideals, perhaps as an intentional affront to the growing socialist orientation of the local women's movement.[42] At the 1914 Baltic Exhibition in Malmö, Swedish women appropriated a well-known national monument, Årsta, a seventeenth-century castle located on the outskirts of Stockholm, for their Pavilion of Swedish Women's Work. During the first half of the nineteenth century, the writer Fredrika Bremer, known as the "mother of the Swedish women's movement" for her impassioned arguments in defense of women's self-determination, had occupied the castle, and it was closely associated with her memory. While Årsta's massive facades, high-pitched roof, and representative entry vestibule were faithfully reconstructed, the residual interiors were executed in a contemporary manner to accommodate various functions—a tearoom, library, exhibits of professional women's work and trade schools, even resting rooms for weary female fairgoers—in support of women as they tested public life.[43]

While the selection of generic domestic architecture broadly referred to normative attitudes about women and the private sphere, the specific citations found in Nashville, Liège, and Malmö proposed more limited interpretations and narrowly defined femininity in relation to class affiliation and local identity. The Nashville pavilion idealized the values of white women in the postbellum South, the one in Liège alluded to the wealth and sophistication of the French aristocracy, and Malmö's reproduction embodied the pragmatic aspirations of Swedish feminists. These three metaphors also excluded overt references to traditional feminine roles (motherhood, familial duties) and drew attention to women's contributions to the public sphere, defined as assuming social responsibilities, supporting culture and education, or undertaking remunerative work. As a strategy serving to "gender" an exhibition building, metaphors exploited the communicative power of architecture to convey meaning about modern identity. Placing these symbols at a major fair overlaid them with notions of progress, proposing that the uncommon feminine ideals presented in these buildings were compatible with the goals of the modern state.

Narratives

The Woman's Buildings discussed above manipulated architectural symbols to communicate broad notions about gender and identity. At the same time, organizers of Woman's Buildings also assembled diverse visual materials and coordinated select spatial practices to construct tightly focused arguments about femininity—what I see as the narratives animating their organizational designs. Like historical or literary narrative, architectural narrative does not rely on the straightforward presentation of statistics or documentation to espouse a particular point of view but instead exploits more evocative and suggestive evidence—in this case the decorations, exhibits, films, performances, landscaping, even the themes of successive exhibition rooms or a series of pavilions—to construct a compelling account or advance a convincing set of relationships developing over time.[44]

In describing the 1893 Woman's Building, Maud Howe Elliot identified several narratives that posited the American woman as a sophisticated persona whose artistic accomplishments and capacity for leadership contributed to her nation's progress. One narrative commenced at the pavilion's northern entry, amid the exhibit of American decorative arts. Surveying the work on display, Elliott declared, "The impression we carry away from it is that we are no longer pensioners of Europe in the matter of design. To-day we have an American School of Design, with a distinct national character of its own, and women are to the fore in every one of its branches." Leaving this exhibit, one's passage through the Hall of Honor toward the south wing was the equivalent of a voyage across the ocean, where the point of arrival was not one country or even one continent, but feminine production from the rest of the world. Elliot declared, "We have crossed the seas. Spain is before us; India, Germany, Austria, Belgium are upon our left; Sweden, Mexico, Italy, France upon the right." She concluded that the achievements of the cultivated American woman, who had developed her own aesthetic sensibility and had inspired her sisters from around the world to display their accomplishments in this pavilion, ultimately served national interests: "In this miniature we have tasted the world's citizenship, we have learned that nothing that is not for the good of humanity at large can benefit us or our country."[45]

Maud Howe Elliott interpreted the arrangements of decorative arts and material culture placed throughout the 1893 Woman's Building to suggest a correlation between the progress of American women and the welfare of her nation. Narratives found in subsequent Woman's Buildings echoed this argument, positing women's labors as necessary contributions to a state's social and economic interests. Because feminist movements in the nineteenth century viewed access to adequate remunerative work as being essential for emancipation, prior to 1914 many Woman's Buildings included exhibits of feminine labor, such as handwork and documentation from female educational institutions. (By implication, self-sufficient women would not burden the state, while those not in need of remuneration could nurture their children's intellectual development or become more sophisticated consumers.) The Woman's Building in Nashville and the Woman's House in Leipzig contrasted historical artifacts with present-day accomplishments,[46] while in the Woman's House in Cologne and the Pavilion of Swedish Women's Work in Malmö, exhibits from female industrial schools and design academies were arranged as a prelude to the achievements of established women professionals.[47]

By the late 1930s, narratives conveyed by Woman's Buildings ceased to promote feminine labor and championed more traditional womanly roles instead. Alarmed by declining birthrates, European governments now defined female citizenship in relation to feminine biology and aggressively supported pronatal and profamily policies.[48] Exhibits in some Woman's Buildings celebrated maternity by implying that child rearing (either at home or in the social service and childcare professions) ultimately supported national interests. At the 1937 World Exposition in Paris, a Woman's Building was located in the building ensemble, Social Issues, a collection of striking international-style pavilions dedicated to social welfare, employment, and labor concerns. Approaching this group of buildings, visitors first encountered The Woman, the Child, and the Family pavilion and then proceeded to two additional buildings that contained exhibits illustrating the effectiveness of worker cooperatives and the national insurance system, respectively. In this scheme, women played a preliminary role, nurturing the nation's offspring who would one day become productive laborers for the state. Upon entering the Woman, the Child, and the Family pavilion, fairgoers experienced a multi-faceted depiction of motherhood. At the center of the building, experts dispersed advice on childcare in a lecture hall, while the surrounding galleries displayed documentation of women's efforts in day nurseries, schools, and the social service professions. Moving farther on, visitors passed by an alcove that was reserved for breast-feeding mothers; they then proceeded outside to observe children frolicking in the adjoining play area.[49]

Two years later, as war clouds gathered across Europe, a narrative displayed at the 1939 Swiss National Exhibition in Zurich argued that although maternity was essential, women contributed other vital labors to insure the state's survival and security. A small pavilion dedicated to the Swiss woman was included in a division of the exhibition entitled Land and People. This division, a collection of buildings and exhibits celebrating the Swiss people, was housed in inventive wooden structures that were connected to one another by an enclosed, elevated boardwalk. The boardwalk shepherded visitors from one display to another, directing them to visit the exhibits sequentially to better grasp the intended connections between the content of successive pavilions.[50] At the entrance to this division, fairgoers encountered dramatic, oversized photographs (suspended from the boardwalk's ceiling) of individual faces, illustrating Switzerland's ethnic diversity, while an adjacent cinema screened short films documenting regional life. In the next pavilion, The Woman, drawings of large female figures (nurse, farmer, homemaker/consumer, artist), representing distinct spheres of feminine labor, delineated on the pavilion's rear interior wall. Continuing along to an area where roof sections of the boardwalk were removed, fairgoers could glimpse the adjoining outdoor recreational play area, where a children's building and a model youth center were also located. Farther along the boardwalk, the final two buildings in this sequence contained exhibits of women's participation in the social services and documentation of Swiss nationals living abroad. As impending war threatened to disrupt everyday life, this narrative drew attention to the Swiss woman who performed selective labor and nurtured her nation's diverse peoples at home or in the diaspora.[51]

Fig. 10.4. The Woman, Swiss National Exhibition, Zurich, 1939. Author's collection.

Compared to metaphors and inventions, which relied on one signifier (an architectural symbol or the female architect) to "gender" a building, narratives required multiple components to explore the feminine experience and advance an argument about difference. The narrative either found in or encompassing a Woman's Building depended on the sequential arrangement of visual materials (buildings, displays, films) and performances (experts lecturing, mothers breastfeeding, children at play). Such planning also necessitated a visitor's linear movement either through a building or along a specific path in a fairground to comprehend the intended connections between the exhibits and activities on display. As time wore on, the narratives promoted by such artifacts and performances in accordance with the directed movements of fairgoers tended more and more to emphasize a highly selective, more traditional feminine contribution to the modern state and were no longer organized to affirm women's self-determination.

Consider the narratives found in the 1893 Chicago Woman's Building compared to those conveyed more than four decades later in the pavilion erected in Paris in 1937 and to a lesser extent the one in Zurich in 1939. Whereas the Chicago Board of Lady Managers compiled artifacts and documentation to support greater feminine public participation, women were less engaged in preparing the later European examples, where this strategy was usurped by the state—quite explicitly in Paris, more subtly in Zurich—to impress upon women the importance of motherhood. Whereas the gender difference that the

1893 Woman's Building proclaimed appeared to be a celebration of woman's progress on behalf of Woman (with her nation benefiting as a result of her advancement), the progress of women expressed in the narratives of these later buildings declared women's primary allegiance to the state through her adherence to traditional roles.

Spaces

Like inventions and metaphors, narratives relied on a more ambiguous aspect of architectural production—namely, space—to propose meanings. Although space can be regarded as a physical dimension or a quantifiable volume (the distance between displays or the volume of an exhibition hall), it can also be understood as a more ephemeral quality, the product of three somewhat interconnected processes: the manner in which a building is used; the representations created to depict it (texts, drawings, photographs); and the memories associated with it, embodied in texts that might range from personal recollections to published criticisms.[52] Space defined in this way allows the more subjective and temporal aspects of a building—experience, depiction, and remembrance—to assume greater significance, and the tangible and quantifiable attributes to recede in importance. A building can be regarded as a gendered space when women and their concerns, for example, dominate the images and language produced to describe it, the manner in which it is used and appropriated, and the memories and associations arising from its use. In this sense, the 1893 Woman's Building can be seen as a gendered space. Women selected a name ("Woman's Building," "Pavilion of the Female Farmers and Estate Owners," "Woman's House," "Palace of Woman and Lacework") to represent their pavilion, they inhabited the building (as organizers, visitors, and performers), and they recalled it in texts ranging from intimate correspondence to published accounts, where they depicted it as the focus of feminine interests and activities. This strategy, the gendered space, informed the production of all the Woman's Buildings. As we have seen, many pavilions were overlaid with additional strategies that enhanced their arguments about gender.

It is wrong to assume that engaged individuals freely and independently elected to construct a gendered space, that is, a Woman's Building at a world or national fair, as organizers (sometimes, but not always, female) normally required official permission to allow such a building to come into existence. Writing about the "growth" of the idea of the 1893 Woman's Building, Bertha Honoré Palmer recalled the United States Government's authorization of feminine representation at the Chicago fair and praised "the valuable work" undertaken by women at the 1876 Philadelphia Centennial and the 1884–85 New Orleans Cotton Centennial, "who had prepared the public mind so thoroughly for the cooperation of women in exhibition work."[53] Judy Sund has labeled this logic "validation by patriarchal approbation,"[54] and her pronouncement does suggest one problem inherent to all these pavilions, namely, that a Woman's Building could only present an effective argument about femininity when it was able to exploit its status as a gendered space, either by strenuously challenging or deliberately reinforcing the expectations imposed on it by a sponsoring authority. In other words, authorization many have granted a Woman's Building a certain status, but this position alone was not sufficient to guarantee that the pavilion would convey a forceful argument about gender. When viewed in isolation, the gendered space can be seen as an ambivalent, or a weak, strategy to impart ideas about femininity through exhibition architecture.

Several Woman's Buildings not previously discussed can be regarded as gendered spaces because they were designated as a Woman's Building by a fair's administration, were predominantly used by women, and were remembered as places devoted to feminine interests. Their architecture and exhibits, however, failed to produce a compelling argument about femininity. In the United States, this would include the Woman's Buildings found at fairs held in Buffalo (1901),[55] Charleston (1901–2),[56] and St. Louis (1904).[57] In all these instances, an extant structure, already located on or near to a fairground, was designated as a Woman's Building by a supervising authority. A women's board subsequently organized events in it, largely social in nature, to appeal to female fairgoers, and chroniclers recorded the activities that were staged inside. Yet contemporary women often recalled these gendered spaces with regret, feeling the loss of deliberate architectural signifiers, the lack of complex displays, and the absence of the female architect rendered these buildings less significant (and more trivial) public architecture.[58]

In contrast, two European examples, the Palace of Women's Work at the 1908 Franco-British Exhibition in London and the Palace of Feminine Work at the 1910 International Exposition in Brussels, actually occupied new buildings, although these pavilions neither possessed a compelling architectural identity, nor did their contents advance a convincing argument about gender. Both were prominently situated buildings, articulated with elaborate facades to compliment the prevailing architectural styles at their respective fairs, Yet their contents failed to provoke speculation about femininity. The pavilion in Brussels, for example, displayed textiles and included a small international exhibition of decorative arts,[59] while the British Palace of Women's Work housed unrelated arrangements of decorative and fine arts, literature and fashion, social welfare work and philanthropy. Regarding this building, one observer noted, "It is rather the housing of women's filling up of time."[60] These gendered spaces were subordinate to the host nation's presentation at a fair and did not convincingly probe or affirm prevailing attitudes toward women.

The gendered space required women to dominate the use, representation, and memory of a Woman's Building. Paradoxically, while it provided the essential means to render exhibition architecture feminine, when it was not overlaid with additional strategies (inventions, metaphors, narratives), its impact waned. The gendered space also demonstrates how the production of a meaningful Woman's Building required more than official authorization or the construction of a new pavilion to produce compelling architecture that explored gender identity.

Conclusion

The four strategies that have been discussed—the invention (the building designed by a female architect who appeared to be personified in her creation), the metaphor (the use of architectural symbols to confer meaning), the narrative (the sequential arrangement of visual materials and selected performances to propose an argument about femininity), and the gendered space (the permission to erect a building dedicated to women and their concerns, reinforced by use, representation, and memory)—can be most vividly seen in the celebrated 1893 Woman's Building, yet these strategies were freely adapted by the producers of Woman's Buildings at subsequent national and world's fairs as well. More than an architectural archetype in the conventional sense, the 1893 Woman's Building offered an alternative paradigm or "a sort of expanding universe to which no limits could be fixed and which would not be incoherence nonetheless."[61] It allowed for diversity and interpretation, although this also gave rise to pavilions, particularly those constructed in Europe in the 1930s, conveying arguments that diverged from those put forth by the Board of Lady Managers in their building at the Columbian Exposition.

As we have seen, Woman's Buildings were not sufficiently technically innovative or artistically daring to be considered as stellar examples of modern architecture. While their heterogeneity challenges notions of architectural typology, their reliance on authorship, symbols, narrative organization, and spatial strategies to inscribe meaning about gender prompts historians to reconsider their reliance on technological and aesthetic novelty as a measure to identify the significant buildings of the late nineteenth and early twentieth centuries. While the architectural canon excludes the Woman's Buildings produced between 1893 and 1939 for their dearth of inventiveness or their abundance of diversity, it is more difficult to eliminate them from histories that explore women's lives, consider gender, or document the world and national fairs. The precepts of identity, and in particular gender identity, which are so difficult to render in brick and stone or glass and steel, were central to the creation, heterogeneity, and longevity of the Woman's Buildings that were constructed with great conviction at the fairs of the late nineteenth and early twentieth centuries.

NOTES

1 Among others, woman's pavilions and divisions were at fairs in Vienna (1873), Philadelphia (1876), New Orleans (1884–1885) and Glasgow (1888).

2 Mary Pepchinski, "The Woman's Building and the World Exhibitions: Exhibition Architecture and Conflicting Feminine Ideals at European and American World Exhibitions, 1873–1915," in *Wolkenkuckucksheim* 5, no. 1 (2000), available at http://www.tucottbus. de/BTU/Fak2/TheoArch/Wolke/eng/Subjects/001/Pepchinski/pepchinski.htm (last accessed January 20, 2010).

3 *Wasmuths Lexicon der Baukunst* [*Wasmuth's Lexicon of Architecture*], vol. 4 (Berlin: Wasmuth, 1932), 578.

4 For example, Kenneth Frampton, *Modern Architecture*, 3rd ed. (London: Thames and Hudson, 1992).

5 Mark Pimlott, *Without and Within* (Rotterdam: Episode Publishers, 2007), 122–38.

6 Mary Pepchinski, *Feminist Space* (Weimar: Verlag und Datenbank fur Geisteswissenschaften, 2007), 74.

7 Thomas Markus and Deborah Cameron, *The Words Between the Spaces* (London: Routledge, 2002), 15–16.

8 Nikolaus Pevsner, *A History of Building Type* (1976; repr., London: Thames and Hudson, 1984), 9.

9 Bertha Honoré Palmer, "The Growth of the Woman's Building" in *Art and Handicraft in the Woman's Building*, ed. Maud Howe Elliott, 27 (Chicago: Rand McNally, 1894).

10 Erik Mattie, *World's Fairs* (New York: Princeton Architectural Press, 1998), 9.

11 Jeanne Madeleine Weimann, *The Fair Women* (Chicago: Academy Chicago, 1981), 141–214.

12 Ibid., 27–30, 50; Bertha Honoré Palmer, "The Growth of the Woman's Building" in Elliott, 30.

13 Maud Howe Elliott, "The Building and its Decoration," in Elliott, 38.

14 Ibid., 35–40.

15 Bruce G. Harvey, "World's Fairs in a Southern Accent: Atlanta, Nashville, Charleston, 1895–1902" (PhD diss., Vanderbilt University, 1998), 246–85.

16 Frank Morton Todd, *The Story of the Exhibition*, vol. 5 (New York: Panama-Pacific International Exposition, 1920), 125–29.

17 Women were admitted to the Academy of Fine Arts in Paris in 1898; to German technical universities in 1908; to Amsterdam's Academy of Building Arts in 1914; to Vienna's Academy of Applied Arts in 1915; and to the Swiss Federal Institute of Technology around 1920.

18 Mary Pepchinski, "Vom Woman's Building zum Haus der Frau: Kulturexport, Typologie und das Problem der Repräsentation, 1893–1914" [From the Woman's Building to the Woman's House: Cultural Export, Typology, and the Problem of Representation, 1893–1914] in *Building America: eine große Erzählung* [*Building America: A Great Narrative*] ed. Hans-Georg Lippert, et al. vol. 3, 183–205 (Dresden: Thelem, 2008).

19 Olgierd Czerner and Hieronim Listowski, eds., *The Polish Avant-Garde: Architecture and Town Planning, 1918–1933* (exhibition catalog) (Paris: Editions du Moniteur, 1981), 64–65, 86.

20 Perilla Kinchin and Juliet Kinchin, *Glasgow's Great Exhibitions* (Oxon: White Cockade, 1988), 127–30, 148–50.

21 Georg Krawietz, *Peter Behrens im Dritten Reich* [Peter Behrens in the Third Reich] (Weimar: Verlag und Datenbank fur Geisteswissenschaften, 1995), 20–23, 58–60; *Zentralblatt der Bauverwaltung* [*Central Report of the Building Administration*] 55 (August 14, 1935): 634, 636.

22 *Atlanta Constitution*, quoted in Harvey, 259.

23 *Die Frau* [*The Woman*] 12 (1913/14): 722.

24 Frances A. Groff, quoted in Sara Holmes Boutelle, *Julia Morgan, Architect* (New York: Abbeville, 1988), 100–105.

25 *Wasmuths Monatshefte für Baukunst* [*Wasmuth's Architecture Monthly*] 4 (1914): 159.

26 *Bauwelt* [Building World] 14 (1914), 24.

27 *Neue Frauenkleidung und Frauenkultur* [*New Women's Clothing and Women's Culture*] 10 (1914): 80.

28 Karen Offen, *European Feminisms* (Stanford: Stanford University Press, 2000), 251–79.

29 *The Builder*, May 20, 1938, 988.

30 Katarzyna Sierakowska, "From Partitions to an Independent State: The Feminist Movement in Poland in the First Half of the 20th Century" in *Women's Movements*, ed. Edith Saurer, et al., 489–93 (Cologne: Böhlau, 2006).

31 Stefania Podhorska-Okolow, quoted in Szymon Piotr Kubiak, "Architektura i płeć. 'Pawilon Pracy Kobiet' na Powszechnej Wystawie Krajowej w 1929 roku" [Architecture and Gender: The "Pavilion of Women's Work" at the General National Exhibition in 1929], in *UniGender* 1:3 (2007), available at http://www.unigender.org /?page=biezac y&issue=02&article=04 (last accessed January 20, 2010).

32 George Lakoff and Mark Johnson, *Metaphors We Live By* (Chicago: University of Chicago Press, 1980), 140–46, 157–58.

33 Maud Howe Elliott, "The Building and its Decoration," in Elliott, 38.

34 Sophia Hayden, quoted in Susanna Torre, ed., *Women in American Architecture* (New York: Watson-Guptill, 1977), 74.

35 *Neue Bahnen* [*New Paths*] 18 (September 1900): 217.

36 *Köln 1906. Ausstellung des Verbandes der Kunstfreunde in den Ländern am Rhein* [*Cologne 1906. Exhibition of the Association of Friends of Art in the Lands along the Rhine*] (catalog) (Cologne: 1906); *Kunstchronik* [Art Chronicle] 26 (1905/06): 96; *Die Werkkunst* [*The Craft Art*] 18 (1905): 273.

37 Amy Yarsinke, *Jamestown Exposition*, vol. 2 (Charleston: Arcadia, 1999), 39.

38 Stanisław Wachowiak (ed.), *Powszechna Wystawa Krajowa w Poznaniu w roku 1929* [General National Exhibition in Poznań, 1929] vol. 5 (Poznań: Wystawa, 1930), 131–47.

39 *New York Times*, May 2, 1897; *New York Times*, June 20, 1897.

40 See http://www.whitehouse.gov/history/about/first-ladies/racheljackson (The White House/Presidents and First Ladies/Rachel Donelson Jackson) (accessed January 20, 2010).

41 Wolfgang Schivelbusch, *Die Kultur der Niederlage* [*The Culture of Defeat*] (Frankfurt am Main: Fischer, 2003), 51–122.

42 Christine Renardy and Sébastian Charlier, "L'architecture en ville et à l'Exposition" [Architecture in the City and the Exhibition] in *Liège et l'Exposition universelle de 1905* [Liège and the Universal Exposition of 1905], ed. Christine Renardy, 188–99 (Brussels: La Renaissance du Livre, 2005).

43 *Årsta. Svenska Kvinnornas utställning* [Årsta Swedish Women's Exhibition] (catalog) (Malmö: Landby and Lundgrens, 1914).

44 Lawrence Stone, *The Past and the Present Revisited* (London: Routledge, 1987), 74.

45 Maud Howe Elliott, "The Building and its Decoration" in Elliott, 49, 63–65.

46 Herman Justi, ed., *Official History of the Tennessee Centennial Exposition* (Nashville: Centennial Committee on Publications, 1898), 143–52; *Das Haus der Frau auf der Weltausstellung für Buchgewerbe und Graphik Leipzig 1914* [*The Woman's House at the World's Fair for Book Trades and Graphics, Leipzig 1914*] (catalog) (Leipzig, 1914).

47 Årsta. *Svenska Kvinnornas utställning* (catalog) (Malmö: Landby and Lundgrens, 1914).

48 Ann Taylor Allen, *Feminism and Motherhood in Western Europe, 1890–1970* (New York: Palgrave Macmillan, 2007), 137–208.

49 Robert Lange, *Merveilles de L'Exposition de 1937* [*Wonders of the 1937 Exposition*] (Paris: Éditions Denoël, 1937), 147–55; *Exposition Internationale des Arts et des Technologies dans la Vie Moderne Paris 1937, Catalogue Général Officiel,* [*International Exposition of Art and Technology in Modern Life: The Official General Catalog*] vol. 1 (Paris 1937), 16–20, 83–87, 202–15.

50 *Die Schweiz im Spiegel der Landesausstellung* [*Switzerland in the Mirror of the National Exposition*] (catalog), vol. 2 (Zurich: Atlantis, 1939), 595–608.

51 Ibid., vol. 1 (Zurich 1939), 130–36. During wartime, neutral Switzerland intensified border security, endured shortages, and accommodated refugees.

52 Henri Lefebvre, *The Production of Space*, trans. Donald Nicholson Smith (1991; repr., Oxford: Blackwell, 2001).

53 Bertha Honoré Palmer, "The Growth of the Woman's Building" in Elliott, 17–19.

54 Judy Sund, "Columbus and Columbia in Chicago, 1893: Man of Genius Meets Generic Woman," *Art Bulletin* 75, no. 3 (1993): 446.

55 *New York Times*, May 22, 1901.

56 Anthony Chibbaro, *The Charleston Exposition* (Charleston: Arcadia, 2001), 28–29, 47.

57 *Amtlicher Bericht über die Weltausstellung in Saint Louis 1904* [*Official Report on the Worlds Fair in St. Louis*] (Berlin: Reichsdruckerei, 1906), 67.

58 Mary B. Mullet, "Women and the Pan-American," *Harper's Weekly* 45 (August 3, 1901): 782.

59 Marjan Groot, *Vrouwen in de vormgeving in Nederland 1880–1940* [*Women in Design in the Netherlands, 1880–1940*] (Rotterdam: Uitgeverij, 2007), 107–10; Commissariat Général du Gouvernment (ed.), *Exposition Universelle et Internationale Bruxelles 1910, Catalogue Spécial de la Section Belge* [*Universal and International Exposition Brussels 1910: Special Belgian Section*] (Brussels: Commissariat Général du Gouvernment, 1910), 8, 108–9, 395–97.

60 D. H. M., "Palace of Women's Work," *Franco-British Exhibition Illustrated Review* (London: Chatto and Windus, 1909), 231–32; *Journal of the Royal Institute of British Architects* 25 (July 25, 1908): 546–56.

61 Luce Irigaray, "This Sex Which Is Not One," in *This Sex Which Is Not One*, trans. Catherine Porter, 31 (Ithaca: Cornell University Press, 1977).

CHAPTER II

Policing Masculine Festivity at London's Early Modern Fairs

Anne Wohlcke

In the early eighteenth century, William Adams was apprenticed to Joseph Bidwell, a carpenter from St. Giles-in-the-Fields. Adams's parents likely hoped their son would learn his trade and eventually embark on an industrious career. By 1732, however, it was obvious to both Adams and his parents that his training was not proceeding as planned; not only did he fail to receive clothes promised him according to his indenture, but he was also not given the opportunity to learn carpentry. Perhaps enticed by easy summertime profits, William's master instead "employed him in driving a chair, with boys and girles [*sic*] in it for halfe pence a piece, drawn by two or three dogs . . . [at] most of the little fairs about town."[1] The Middlesex county justices found this work troubling, and they viewed Bidwell's misuse of his apprentice with concern. When they heard this case, the justices were engaged in a campaign to contain the often disorderly amusement of fairs, many of which extended well beyond their chartered days or, worse, were held with no charters. This fraudulent apprenticeship represented to the justices exactly the type of improper masculine commerce that fairs encouraged in and around London. Without hesitation, the magistrates discharged William Adams from his indenture.

The story of William Adams and his problematic apprenticeship predates the modern world of national fairs and exhibitions. Prior to the emergence of fairs as suitable venues to showcase national values or economic strength, they needed to be understood by potential exhibition organizers as orderly occasions capable of both containing and projecting the values of exhibition organizers. The organizers at modern fairs concerned themselves with drawing audiences through publicity departments.[2] By the late nineteenth century, exposition organizers could assume that their potential audience shared organizers' understandings of the "semiotics of commodity spectacle," but the emergence of fairgrounds as a space that could host such a mass audience has a history.

Gendering fairs was the first step in making fairgrounds useable venues for the promotion of national or economic interests. Fairs not only needed to become appropriate spaces for female viewers, as Lauren Rabinowitz demonstrates; they also had to emerge as spaces suited to the use of respectable men.[3] Harnessing masculinity and orienting its expression toward furthering the public good (as well as that of the nation and empire) sanitized the early modern institution of fair going. Controlled masculine conduct at fairs created stable boundaries that encircled this type of public expression. So confined, fairgrounds became a predictable slate on which visions of the present and future could be drawn. Once fair organizers as well as the public understood fairs as orderly spaces, "consuming subjects" could safely interact with fair spectacles and perceive the messages delivered by organizers at national expositions.[4]

This chapter explores public efforts to contain masculinity at London fairs during the early modern era. Earlier fairs are one precursor to the national and international exhibitions examined in this book.[5] Early modern fairs themselves evolved from the Middle Ages and were, in early industrial England, becoming more separated from the medieval marketing structures that governed their original charters. By the late seventeenth century, social critics in England already wondered what to make of large gatherings located within regular commercial spaces in London and devoted to frivolity. No longer tied to the Roman Catholic Church, under which most were founded and increasingly targeted as immoral by good Anglicans, London's fairs were reconfigured as their opponents and supporters both looked for ways to shape the events into institutions reflecting their own idealized notions of early-modern urban order. Central to that reconfiguration was renegotiating gender order. Reform-minded Londoners worried that urban fairs had power to corrupt men, making them unproductive and, therefore, unfit citizens and subjects. Mannered men took up the cause to transform fairs into spaces fit for respectable sociability. Examining the contest over early modern fairgrounds reveals that it was only when early modern fairgrounds had been reconceived as polite and productive that world fairs were imaginable as appropriate venues to educate and inspire nations or the world.

This transformation was not smooth. London's early modern officials, social reformers, businessmen and women, and fairgoers all struggled to define urban festivity. Evidence of this struggle is found in court records, pamphlet literature, art, and newspapers—all sources that reveal groups and individuals with divergent interests. For over a century, opposed interests debated the suitability of fairs in the capital city and in the process helped shape these institutions into arenas fit for productive purposes. Polite fairgrounds maintained a festive atmosphere, but under the watchful eye of mannered men who embodied control and policed themselves and others while in pursuit of festivity.

City and county authorities spent a good deal of the late seventeenth through mid-eighteenth centuries proposing legislation they believed would create an orderly and productive city. Their reform efforts reveal shared understandings that urban space best served Londoners when it was used to undertake appropriate commerce. Appropriate, for these men, meant commerce that reflected the sort of polite and controlled masculinity expounded by reform societies and religious discourse. Commercial exchanges were orderly when they occurred in urban spaces dedicated to trade and free of festivities that might divert Londoners from their usual business.[6] Crime encouraged by city "temptations," such as fairs, corrupted servants and apprentices, and authorities thought that fair entertainments not only encouraged social disruptions attending drinking and festivity, but that fairs were also spectacles that distracted men from their occupations, obligations, and proper social place.[7] In the justices' view, festivals lessened the overall commercial and moral strength of London.

An analysis of urban reform efforts targeting fairs reveals that the campaign to regulate festivity was a gendered project. City fathers and social reformers informed by emerging ideas of "polite" masculinity wanted to shape London into a mannered metropolis, but their reform efforts met repeated resistance from fairgoers. Young men who used fairs for leisure or income (both legitimate and illicit) held contrary views regarding urban festivity. Their customary use of fair space as a location for drinking, carousing, profit, and/or sociability did not conform to new ideas about appropriate male urban behavior. Despite regulation, many male and female business owners and peddlers continued to see fairs as commercial venues where they worked despite official regulation. Contrary views of the purpose and suitability of fairs worked against each other, and the campaign to regulate fairs was not easy.

Here, I view the efforts of London authorities and reform-minded individuals to regulate and control London's many fairs in terms of emerging notions of polite masculinity, which often reflected religious belief and theories of urban and social order. London courts, including the Court of Aldermen and Common Council as well as the Middlesex Sessions of the Peace, had focused on curtailing disorder in city fairs since a series of royal decrees issued during the late seventeenth century. Through legislation of fairs, London's aldermen and other city officials hoped to "procure a thorough Reformation of Manners."[8] A reformation of traditional public amusement was no easy task, however. Until the mid-eighteenth century, fairs, illegal play booths, and curious spectacles exhibited in the city seemed only to increase. City officials, social reformers, and critics informed by discourses of religious reform, politeness, and notions of urban order and social control all desired to regulate the duration and frequency of public amusements. In so doing, they hoped also to circumscribe individuals' gender-specific behavior in ways that would have lasting effect on the way that fairs such as these were experienced for some time.

Men and a Mannered Metropolis

Metropolitan efforts to control fairs reflected royal concern with unruly public behavior. In the early 1690s, Queen Mary wrote a letter to the Middlesex justices in which she appealed to parish officers and "all other officers and persons whatsoever, to do their part in their several stations, by timely and impartial informations and prosecutions," to prevent disorderly and ungodly public behavior.[9] In 1692, her husband, King William III, delivered a "Proclamation against Vicious, Debauched and Profane Persons," calling for the regulation and suppression of "blasphemy, profane swearing and cursing, drunkenness, lewdness, breaking the Sabbath and 'other dissolute, immoral or disorderly practice.'"[10] This royal trend of heightened concern that English subjects were far too immoral continued under Queen Anne, who wrote a letter to the Westminster Quarter Sessions in January 1712 encouraging the justices to enforce laws against "irreligion," including those prohibiting "Blasphemy, Prophane swearing and cursing, Prophanation of the Lord's Day, Excessive Drinking, Gaming, Lewdness and all other dissolute immoral and disorderly practices."[11] Beyond royal decrees, two parallel impulses influenced urban reform efforts: politeness and renewed religious zeal. Motivated by crown and religion, reformers turned their critical gaze onto the capital city's fairs. In and around London, a series of fairs operated both legally and without charters; unchartered fairs were dubbed "pretend fairs" by the Middlesex justices. Licensed or not, most city officials thought fairs were disorderly and all became central targets of efforts to order the metropolis.

Much recent scholarship explores emerging polite society in the later Stuart years.[12] This literature views "politeness" as a movement undertaken by middling to elite men and women to become "well-polished," ordered, or accomplished in appropriate skills or personality traits according to one's sex.[13] Efforts to exhibit politeness were influenced by many factors, including the growth of commerce and an infrastructure of shops devoted to fashion and sociability, as well as emerging feelings of nationalism, civic virtue, morality, and religion. Polite ideas stemmed from a growing body of conduct literature aimed at both men and women, although the most recent studies on the subject focus especially on the creation of a specifically masculine and polite identity in the eighteenth century.

Men who conformed to a polite sensibility applied these notions to themselves or to their environments. Fears of urban disorder were voiced by city designers and leading political philosophers. The Earl of Shaftesbury, Bernard Mandeville, and David Hume all shared concerns regarding the disorderly state of the city, especially its streets. These men believed that city streets were "a matter of government, civility and self-control."[14] Physically ordering streets meant cleaning, paving, and lighting them. But creating paved, straight, and aesthetically pleasing streets only altered London's topography—unsavory practices remained. The city could only be made civil if unruly public gatherings such as fairs could be contained.

Urban authorities also believed that fairs upset the city's usual commerce.[15] Popular recreations based around an agricultural calendar did not make sense in an emerging world of wage laborers more oriented on industrial time.[16] City officials struggled to discipline and regulate London's influx of working people, who had left the paternalist rule of their parishes and families behind in the country. Concern about how order would be imposed was particularly acute in a metropolis the size of London, a space in which thousands of people carried out their lives free of "natural" sources of discipline.[17]

Economic trends between 1690 and 1750 contributed to urbanization and also benefited Londoners involved in trade, industry, and commercial agriculture. Prosperous "middling people," who now outnumbered England's traditional landed elite, empowered a rising consumer society.[18] Those who prospered from trade, industry, and the professions made up this new group of neither gentlemen nor traditional laboring people. Such prospering folk were referred to by contemporaries as constituting "the middling sort" or a "middle station."[19] Middling men and women avidly consumed entertainment, services, and a new genre of print culture including novels, newspapers, and periodical journals, through which they developed shared understandings and looked for ideas about self-improvement.[20]

During the late seventeenth century, writers targeted a middling audience with literature focused on themes of self-improvement, economics, religion, and politics.[21] Improvement-minded men might participate in such groups as the Societies for Reformation of Manners. Ideas of such reform groups reflected themes repeated in sermons heard by members and available to a wider audience in print. Improvement-oriented concerns consolidated by this literature contributed to middling readers' conceptions of mannered and acceptable urban behavior. Worried by a growing and unruly metropolis with no institutional means to enforce laws, reform-minded middling men stepped into the role of urban patriarchs in groups such as the Societies for Reformation of Manners. Sermons delivered to gatherings of these would-be polite reformers were printed widely, as were tracts describing the societies' agenda, such as Josiah Woodward's *An Account of the Rise and Progress of the Religious Societies in the City of London* (1698).[22]

Reforming Londoners altered surveillance techniques of "traditional" agricultural-based society to accommodate the urban setting. In smaller towns, neighbors were aware of the actions of neighbors and might intervene if individual behavior crossed legal or moral boundaries. Community policing worked in villages, but early-eighteenth-century London had long grown past manageable enforcement. Though volunteer constables policed city streets to "see the Queen's [or King's] Peace to be well and truly kept," they were overwhelmed by the level of illegal activity in the metropolis.[23] As a remedy, the Societies for Reformation of Manners called for policing by ordinary individuals. If enough men embraced theories of mannered urban behavior, they could assist constables in preventing dangerous behavior. Controlled men could survey the urban landscape and intervene when they witnessed behaviors they recognized as immoral.[24] A sermon delivered by Thomas Bray in 1708 exemplifies this impulse. Bray sees London societies as the only means to curtail "Sins of Uncleanness," such as cursing or sodomy, offenses magistrates should "countenance and encourage" any people to "inform against."[25]

The Challenge of Policing London's Fairs

Members of the London societies understood the capital's fairs as areas that harbored the city's worst moral and religious offenders. The most dangerous fairs included May Fair, held in early May, and Bartholomew Fair, held in late August. Both fairs were under local scrutiny in 1708. In the same year Bray addressed the Societies for Reformation of Manners, London's Aldermen issued an order regulating Bartholomew Fair. Bray's sermon reflects a wider concern about "outrages" committed at Bartholomew and May Fairs against civic and religious law.[26] He presents an optimistic view that city regulation of Bartholomew Fair indicated a triumph against this sort of amusement. However, Bray was premature in proclaiming that the city regulation had successfully "[overthrown . . . and routed] that Seminary of Impiety and Debauchery Annually held in [Bartholomew Fair], *to the undoing* of the Youth, both of Town and Country."[27] Though temporarily curtailed, both Bartholomew Fair and May Fair continued well past 1709 (when Bray's sermon appeared in print). Bray preached about this civic triumph (however temporary) as a reminder to the society of the tangible social benefits of promoting good manners in the city.

Reformers who heard and acted according to this sermon hoped to purge London of social and moral disorder while ensuring stable religious and political order. Bray evokes the image of the once Roman Catholic priory of St. Bartholomew, the grounds of which hosted the yearly impious and debauched "seminary" of Bartholomew Fair. Reform-minded Anglicans, Bray argued, ought to be suspicious of a fair held in these papist surroundings because they hindered the "cause of God against the Powers of Darkness."[28] Though in his speech Bray applauds city officials who regulated fairs for "taking the *Outworks* of Satan's fortified Place among us," he warned that the *"Citadel* it self" was actually the playhouse found both within fairs and without; the place to which Satan's *"Militia* have now a Place to retreat."[29]

Bolstering his militaristic message and conjuring an army full of manly Christian soldiers, Bray called for his parishioners to assault the *"Spiritual Enemies"* of London fairs and their entertainments.[30] With the help of the *"Society for Reformation of Manners,* and their noble Band of *Heroick Informers,"* Christ's "Kingdom" would triumph and these warriors would meet the approval not only of their Church and nation, but also of "so many Kingdoms and States Abroad."[31] Combating the entertainments of fairs and play houses seemed a tangible way for reform-minded Anglican men to maintain the nation's, London's, and their own providence while also ensuring social stability. This process also provided them vital roles in their city's and nation's governance. As actively engaged local informers, urban reformers made themselves essential to the reliable and peaceful functioning of their local community.

Sermons delivered to Societies for Reformation of Manners reinforced middling men's belief that they had a special policing function in their city, while also revealing specific areas and behaviors on which to focus their reform efforts. Reforming the city with godly intent is a trope repeated again and again in these sermons. Though informed primarily by religious belief, these sermons also reflect emerging notions of politeness and proper urban behavior held by their audience. Making a mannered city was one way middling men influenced their urban landscape while in the process portraying themselves as actors in an important political debate.

While some urban reformers attended sermons and walked city streets as "Heroick Informers," other Londoners attempted to curtail city fairs from positions of formal legal authority. When St. Bartholomew Fair's lease was up for renewal in 1708, city officials debated how to modify, or possibly stop, this festival. After the Restoration, the fair grew from its original length of three days to a full fourteen days, and officials hoped at the very least to return it to three. The public debate surrounding attempts to regulate this longstanding fair with origins in the twelfth-century reveals economic and social concerns that motivated efforts to reform fairs. It also demonstrates that those who governed and legislated in London shared the concerns of urban reformers regarding appropriate use of urban space.

Whether or not the lease of Bartholomew Fair should be renewed, and in what manner, was the subject of an anonymous tract, *Reasons for the Limiting of Bartholomew-Fair*, directed at London's Lord Mayor and the Court of Aldermen and Common Council. This pamphlet justified the limiting of Bartholomew Fair for some of the same reasons accentuated by the Societies for the Reformation of Manners—fair space proved too disorderly for a polite city. Echoing the societies' concerns, the *Reasons for the Limiting of Bartholomew-Fair* finds London's order instrumental to England's strength: "The Happiness and Prosperity of the *Great* and *Wealthy* City of *London,* our August *Metropolis,* are so much the Interest and Honour of this whole *Island,* that every Inhabitant thereof is, by *Self-love* as well as *Duty,* bound to promote the Welfare of it, as he is capable."[32]

Promoting London's—and by extension, England's—welfare meant to London's city officials the promotion of "good order and good manners," established only when "honest citizens" assisted magistrates in restoring order to the "visible occasions of Disorder and Misdemeanor" in such places as Bartholomew Fair. The pamphlet's author labeled the fair a "meer *Carnival,* a season of the utmost *Disorder* and *Debauchery* by reason of the *Booths* for Drinking, Musick, Gaming, Raffling, and what not."[33] By referring to the fair as being merely a carnival, the author pointed out a foundational problem with the event. The fair, originally established as a marketing opportunity, now revolved around entertainment.

As this tract debating the regulation of Bartholomew Fair circulated, a similar pamphlet launched an attack against May Fair, which also notoriously withstood regulation attempts. The author of this 1709 tract, *Reasons for Suppressing the Yearly Fair in Brook-Field, Westminster; Commonly Called May-Fair,* depicts the fair as breeding disorder and calls it "a pregnant Nursery of *Treason* and *Rebellion.*" In 1702, fairgoers violently attacked the special force of constables sent to preserve order at the fair and its surrounding areas, demonstrating how helpless London's constables could be against large crowds. This force could do little against a riot of "30 Persons with drawn Swords," and the "Mob" wielding "Stones and Dirt." One constable, John Cooper, was killed in the affray and eight other people were injured.[34] During a later attempt to quell the fair, a constable was, "drag'd thro' a Horse-Pond" while policing the fair. Other constables had even been pursued, "to the very Doors of the neighboring *Justices* of the Peace; and the *Justices* themselves have not been able to protect them, by reason of the *Numbers* and *Insolence* of the riotous Mob."[35] Clearly, Middlesex policing efforts represented a drop in the bucket of what would have been required to effectively suppress this popular yearly festival. Rowdy fairgoers, it seemed, turned the tables of authority on constables, whom they chased out of the fair, instead of the reverse. Scenarios such as these deeply troubled authorities. By failing to restore order at May Fair, the anonymous writer argued, government itself, both local and national, was made to seem like a *"May-Game."*[36]

According to critics, May Fair was troubling because it sheltered unruly masculinity. Literally protected within this "nursery," the author believes young men found sustenance for socially destructive behavior. The author draws insightful conclusions about causes behind the complicated regulation of this fair and lists several explanations for why the fair had become so dangerously disruptive. The underlying difficulty was not only that fairgoers were young and male but also that the fair was the first festival of the spring and summer fair season. Young men were encouraged to "licentiousness" by the time of the year—early May. A mixture of seasonal feelings and festivity was so potent that the pamphlet's author describes how even innocent youth might spot the fair and decide to walk through it for "curiosity." Young Londoners lacking fully formed notions of godly and productive behavior could then "fall in" with the fair and into the downward spiraling *"Circle* of Temptation."[37] Once young people, primarily men, succumbed to the initial lure of the fair, they faced ruin at the endless variety of fair entertainments. Worst, the author proclaims, were gaming booths, which drew in and "decoy'd" apprentices and other young people and then cheated them out of their money. As a means to repair their fortunes, these financially ruined victims would have to go "home to the *Cash* of their *Parents* and *Masters*."[38]

Throughout the tract, the author avoids laying all blame with festive young men and instead looks for a way to counter disorderly masculinity with polite male behavior. Certainly, the author argues that there would always be "vain and wicked Persons [who] will not fail to partake of [fair entertainment], tho' they beggar themselves, starve their Families, and ruine their Souls thereby."[39] Young men will be young men, and what they required were godly and mannered older men to steer them away from this temptation. Wiser men comprehended the ill effects of fairs on all sorts of young people, from novice apprentices to the "meaner sort" of people, whom authorities did not expect to behave reasonably. This pamphleteer calls upon local residents of, "true *Honour* and *Virtue*," asking them to assist in the fair's suppression.[40] With the help of local notables, the author of this pamphlet believed the fair might be finally contained. This is similar to conclusions drawn in the tract on Bartholomew Fair and by members of London's Societies for the Reformation of Manners. Without a viable police force, there was no other solution but to rely on traditional notions of order—

respected authorities with understandings of their own self-control and governed by religious principles would shepherd Londoners they believed lacked both. Central to this order was deploying men who embodied civility and controlled behavior as moral models for London's youth.

Concerns about the dangerous potential of unrestrained masculinity prompted London's Court of Aldermen and Common Council as well as the Middlesex county authorities (one of the counties bordering London) to debate possible regulation of London's fairs for nearly twenty years prior to this tract. Court records reveal urban authorities' concerns that fair booths were places "to which the Worst and Lewdest of both Sexes resort." They also believed that fairs were sites of "frequent Bloodsheds, Tumults and Disorders [that] daily happen to the terror of the Inhabitants and others," and that at fairs, "the Apprentices, Servants and Youth of and about this City are debauched."[41] Their orders reveal officials' fears that apprentices, servants, soldiers, and other young men were an ominous and unpredictable force if authorities failed to contain them. Such men threatened the security of all Londoners if their celebrations outgrew the spatial and temporal boundaries of fairs. Drunken revelers, seduced by the temptations of gaming and women (such as ropedancers or actresses), threatened the peace and safety of more controlled fairgoers as well as the neighborhoods surrounding fairs. Worse for authorities, unruly groups of men might become susceptible to political movements, such as Jacobitism, which threatened the peace and security of the nation.[42]

Polite Patriarchs vs. "Evil Disposed Persons"

One incident demonstrates directly how fairgrounds could become arenas in which new ideas of polite masculinity conflicted with alternative practices. Joseph Underwood, the Duke of Montrose's cook, met the potential terror of fairs face to face one evening at Bartholomew Fair. There to serve as an escort to his sister and her female friends, he had graciously stopped to help one of the women cross a ditch when he was torn from his party, shoved into the crowd, and violently assaulted. In the affray, he was robbed of his walking stick, watch, and wig.[43] This man's manners and comportment meant nothing to rowdy and seemingly fearless criminals in Bartholomew Fair. If anything, these men took advantage of Underwood's manners—assaulting him just at the moment when his actions made him most vulnerable. While he protected a female companion from harm across a dirty and uneven street, he failed to protect himself. This incident exemplifies that in the everyday practice of fairs, manners mattered very little. Though men like Underwood may have hoped to use fair space to showcase their finery or manners, many more men, such as William Brister, James Page, Theophilus Watson, and others (such as those indicted for assaulting and robbing him) recognized fairs as a hunting ground for polite, easy prey.

While London's aldermen and lord mayor debated their options for limiting Bartholomew Fair, the magistrates in the county of Middlesex launched their own campaign against disorderly public amusements. They, too, believed they combated "vice" in their repeated attempts at regulation, although what they faced was a much more difficult situation. Throughout the early eighteenth century, Middlesex officials confronted the problem of unlicensed play booths and playhouses, as well as many unchartered and illegal "pretend fairs" sprouting up in diverse locations throughout growing suburbs. These spontaneous occasions were much more difficult to contain and had the potential to become more dangerous and disorderly than licensed fairs. Records of magistrates' attempts to regulate these fairs note more frequent and severe disturbances than the London city records or the existing court rolls from Bartholomew Fair's Pie Powder Court reveal.[44]

Pretend fairs became customary festivals not because an authority established them for a given purpose but because common people took it upon themselves to establish them. These informal traditions threatened the root of order in London, and county officials viewed them as sites of potential social disturbance. Gaming, theatrical shows, music, and festivity all encouraged drinking, which, in turn, promoted unruly or uninhibited actions. Coupled with this was the fact that festive places might become gathering spaces for young and potentially disruptive men not engaged in any sort of commerce or trade.

At the crux of this regulation campaign were competing notions of commerce and different understandings of public safety. Some Londoners profited from running booths featuring music, theater, gaming or drinking, but others were assaulted or robbed at these gatherings. One notorious pretend fair was held at Tottenham Court, which continued year after year regardless of attempts by Middlesex authorities' to regulate it. An order made in July 1718 is typical of their approach, which usually entailed prohibiting the festival while concurrently informing Londoners of why this festival was dangerous: they argued that it encouraged "vice" and "immorality," that people were often defrauded of their money there and that such fairs led to "the debauching and ruining of Servants and Apprentices."[45] Orders against the fair had little effect, and in 1724 the Middlesex magistrates undertook their most decisive action against this festival, ordering the high constable of Holborn to assemble with his petty constables at Tottenham Court. So assembled, this force was to apprehend illegal exhibitors. If this raid was successful, it was only temporary. The "evil disposed persons" returned year after year, continuing the informal tradition of this unruly public assembly.[46] Gathering a force to police county orders was logistically difficult, particularly because in order to suppress a fair of this size, large numbers of men (who would not, themselves, join in the festivity) would be required to police the area continually for the duration of the festival. Not only was such a force difficult to gather with consistency, but once raised, it also drained constables from surrounding areas, thereby threatening order there.

Though the Middlesex orders were printed in newspapers and posted throughout town, these spontaneous festivals continued and spread. One of the most disorderly fairs in Middlesex was Welch Fair, held in the Parish of St. James, Clerkenwell. It reached the height of its unruliness in 1744, when one of the few people to be indicted at a fair and have his case recorded in the sessions' books was apprehended. William Griffiths "unlawfully maliciously and contemptuously utter[ed] and [spoke] of and concerning John Elliott . . . one of his Majesty's Justices of the Peace . . . (being in the Execution of his office for Preservation of the King's Peace and to Suppress any unlawful assembly of loose, idle and disorderly Persons [at] Welch Fair)." Griffiths was convicted for challenging this man's authority as well as his masculinity. Reportedly, he called the justice of the peace a "scoundrel" and told him, "I am a better man than you . . . you may kiss my Arse." He was also indicted, but not convicted, of assaulting and beating Francis Hole, another Justice of the Peace.[47] Griffith's blatant contempt for local authority had significance beyond his insults and physical attacks. His disregard for urban authority and disorderly masculinity represented the wider threat these illegal festivals posed to the foundations of metropolitan order. The continued presence of such fairs for a significant amount of the year illustrates local officials' loss of control over policing urban space.

Officials usually argued that the force behind unchartered fairs were primarily young men seeking to amuse themselves or avoid labor. This was not always the case. Businessmen and women whose enterprises prospered from the fairs also resisted urban authorities' regulatory efforts. In 1735, for example, a group of London citizens and inhabitants of West Smithfield petitioned the aldermen who were in the process of considering their legal rights to regulate Bartholomew and Southwark Fairs. These inhabitants asked the court to continue Bartholomew Fair for fourteen days. Their petition was denied, but it is clear that continuing this fair for longer than three days benefited many Londoners, particularly those who profited by living near the center of fairs or who had property let during the fairs tenure.[48]

The struggle to regulate London's fairs reveals a contest between the authority of local government and traditional elite male authority. Urban authorities seemed most frustrated by elite defiance of their orders to curtail fairs. Bartholomew Fair, for example, continued to be held at least in part because the heirs to Richard Rich (by the early eighteenth century, the Lord Kensington) held a portion of the rights to the fair. When in 1761 the city lands committee investigated closing this fair, the city attorney advised them against it, because the current Lord Kensington, William Edwards (an absentee landlord residing in Wales), refused to sell his rights to the fair.[49] London's Aldermen viewed this with suspicion and thought it revealed Edwards's contempt of civic officials because he derived only a small profit from continuing the fair.[50] Legally, London's officials were powerless to prevent Edwards from continuing Bartholomew Fair.

Middlesex justices faced their own struggle with elite landowners who lived near May Fair. County officials blamed the elite men who lived with their families in the new and prestigious housing developments around May Fair (an area known collectively by that name). They believed the "Gentlemen and others in Office and Authority within the City of Westminster" who lived near where May Fair was kept should have been obliged "to act with the utmost Vigour" to regulate the disorderly fair. The justices believed that influential and elite men had a duty to promote social order by encouraging Londoners in proper comportment, but their notion was confounded by elite behavior. While the May Fair gentlemen apparently ignored the fair, absolved themselves of the responsibility to curtail it, or were elsewhere during its tenure, voluntary constables and magistrates assumed the role of the area's patriarchs.

Fig 11.1. View of Southwark Fair, William Hogarth. City of London, London Metropolitan Archives.

As London fairs continued, social critics and local officials blamed them in part for a gender order gone awry. At both popular and elite levels, fairs destabilized masculine authority in London and tempted men from various backgrounds and ages to neglect their proper sphere. Distracted from their labor or responsibility, wayward men allowed London to fall into disorder and disrepair. This was best represented in a famous painting by William Hogarth, *Southwark Fair*. Completed in 1733, this painting depicts similar concerns about urban amusement repeated in common critiques of fairs. In his picture, Hogarth represents the fear that fairs threatened London if they spilled out of their physical and temporal confines, just like the Greek army's spilling out of the Trojan horse depicted on the centrally located advertisement for Lee and Harper's "Siege of Troy." Art historians often refer to the theme of a "fall" or "descent from good fortune to calamity" in this painting.[51] Not only is Troy about to fall, but this theme is reinforced again to the right of that poster, where an advertisement for a puppet show depicts the fall of Adam and Eve. Under the original Biblical father and mother who strayed is an image of Punch pushing Judy toward the jaws of Hell.[52] This is echoed on a lantern advertisement for *The Fall of Bajazet*, located metaphorically just below a collapsing platform of theater players. The ill effects of unruly male behavior are repeatedly represented across the picture, from a "procurer . . . enticing a pair of country girls to their ruin" to a farmer losing money in a game of dice.[53] Hogarth's portrait of Southwark Fair underscored the general fear that fairs threatened to swallow up rational commerce, overtake the urban environment, and lead to the destruction of London (and, by extension, the nation) if not properly contained.[54] All of this was done under the authority of men who succumbed to the temptations of fairs, endangering fairgoers and the wider residents of London.

City and county attacks on fairs continued for decades and were finally successful in some cases by the middle of the eighteenth century. Middlesex authorities continued to battle both May Fair and the county's "pretend fairs" through the early 1760s. After repeated attempts to suppress the chartered May Fair, it was finally abolished in 1764. In the city of London's jurisdiction, Southwark Fair was abolished in 1762 and Bartholomew Fair continued until 1854. Small area fairs continued sporadically until the mid-nineteenth century, but after the mid-eighteenth century, these festivals were frequented by fewer people. This relates to the emergence of class-specific amusements that featured some of the same offerings of fairs—music, dancing, and sociability. For example, pleasure gardens—another summertime amusement held at night and often during the day—emerged in a variety of contexts. Some, such as Vauxhall or Ranelagh, catered to "polite" audiences who enjoyed features such as controlled garden paths, classical music, and promenading, but other gardens, such as Cuper's Gardens or Baginnine Wells, catered to working people. Even the most polite gardens retained many popular and legendary features of fairs—dark walks in which one might encounter "rakes" or prostitutes as well as mechanical pictures, spectacular entertainment, and popular songs.[55]

William Adams, whose story opened this chapter, experienced first hand the cultural debate regarding changing urban conditions from the seventeenth to eighteenth centuries in London. Two conflicting perspectives of what was productive masculinity undermined his apprenticeship. To Adams's parents, driving a dog-drawn cart at fairs seemed a ludicrous and useless skill for a future carpenter to learn. They expected their son to receive training that would make him into a respectable working man. These parents believed that providing amusement at fairs, even for a profit, did not qualify as proper training for a young man, and city and county magistrates agreed. Adams's fraudulent master worked from a different understanding of the great profit to be made in providing entertainment to the city's children and anyone else with a few pence to spare for amusement. Customary urban entertainment was changing, reflected by revelers' concerted resistance to orders against their play. Young men expected amusement to be part of their lives, and people of all classes sought more opportunities for leisure. Those who participated in informal opportunities for urban amusement did not care that it required charters or licenses (evidenced by the numerous "pretend fairs" emerging during this time). Through their vigorous participation in urban amusement, Londoners helped create a new type of festivity. By the middle of the eighteenth century, authorities gradually relented, or at least realized the profitability of these occasions when they began issuing licenses approving a new type of outdoor urban entertainment at London's many pleasure gardens and outdoor tea rooms. From these new entertainments directed both at middle- and lower-class Londoners emerged a new form of polite urban amusement. This new amusement combined elements of the old fairs with new understandings of commercially confined—and often polite—urban play.

Anxiety over unstable masculinity at London's early modern fairs stemmed from urban officials' concerns that unregulated festivity could undermine order throughout the capital city. Efforts to curtail public festivity were met with resistance, and when consumers refused to abandon the customs they expected to enjoy on a seasonal basis, entrepreneurs stepped up and created confined, predictable, and polite venues to meet the demand. Laws were changed to license these new entertainments, and fair festivity was molded into a more manageable urban expression. Contained by notions of civility and legality defined by an emerging cohort of middle-class men, fairgrounds survived the early modern era. The remnants of early modern fairs disappeared with the curtailment of Bartholomew

Fair in 1854—not coincidentally just two years after industrious masculinity had been encased in London for the world to see at the Great Exhibition.

At national and world exhibitions, mannered fairs emerged with boundaries solid enough to contain and celebrate the artifacts of masculine civility while also maintaining elements of the "show" in safely controlled exhibits intended to reinforce national values by instructing viewers in what existed just beyond those bounds. Only when exposition organizers believed fairgoers embodied a stable and appropriately gendered national hierarchy could they place midways safely within that symbolic space.[56] Organizers could comfortably feature national or social "outsiders" in nineteenth- and twentieth-century midways to instruct or merely entertain because they no longer feared, as their early modern predecessors did, that these spectacles could tempt viewers to abandon a productive or accepted way of life. Shaping fair going into an orderly pursuit overseen by mannered, masculine consumers was essential to the creation of modern national expositions.

NOTES

1 Middlesex and Westminster Sessions of the Peace, No. 903, 56–57, August, 1732. London Metropolitan Archives, MJ/SB/B/89.

2 Robert Rydell, *A World of Fairs: The Century-of-Progress Expositions* (Chicago: The University of Chicago Press, 1993), 22.

3 Lauren Rabinowitz, *For the Love of Pleasure: Women, Movies and Culture in Turn-of-the-Century Chicago* (New Brunswick, N.J.: Rutgers University Press, 1998).

4 Thomas Richards, *The Commodity Culture of Victorian England: Advertising and Spectacle, 1851–1914* (Stanford, Calif.: Stanford University Press, 1990), 64–5.

5 Jeffery Auerbach discusses how early modern fairs contributed to the idea of national industrial exhibitions in *The Great Exhibition of 1851* (New Haven, Conn.: Yale University Press, 1999), 13. See also Jeffery Auerbach and Peter Hoffenberg, eds., *Britain, the Empire, and the World at the Great Exhibition of 1851* (Hampshire, UK: Ashgate, 2008).

6 Emerging "polite" commerce is explored in David Alexander, *Retailing in England During the Industrial Revolution* (London: Athlone, 1970); Neil McKendrick, John Brewer and J. H. Plumb, *The Birth of Consumer Society: The Commercialization of Eighteenth-Century England* (London: Europa, 1982); and Paul Langford, *A Polite and Commercial People: England 1727–1783* (Oxford: Clarendon, 1989). See also Peter Earle, *A City Full of People: Men and Women of London, 1650–1750* (London: Methuen, 1994).

7 James Beattie, *Policing and Punishment in London, 1660–1750* (Oxford: University Press, 2001), 55–57.

8 Repertory of the Court of Aldermen (hereafter as Rep.), 98, 303 (1693–1694). Corporation of London Records Office.

9 Robert Shoemaker, "Reforming the City: The Reformation of Manners Campaign in London, 1690–1738," in *Stilling the Grumbling Hive: The Response to Social and Economic Problems in England, 1689–1750*, ed. Lee Davison, Tim Hitchcock, et al., 101 (New York: St. Martin's, 1992).

10 Ibid., 103.

11 Middlesex Sessions, No. 700, 21, January 1711–12, MJ/SB/B/069.

12 This literature includes Lawrence Klein, *Shaftesbury and the Culture of Politeness: Moral Discourse and Cultural Politics in Early Eighteenth-Century England* (Cambridge: Cam-

bridge University Press, 1994); Paul Langford, *A Polite and Commercial People: England 1727–1783* (Oxford: Clarendon, 1989); J. G. A. Pocock, *Virtue, Commerce and History* (Cambridge: Cambridge University Press, 1985); and Elizabeth A. Foyster, *Manhood in Early Modern England: Honour, Sex, and Marriage* (London: Longman, 1999).

13 Philip Carter, *Men and the Emergence of Polite Society, Britain, 1660–1800* (Harlow, Essex: Pearson Education, 2001), 35.

14 Miles Ogborn, *Spaces of Modernity: London's Geographies, 1680–1780* (New York: Guilford, 1998), 78–9.

15 These concerns are featured in *Reasons for Suppressing the Yearly Fair in Brook-Field, Westminster; Commonly Called May-Fair* (London, 1709), British Library and *Reasons Formerly Published for the Punctual Limiting of Bartholomew Fair* (London, 1711), British Library.

16 Robert W. Malcomson, *Popular Recreations in English Society, 1700–1850* (Cambridge: Cambridge University Press, 1973), 89.

17 Ibid., 160–61. See also Susan Dwyer Amussen, *An Ordered Society: Gender and Class in Early Modern England* (New York: Columbia University Press, 1988).

18 Davison, Hitchcock, et al., xxvi–xxvii.

19 Peter Earle, *The Making of the English Middle Class, Business, Society and Family Life in London, 1660–1730* (Berkeley: University of California Press, 1989). Margaret R. Hunt, *The Middling Sort: Commerce, Gender and the Family in England, 1680–1780* (Berkeley: University of California Press, 1996).

20 Earle, 10.

21 Ibid., 10–11.

22 Josiah Woodward, *An Account of the Rise and Progress of the Religious Societies in the City of London, & etc., and of the Endeavours for Reformation of Manners Which Have Been Made Therein* (London, 1698). Huntington Library Rare Books, San Marino, Calif.

23 *The Compleat Constable* (London: Thomas Bever, 1710), 10.

24 Julia Hoppit, *A Land of Liberty? England, 1689–1727* (Oxford: Clarendon, 2000) 237–39.

25 Thomas Bray, *For God, or for Satan: Being a Sermon Preach'd at St. Mary le Bow, Before the Societies for Reformation of Manners, December 27, 1708* (London, 1709), 10–11. Huntington Library Rare Books, San Marino, Calif.

26 Ibid., 11.

27 Ibid., 11–12.

28 Ibid.

29 Ibid., 12.

30 Ibid.

31 Ibid., 13.

32 *Reasons Formerly Published for the Punctual Limiting of Bartholomew-Fair* (London, 1711), 3.

33 Ibid., 9.

34 *Reasons for Suppressing the Yearly Fair in Brook-Field, Westminster; Commonly Called May-Fair* (London, 1709), 12–13.

35 Ibid.

36 Ibid., 13.

37 Ibid., 8–9.

38 Ibid., 7–8.

39 Ibid., 10.

40 Ibid., 31–32.

41 Rep. 98, f. 410.

42 Jacobites supported the Stuart over the Hanoverian claim to the throne. See: Evelyn Cruickshanks and Howard Erskine-Hill, *The Atterbury Plot* (New York: Palgrave Macmillan, 2004); Evelyn Lord, *The Stuarts' Secret Army: English Jacobites, 1689–1752* (New York: Pearson Longman, 2004).

43 The Proceedings of the Old Bailey (OBP), December 5, 1744. Ref: T17441205-34.

44 Pie Powder Court Rolls, HB.C6, Highclere Castle Archive.

45 This earlier order is mentioned and reissued in the Middlesex Sessions, Orders of Court, August 1724, MJ/o/oo1.

46 Ibid.

47 Middlesex Sessions, Orders of Court, January, 1744, MJ/o/C/oo4.

48 Rep 139. Petitioners against the limitation of Bartholomew Fair also appeared in court in 1744 (Rep 148, f385).

49 Journal of the City Lands Committee, August 19, 1761, vol. 53, 162.

50 Ibid.

51 E. D. H. Johnson, *Paintings of the British Social Scene from Hogarth to Sickert* (London: Weidenfeld and Nicolson, 1986), 26.

52 Ibid.

53 Ibid., 26–27.

54 Christina Kiaer, "Professional Femininity in Hogarth's *Strolling Actresses Dressing in a Barn*," in *The Other Hogarth, Aesthetics of Difference,* Bernadette Fort and Angela Rosenthal, eds. (Princeton, N.J.: Princeton University Press, 2001).

55 See Warwick Wroth, *The London Pleasure Gardens of the Eighteenth Century* (London: Macmillian, 1896/Hamden, Conn.: Archon, 1979).

56 The cultural use and significance of midways is discussed by Robert Rydell, *Visions of Empire at American International Expositions, 1876–1916* (Chicago: University of Chicago Press, 1987); James Gilbert, *Perfect Cities: Chicago Utopias of 1893* (Chicago: University of Chicago Press, 1991); Gail Bederman, *Manliness and Civilization: A Cultural History of Gender and Race in the United States 1880–1917* (Chicago: University of Chicago Press, 1995); and Barbara J. Ballard, "African-American Protest and the Role of the Haitian Pavilion at the 1893 Chicago World's Fair," in *Multiculturalism: Roots and Realities,* ed. C. James Trotman (Bloomington: Indiana University Press, 2002).

SUGGESTIONS FOR FURTHER READING

Andrews, William D. "Women and the Fairs of 1876 and 1893." *Hayes Historical Journal* 1 (1977): 173–83.

Banta, Martha. *Imaging American Women: Ideas and Ideals in Cultural History.* New York: Columbia University Press, 1989.

Barth-Scalmani, Gunda, and Margret Friedrich. "Frauen auf der Wiener Weltausstellung von 1873: Blick auf die Bühne und hinter die Kulissen" [Women at the Vienna World Exhibition of 1873: View of the Stage and behind the Scenes]. In *Bürgerliche Frauenkultur im 19. Jahrhundert,* edited by Brigitte Mazohl-Wallnig, 175–232. Vienna: Böhlau, 1995.

Beckett, Jane. "Engendering the Spaces of Modernity: The Women's Exhibition, Amsterdam 1913." In *Women Artists and the Decorative Arts 1880–1935,* edited by Bridget Elliott and Janice Helland, 155–69. Surrey: Ashgate, 2002.

Bederman, Gail. *Manliness and Civilization: A Cultural History of Gender and Race in the United States, 1880–1917.* Chicago: University of Chicago Press, 1995.

Bergland, Barbara. *Making San Francisco American: Cultural Frontiers in the Urban West, 1846–1906.* Lawrence: University of Kansas Press, 2006.

Blair, Karen J. "The Limits of Sisterhood: The Woman's Building in Seattle, 1908–1921." *Frontiers: A Journal of Women Studies* 8, no. 1 (1984): 45–52.

Blanchard, Mary W. "Queen of a Europeanized World." In *Een Vaderland voor Vrouwen* [A Fatherland for Women], edited by Maria Grever and Fia Dieteren, 30–46. Amsterdam: Stiftung beheer IISG, 2000.

Bland, Sidney. "Women and World's Fairs: The Charleston Story." *South Carolina Historical Magazine* 94, no. 3 (1993): 166–84.

Boisseau, TJ. "Once Again in Chicago: Revisioning Women as Workers at the Chicago Woman's World's Fairs of 1925–1928." *Women's History Review* 18, no. 2 (2009): 58–72.

———. "Where Every Woman May Be a Queen: Gender, Politics, and Visual Space at the Chicago World's Fair, 1893." In *Space in America: Theory, History, Culture,* edited by Klaus Benesch and Kerstin Schmidt, 285–309. Amsterdam: Rodopi Press, 2004.

———. "White Queens at the Chicago's World Fair, 1893: New Womanhood in the Service of Class, Race, and Nation." *Gender and History* 12, no. 1 (2000): 33–81.

Bokovoy, Matthew F. *The San Diego World's Fairs and Southwestern Memory, 1880–1940.* Albuquerque: University of New Mexico Press, 2005.

Brown, Candy Gunther. "Publicizing Domestic Piety: The Cultural Work of Religious Texts in the Woman's Building Library." *Libraries and Culture* 41, no.1 (2006): 35–54.

Brown, Julie. *Contesting Images: Photography and the World's Columbian Exposition.* Tucson: University of Arizona Press, 1994.

Burton, Shirley J. "Obscene, Lewd, and Lascivious: Ida Craddock and the Criminally Obscene Women of Chicago, 1873–1913." *Michigan Historical Review* 19, no. 1 (1993): 1–16.

Canfield, Amy Taipale. "Discovering Woman: Women's Performances at the World's Columbian Exposition Chicago, 1893." PhD diss., Ohio State University, 2002.

Carby, Hazel. *Reconstructing Womanhood: The Emergence of the African American Woman Novelist.* New York: Oxford University Press, 1987.

Carr, Carolyn Kinder, and Sally Webster. "Mary Cassatt and Mary Fairchild MacMonnies: The Search for their 1893 Murals." *American Art* 8, no. 1 (1994): 52–69.

Çelik, Zeynep, and Leila Kinney. "Ethnography and Exhibitionism at the *Exposition Universelles.*" *Assemblage* 13 (1990): 34–59.

Coombs, Annie. *Reinventing Africa.* New Haven, Conn: Yale University Press, 1994.

Cordato, Mary Francis. "Representing the Expansion of Woman's Sphere: Women's Work and Culture at the World's Fairs of 1876, 1893 and 1904." PhD diss., New York University, 1989.

———. "Towards a New Century: Women and the Philadelphia Centennial Exhibition, 1876." *Pennsylvania Magazine of History and Biography* 107, no. 1 (1983): 113–36.

Cressman, Jodi. "Helen Keller and the Mind's Eyewitness." *Western Humanities Review* 54, no. 2 (2000): 108–23.

Dabakis, Melissa. "The Spectacle of Labor: The World's Columbian Exposition of 1893." In *Visualizing Labor in American Sculpture: Monuments, Manliness, and the Work Ethic, 1880–1935,* 62–82. Cambridge: Cambridge University Press, 1999.

Darney, Virginia Grant. "Women and World's Fairs: American International Expositions, 1876–1904." PhD diss., Emory University, 1982.

Derby, Lauren. "The Dictator's Seduction: Gender and State Spectacle during the Trujillo Regime." *Callaloo (Dominican Republic Literature and Culture)* 23, no. 3 (2000): 1112–46.

Downey, Dennis B. *A Season of Renewal: The Columbian Exposition and Victorian America.* Westport, Conn.: Praeger, 2002.

Falke, Wayne. "Samantha at the Centennial." *Hayes Historical Journal* 1 (1977): 165–71.

Feldman, Ann E. "Being Heard: Women Composers and Patrons at the 1893 World's Columbian Exposition." *Notes* [Music Library Association] 47 (1990): 7–20.

Ferry, Emma. "'A Novelty among Exhibitions': The Loan Exhibition of Women's Industries, Bristol 1885." In *Women and the Making of Built Space in England, 1870–1950,* edited by Elizabeth Darling and Lesley Whitworth. Surrey: Ashgate, 2007.

Floré, Fredie, and Mil de Kooning. "The Representation of Modern Domesticity in the Belgian Sector of the Brussels' World's Fair of 1958." *Journal of Design History* 16, no. 4 (2003): 319–40.

Ganz, Cheryl. *The 1933 Chicago World's Fair: A Century of Progress.* Urbana: University of Illinois Press, 2008.

Garfinkle, Charlene G. "Lucia Fairchild Fuller's 'Lost' Woman's Building Mural." *American Art* 7, no. 1 (1993): 2–7.

Gautier, Amina. "African American Women's Writings in the Woman's Building Library." *Libraries and Culture* 41, no. 1 (2006): 55–81.

Giddings, Paula. *When and Where I Enter: The Impact of Black Women on Race and Sex in America.* New York: William Morrow, 1984.

Golomb, Deborah Grand. "The 1893 Congress of Jewish Women: Evolution or Revolution in American Jewish Women's History?" *American Jewish History* 70, no. 1 (1980): 52–67.

Grabenhorst-Randall, Terree. "The Woman's Building." *Heresies* 1 (1978): 44–46.

Greenhalgh, Paul. *Ephemeral Vistas: The Expositions Universelles, Great Exhibitions and World's Fairs, 1851–1939.* Manchester: Manchester University Press, 1988. (See esp. 174–97.)

Grever, Maria. *Een Vaderland voor Vrouwen* [A Fatherland for Women]. Amsterdam: Stichting beheer IISG/VVG, 2000.

Grever, Maria, and Berteke Waaldijk. *Transforming the Public Sphere: The Dutch National Exhibition of Women's Labor in 1898.* Durham, N.C.: Duke University Press, 2004.

Groot, Marjan. *Vrouwen in de vormgeving 1880–1940* [Women in Design in the Netherlands]. Rotterdam: 010 Publishers, 2007.

Gullett, Gayle. "'Our Great Opportunity': Organized Women Advance Women's Work at the World's Columbian Exposition of 1893." *Illinois Historical Journal* 87, no. 4 (1994): 259–76.

Harvey, Bruce G. "World's Fairs in a Southern Accent: Atlanta, Nashville, Charleston, 1895–1902." PhD diss., Vanderbilt University, 1998.

Heaman, Elsbeth Anne. "Taking the World by Show: Canadian Women as Exhibitors to 1900." *Canadian Historical Review* 78, no. 4 (1997): 599–631.

Hoffenberg, Peter H. *An Empire on Display: English, Indian and Australian Exhibitions from the Crystal Palace to the Great War.* Berkeley: University of California Press, 2001.

Hunt, Sylvia. "Throw Aside the Veil of Helplessness: A Southern Feminist at the 1893 World's Fair." *Southwestern Historical Quarterly* 100, no. 1 (1996): 48–62.

Hutton, John. "Picking Fruit: Mary Cassatt's Modern Woman and the Woman's Building of 1893." *Feminist Studies* 20, no. 2 (1994): 318–48.

Iskin, Ruth E. "The Chic Parisienne: A National Brand of French Fashion and Femininity." In *Modern Women and Parisian Consumer Culture in Impressionist Painting*, 184–224. Cambridge: Cambridge University Press, 2007.

Jamieson, Duncan R. "Women's Rights at the World's Fair, 1893." *Illinois Quarterly* 37 (1974): 5–20.

Kennedy, Charles A. "When Cairo Met Main Street: Little Egypt, Salome Dancers, and the World's Fairs of 1893 and 1904." In *Music and Culture in America, 1861–1918*, edited by Michael Saffle, 271–298. New York: Garland Publishing, 1998.

Kinchin, Perilla, and Juliet Kinchin. *Glasgow's Great Exhibitions.* Oxon, UK: White Cockade Publishing, 1988.

Kline, Wendy. "Motherhood, Morality and the 'Moron.'" In *Building a Better Race: Gender, Sexuality and Eugenics from the Turn of the Century to the Baby Boom*, 7–31. Berkeley: University of California Press, 2001.

Kubiak, Szymon Piotr. "*Architektura i płeć. 'Pawilon Pracy Kobiet' na Powszechnej Wystawie Krajowej w 1929 roku*" [Architecture and Sex: "Pavilion of Women's Work" at the Universal Exhibition in 1929, the "National"]. *Uni Gender* 1/2007 (3), available online at http://www.unigender.org/?page=biezacy&issue=02&article=04.

Maass, John. *The Glorious Enterprise.* Watkins Glen, N.Y.: American Life Foundation, 1973.

MacDonald, Anne L. "Celebrating Women's Ingenuity: Expositions, Fairs, and Patent Office Lists." In *Feminine Ingenuity: Women and Invention in America*, 71–102. New York: Ballantine Books, 1992.

———. "Centennial Sisterhood." In *Feminine Ingenuity: Women and Invention in America*, 167–90. New York: Ballantine Books, 1992.

Madsen, Carol Cornwall. "'The Power of Combination': Emmeline B. Wells and the National and International Councils of Women." *Brigham Young University Studies* 33, no. 4 (1993): 646–73.

Markwyn, Abigail. "Constructing 'An Epitome of Civilization': Local Politics and Visions of Progressive-Era America at San Francisco's Panama-Pacific International Exposition." PhD diss., University of Wisconsin-Madison, 2006.

Massa, Ann. "Black Women in the 'White City.'" *Journal of American Studies* 8 (1974), 319–37.

McElya, Micki. *Clinging to Mammy: The Faithful Slave in Twentieth-Century America*. Cambridge, Mass.: Harvard University Press, 2007.

McQuaid, Matilda, ed. *Lilly Reich, Designer and Architect*. New York: Museum of Modern Art, 1996.

Meyer, Esther da Costa. "Cruel Metonymies: Lilly Reich's Designs for the 1937 World's Fair." *New German Critique* 76 (1999): 161–89.

Miller, Kristie. "Of the Women, For the Women, and By the Women." *Chicago History* 24, no. 2 (1995): 58–72.

Muccigrosso, Robert. *Celebrating the New World: Chicago's Columbian Exposition of 1893*. Chicago: Ivan R. Dee, 1993.

Nathan, Marvin. "Visiting the World's Columbian Exposition at Chicago in July 1893: A Personal View." *Journal of American Culture* 19, no. 2 (1996): 79–102.

Nichols, K. L. "Women's Art at the World's Columbian Exposition, 1893," available online at http://members.cox.net/academia/cassattxx.html (accessed January 24, 2010).

Oldenziel, Ruth. *Making Technology Masculine*. Chicago: University of Chicago Press, 1999.

Owen, Nancy E. "Americanism and the Culture of Crisis." In *Rookwood and the Industry of Art: Women, Culture, and Commerce, 1880–1913*. Athens: The Ohio University Press, 2001.

Paine, Judith. "The Women's Pavilion of 1876." *Feminist Art Journal* 4, no. 4 (1976): 5–12.

Parezo, Nancy J., and Don D. Fowler. *Anthropology Goes to the Fair: The 1904 Louisiana Purchase Exposition*. Lincoln: University of Nebraska Press, 2007.

Patton, Phil. "Mammy: Her Life and Times." *American Heritage* 44, no. 5 (1993): 78–87.

Peck, Amelia, and Carol Irish. *Candace Wheeler*. New York: Metropolitan Museum of Art, 2001.

Peer, Shanny. *France on Display*. Albany: State University of New York Press, 1998.

Pepchinski, Mary. *Feminist Space: Exhibitions and Discourses between Philadelphia and Berlin 1865–1912*. Weimar: Verlag und Datenbank für Geisteswissenschaften/Weimar, 2007. See also Pepchinski, "The Woman's Building and the World's Exhibitions," available online at http://www.tu-cottbus.de/theoriederarchitektur/wolke/eng/Subjects/001/Pepchinski/pepchinski.htm.

Pilato, Denise E. "American Progress: Celebrated or Relegated." In *The Retrieval of a Legacy: Nineteenth Century American Women Inventors*. Westport, Conn.: Praeger, 2000.

Pohl, Frances K. "Historical Reality or Utopian Ideal?" *International Journal of Women's Studies* 5 (1982): 289–311.

Post, Pamela Lee. "East Meets West: The Model Homes Exhibits at the 1939–40 New York and San Francisco's World's Fairs." PhD diss., University of California at Santa Barbara, 2000.

Quizon, Cherubim A. "Two Yankee Women at the St. Louis Fair: The Metcalf Sisters and their Bagobo Sojourn in Mindanao." *Philippine Studies Quarterly* 52, no. 4 (2004): 527–55.

Rabinovitz, Laura. "The Fair View: The 1893 Chicago World's Columbian Exposition." In *For the Love of Pleasure: Women, Movies, and Culture in Turn of the Century Chicago*. New Brunswick, N.J.: Rutgers University Press, 1998.

Rydell, Robert. "A Cultural Frankenstein? The Chicago World's Columbian Exposition of 1893." In *Grand Illusions: Chicago's World's Fair of 1893*, edited by Neil Harris, Wim de Wit, James Gilbert, and Robert Rydell, 87–116. Chicago: Chicago Historical Society, 1993.

———. *World of Fairs: The Century-of-Progress Expositions*. Chicago: University of Chicago Press, 1993.

Sanders, Kimberly Wallace. "Dishing Up Dixie: Recycling the Old South in the Early-Twentieth-Century Domestic Ideal." In *Burning Down the House: Recycling Domesticity*, edited by Rosemary Marangoly George, 215–31. Boulder, Colo.: Westview Press, 1998.

Scobey, David. "What Shall We Do with Our Walls? The Philadelphia Exposition and the Meaning of Household Design." In *Fair Representations: World's Fairs and the Modern World*, edited by Robert Rydell and Nancy Gwinn, 87–120. Amsterdam: VU Press, 1994.

Scott, Ann Firor. *Natural Allies: Women's Associations in American History*. Champaign: University of Illinois Press, 1992.

Scott, Gertrude M. "Village Performance: Villages of the Chicago World's Columbian Exposition of 1893." PhD diss., New York University, 1990.

Sear, Martha. "Unworded Proclamations: Exhibitions of Women's Work in Colonial Australia." PhD diss., University of Sydney, 2000.

Silvermann, Debora. *Art Nouveau in Fin-de-Siécle France*. Berkeley: University of California Press, 1989.

Sklar, Kathryn K., and Erin Shaunessy. "African-American Women and the Chicago World's Fair." In *Women and Social Movements in the United States, 1600–2000*, available online at http://asp6new.alexanderstreet.com/wasm/wasmrestricted/ibw/intro.htm.

Snyder-Ott, Jocelynn. "Woman's Place in the Home (that she built)." *Feminist Art Journal* 3 (1974): 7–8.

Stephenson, William. "How Sallie Southall Cotton Brought North Carolina to the Chicago World's Fair of 1893." *North Carolina Historical Review* 58, no. 4 (1981): 364–83.

Stetson, Erlene. "A Note on the Woman's Building and Black Exclusion." *Heresies* 2 (1979): 45–47.

Steven, Lorenzas, and Karen Kilcup, eds. *From Beacon Hill to the Crystal Palace: The 1851 Travel Diary of a Working Class Woman*. Iowa City: University of Iowa Press, 2002.

Sund, Judy. "Columbus and Columbia in Chicago, 1893: Man of Genius Meets Generic Woman." *Art Bulletin* 75, no. 3 (1993): 443–66.

Todd, Emily B. "Afterword: The Woman's Building Library and History" *Libraries and Culture* 41, no. 1 (2006): 153–61.

Torre, Susanna, ed. *Women in American Architecture*. New York: Whitney Library of Design, 1977.

Trachtenberg, Alan. *The Incorporation of America: Culture and Society in the Gilded Age*. New York: Hill and Wang, 1982.

Trump, Erik. "Primitive Woman—Domesticated Woman: The Image of the Primitive Woman at the 1893 World's Columbian Exposition." *Women's Studies* 27, no. 3 (1998): 215–58.

Tsenes-Hills, Temple Bryonny. "I Am the Utterance of My Name: Black Victorian Feminist Discourse and Intellectual Enterprise at the Columbian Exposition, 1893." PhD diss., Loyola University, 2004.

Valis, Noël. "Women's Culture in 1893: Spanish Nationalism and the Chicago World's Fair." *Letras Peninsulares* 13, no. 2–3 (2001): 633–64.

van Kessel, Ellen, and Marga Kuperus. *Margaret Staal-Kropholler, Architect*. Rotterdam: 010 Publishers, 1992.

Vignocchi, Bernice. "Fair to Look Upon: An Analysis and Annotated Bibliography of Illinois Women's Fiction at the 1893 World's Columbian Exposition in Chicago." PhD diss., Northwestern University, 1990.

von Miller, Manu. "Philadelphia 1876-Chicago 1893-Paris 1900: *Amazonen der Kunst erobern die Weltausstellungen*" [Philadelphia 1876–Chicago 1893–Paris 1900: The Amazons of Art: Women Conquer World Exhibitions]. PhD diss., Universität Salzburg, 1998.

Warner, Deborah J. "Women Inventors at the Centennial." In *Dynamos and Virgins Revisited: Women and Technological Change in History: An Anthology*, edited by Martha Moore Trescott, 102–19. Metuchen, N.J.: Scarecrow, 1979.

Weimann, Jeanne Madeline. "A Dream for the "Age of Discovery": A Woman's Building at Chicago 1992," *World's Fair* 2, no. 3 (1982): 1–7.

———. *The Fair Women*. Chicago: Academy Press, 1981.

———. "A Temple to Woman's Genius: The Woman's Building of 1893," *Chicago History* 6 (1977): 23–33.

———. "Women of Veiled Fire." *World's Fair* 4, no. 4 (1984): 13–7.

Wels, Susan. "Spheres of Influence: The Role of Women at the Chicago World's Columbian Exposition of 1893 and the San Francisco Panama-Pacific International Exposition of 1915." *Ex Post Facto, Journal of San Francisco State History Students* 8 (1999): 6. Available online at http://userwww.sfsu.edu/~epf/1999/wels.html.

Wexler, Laura. "Kasebeir's Indians." In *Tender Violence: Domestic Visions in an Age of U.S. Imperialism*, 177–208. Chapel Hill: University of North Carolina Press, 2000.

Willis, Deborah, and Carla Williams. "The Black Female Body in Photographs from World's Fairs and Expositions." In "Race, Photography, and American Culture," *exposure: the Journal for the Society of Photographic Education*, 33, no. 1/2 (2000). Available online at http://www.carlagirl.net/writing/spe.html (accessed January 24, 2010).

Wood, Andrew E. "Managing the Lady Managers: The Shaping of Heterotopian Spaces in the 1893 Chicago Exposition's Woman's Building." *Southern Communication Journal* 69, no. 4 (2004): 289–302.

Yount, Sylvia. "A 'New Century' for Women: Philadelphia's Centennial Exhibition and Domestic Reform." In *Philadelphia's Cultural Landscape*, edited by Katharine Martinez and Page Talbott, 149–160. Philadelphia: Temple University Press, 2000.

Zipf, Catherine. *Professional Pursuits: Women and the American Arts and Crafts Movement*. Nashville: University of Tennessee, 2007.

Zschokke, Walter, and Dorothee Huber, eds. *Die Architektin Lux Guyer, 1894–1955: Das Risiko, sich in der Mitte zu bewegen* [*The Architect of Lux Guyer: The Risk to Move into the Middle*]. Zürich: gta/ETH Zürich, 1983.

CONTRIBUTORS

TJ BOISSEAU is an associate professor of gender and American cultural history at the University of Akron (Ohio). She is the author of *White Queen: May French-Sheldon and the Imperial Origins of American Feminist Identity*. Her research has been published in *Signs: A Journal of Women and Society; Gender & History; thirdspace: Journal of Feminist Theory and Culture*, and *Women's History Review*. She has recently coedited a special issue of the *National Women's Studies Association Journal* and is coediting (with Tracy Thomas) *Feminist Legal History* (forthcoming from New York University Press).

ANNE CLENDINNING is an associate professor of modern British history at Nipissing University (Ontario). Her research on women, gender, domestic technology, and commercial exhibitions has appeared in the *Canadian Journal of History, Women's History Review*, and *Victorian Review* and is the subject of her book *Demons and Domesticity: Women and the English Gas Industry, 1889–1939*.

LISA K. LANGLOIS is an assistant professor of art history and the director of women's studies at the State University of New York (Oswego). Her research focuses on Japan and gender and national identity at the 1893 Columbian Exposition.

ABIGAIL M. MARKWYN is an assistant professor of history at Carroll University (Waukesha, Wisconsin). Her article, "Economic Partner and Exotic Other: China and Japan at San Francisco's Panama-Pacific International Exposition," appeared in *Western Historical Quarterly*.

SARAH J. MOORE is an associate professor of art history at the University of Arizona. She has published numerous book chapters on American art and constructions of nationalism and is the author of *John White Alexander and the Construction of National Identity: Cosmopolitan American Art, 1880–1915*.

ISABEL MORAIS is an associate professor at the University of Saint Joseph (Macau, Special Administrative Region of China). She is also the co-coordinator of the Center of History and Heritage Studies and the Office of International Relations. Her research has been published in the *Chinese Heritage Centre Bulletin and Review of Culture*.

MARY PEPCHINSKI is a professor of architecture at the University of Applied Sciences in Dresden (Germany). Her research focuses on the relation between gender and modern architecture, urbanism, and public space. She is the author of *Feminist Space: Exhibitions and Discourses between Philadelphia and Berlin, 1865–1912*.

ELISABETH ISRAELS PERRY is a John Francis Bannon Professor of History Emerita and professor of women's studies emerita at Saint Louis University (Missouri). She was president of the Society for Historians of the Gilded Age and Progressive Era and has been an Organization of American Historians Distinguished Lecturer since 2001. Among her many publications is *Belle Moskowitz: Feminine Politics and the Exercise of Power in the Age of Alfred E. Smith*. Her most recent major publication is an edited reissuing of *An American Girl, and Her Four Years in a Boys' College* (1878), by Olive San Louie Anderson.

ANDREA G. RADKE-MOSS holds a faculty appointment in the Department of History at Brigham Young University–Idaho. Her research interests include women and higher education, schoolteachers, rural women, and Mormon women. She has published award-winning articles in *Great Plains Quarterly* and *Brigham Young University Studies* and is the author of *Bright Epoch: Women and Coeducation in the American West*.

ALISON ROWLEY is an associate professor in the Department of History at Concordia University (Montreal). Numerous articles featuring her research on Russian and Soviet women's history have appeared in *Revolutionary Russia; Minerva: A Journal of Women and War; Minerva: Quarterly Report on Women and the Military; Canadian Slavonic Papers; International Journal of the History of Sport; Solanus;* and *Slavonica*.

ROBERT W. RYDELL, widely recognized as a foremost historian of world's fairs and international expositions, is a professor of history and the director of the Montana State University Humanities Institute in Bozeman. Among his numerous articles and books on the subject of world's fairs are *All the World's a Fair; The Books of the Fairs; World of Fairs; Fair America;* and *Buffalo Bill in Bologna: The Americanization of the World, 1869–1922.*

ANNE WOHLCKE is an assistant professor in the Department of History at California State Polytechnic University (Pomona). Her research into the regulation of urban amusements has appeared in the *Journal of Interdisciplinary Feminist Thought.* She is currently working on a comprehensive history of early modern fairs held in London, entitled *Ordering London at Play: Gender, Disorder and Urban Amusement, 1689–1752.*

INDEX

THE UNIVERSITY OF ILLINOIS PRESS
IS A FOUNDING MEMBER OF THE
ASSOCIATION OF AMERICAN UNIVERSITY PRESSES.

_____

COMPOSED IN 9.75/13.5 ICS SCALA
BY BARBARA EVANS
AT THE UNIVERSITY OF ILLINOIS PRESS
MANUFACTURED BY SHERIDAN BOOKS, INC.

UNIVERSITY OF ILLINOIS PRESS
1325 SOUTH OAK STREET
CHAMPAIGN, IL 61820-6903
WWW.PRESS.UILLINOIS.EDU